Advances in Political Science: An International Series

Members of the editorial board: **Asher Arian** (general editor), **Luigi Graziano, William Lafferty, Theodore Lowi** and **Carole Pateman**

As an expression of its commitment to global political science, the International Political Science Association initiated this series to promote the publication of rigorous scholarly research by its members and affiliated groups. Conceptual and theoretical developments in the discipline, and their explication in various settings, represent the special focus of the series.

Titles include:

Advances in Political Science
Series Standing Order ISBN 0–333–71458–X
(*outside North America only*)

You can receive future titles in this series as they are published by placing a standing order. Please contact your bookseller or, in case of difficulty, write to us at the address below with your name and address, the title of the series and the ISBN quoted above.

Customer Services Department, Macmillan Distribution Ltd, Houndmills, Basingstoke, Hampshire RG21 6XS, England

Mediation in the Yugoslav Wars

The Critical Years, 1990–95

Saadia Touval

palgrave

First published 2002 by
PALGRAVE
Houndmills, Basingstoke, Hampshire RG21 6XS and
175 Fifth Avenue, New York, N. Y. 10010
Companies and representatives throughout the world

PALGRAVE is the new global academic imprint of
St. Martin's Press LLC Scholarly and Reference Division and
Palgrave Publishers Ltd (formerly Macmillan Press Ltd).

ISBN 0–333–96503–5

This book is printed on paper suitable for recycling and made from fully managed and sustained forest sources.

A catalogue record for this book is available from the British Library.

Library of Congress Cataloging-in-Publication Data
Touval, Saadia.
  Mediation in the Yugoslav wars ; the critical years, 1990–95 / Saadia Touval.
    p. cm. — (Advances in political science)
  Includes bibliographical references and index.
  ISBN 0–333–96503–5
  1. Yugoslav War, 1991–1995—Diplomatic history. I. Title.
  II. Advances in political science (New York, N. Y.)
  DR1313.7.D58 T678 2001
  949.703—dc21
                                                        2001034804

10   9   8   7   6   5   4   3   2   1
11   10   09   08   07   06   05   04   03   02

Transferred to digital printing in 2006.

Contents

Chronology

1918	Establishment of the Kingdom of Serbs, Croats and Slovenes (name later changed to Yugoslavia).
1941–44	Yugoslavia occupied by Nazi Germany and its allies.
1980	Tito dies.
1987	Milošević becomes leader of Serbia.
1989	Berlin Wall falls.
1990	First free multiparty elections held in the republics. Nationalists rise to power. Growing support for secession in Slovenia and Croatia.
1990–91	Crisis in the Gulf.
1990	US proposal to discuss Yugoslavia at NATO Council opposed by Europeans in November.
1991	
4 April	The EC Troika visits Belgrade.
21 June	US Secretary of State James Baker visits Belgrade for last-minute attempt to prevent the violent disintegration of Yugoslavia.
25 June	Croatia and Slovenia proclaim independence.
27 June	War begins in Slovenia and Croatia.
27 June	European Council meeting in Luxembourg dispatches the Troika to Yugoslavia.
28 June	Yugoslav parties agree to a ceasefire.
30 June	Troika again visits Belgrade. Yugoslav leaders readopt ceasefire.
7 July	The Brioni Declaration, mediated by the EC Troika, ends the war in Slovenia.
18 July	The Yugoslav federal presidency decides to withdraw federal forces from Slovenia.
19 August	Coup attempt against Gorbachev. Disintegration of the Soviet Union accelerates.
27 August	EC foreign ministers decide to convene a peace conference at the Hague.
7 September	The Hague peace conference begins under the chairmanship of Lord Carrington.
25 September	First UN Security Council meeting on Yugoslavia.
4 October	Carrington presents the outlines of his peace plan to Yugoslav leaders.
8 October	Cyrus Vance appointed as UN secretary-general's representative.

23 November	Vance mediates fifteenth ceasefire agreement for Croatia: 'The Vance Plan'.
7 December	The Badinter Commission proclaims that Yugoslavia is in the process of dissolution.
11 December	European leaders meet at Maastricht to conclude negotiations establishing the European Union.
17 December	EC foreign ministers decide to recognise Yugoslav republics upon the meeting of certain criteria. All republics desiring independence invited to apply by 23 December.

1992

15 January	EC foreign ministers formally recognise the independence of Croatia and Slovenia.
21 February	Ceasefire in Croatia found to be holding. Security Council decides to dispatch peacekeeping force.
23 February	All three Bosnian parties accept first version of Cutileiro Plan.
25 February	Izetbegović withdraws his acceptance of the Cutileiro Plan.
29 February	Bosnia holds referendum on independence. Serbs boycott referendum.
March	US and EC agree to recognise Bosnia's independence in April.
18 March	The three Bosnian parties accept revised Cutileiro Plan. Croats and Muslims soon renege.
7 April	EC, US and others recognise Bosnia's independence. War begins.
26 August	Carrington resigns. London Conference meets. ICFY, headed by Vance and Owen, established to help settle all Yugoslav disputes.
October	First version of the Vance–Owen Plan presented to the parties.

1993

30 January	Muslims join Serbs and Croats in accepting the constitutional principles of the Vance–Owen Plan.
25 March	Muslims and Croats accept full plan; Serbs refuse.
3 May	Stoltenberg becomes UN representative on ICFY, replacing Vance.
6 May	Bosnian Serb Assembly finally rejects Vance–Owen Plan, defying Milošević's plea to accept.
August	All three Bosnian parties accept principles of the ICFY's *Invincible* Plan.
20 September	Three Bosnian leaders meet on the *Invincible* but fail to sign the plan.
7 November	Germany and France launch the EU Plan for a Bosnian settlement.

1994

January	EU Plan dropped by its sponsors.
February	The US, assisted by Germany, mediates Muslim–Croat agreement establishing the Bosnian Federation.
April	Contact Group established.

6 July	Contact Group Plan presented to the parties.
19 July	Croat–Muslim Bosnian Federation accepts the Contact Group Plan; Serbs' ambiguous response taken as rejection.

1995

May	US resumes negotiations with Milošević. Croatia occupies Serb-held western Slavonia in Croatia. NATO airstrikes against the Bosnian Serbs, who respond by taking hundreds of UNPROFOR prisoners and using them as 'human shields'.
June	Bildt becomes EU representative on ICFY, replacing Owen.
July	Bosnian Serb army occupies UN-proclaimed safe areas and massacres thousands of Muslims at Srebrenica.
23 July	Croatia and Bosnian Muslims begin joint military operation against Serbs.
August	US launches a new diplomatic initiative, taking the lead in the negotiations. Croatia occupies additional Serb-populated area in Croatia, 'cleanses' area of Serbs.
28 August	Start of NATO airstrikes against Bosnian Serbs after explosion of another mortar shell in Sarajevo.
30 August	Holbrooke in Belgrade. Bosnian Serbs agree to authorise Milošević to negotiate on their behalf.
8 September	Holbrooke brokers Geneva agreement between the three parties' foreign ministers on the principles for a settlement.
25 September	Holbrooke mediates New York agreement between the three parties' foreign ministers on additional principles.
14 October	Ceasefire comes into effect in Bosnia.
1 November	Dayton conference begins.
20 November	Dayton Accords signed.

Preface

This book arose out of my long-term interest in the mediation of international conflicts. While mediation is usually looked at from the peacemaking perspective, I argue that mediation by states is also a form of intervention, motivated by broad strategic objectives. An understanding of international mediation therefore, requires an examination of both perspectives. I have tried to contribute to our understanding of mediation within the broader context of international politics through case studies as well as conceptual–theoretical writings. Previous cases I have written about concern the mediation of African territorial disputes and the Arab–Israeli conflict. When fighting erupted in Yugoslavia in 1991 I turned my attention to third parties' attempts to stop that war.

It was more than pure intellectual curiosity that drew my attention. I was born in 1932 in what was then the Kingdom of Yugoslavia. Even in the first year of primary school in Novi Sad I was acutely aware of the ethnic–national distinctions between people, and sensed the latent tension between them. I knew my classmates not only by their names, but also by their national identity – Serb, Croat, Hungarian, German and Jewish.

From 1991, when the war erupted, several major powers attempted to mediate between the parties, sometimes acting alone and sometimes jointly with others, under the aegis of international organisations. Unfortunately it took a very long time to end the fighting. And in Bosnia we witnessed the unusual process of the West combining military action with mediation. When trying to understand the difficulties encountered during that mediation effort I focused on the political considerations and the relationships among the mediating entities – states and intergovernmental organisations. I assumed that (besides the obvious obstacles posed by the policies of the disputing parties) an examination of the complex motives of the mediating governments and the tangled relationships between them would significantly help to explain the disappointing results of the mediation efforts.

I drew on a variety of sources when preparing this study. The abundant secondary literature provides an enormous amount of information, but it leaves many questions unanswered. To fill the gaps I utilised the published memoirs of several participants, and learned much from interviews with policy makers and negotiators. The interviews were especially useful for verifying information obtained from secondary sources and press accounts. As requested by the persons interviewed, I have not cited their names. I am beholden to them all.

I wish to thank a number of individuals and institutions for help along the way. Initial encouragement came from the United States Institute of Peace, which invited me to spend a year as Jennings Randolph Fellow at the Institute. Among the Institute's staff I particularly wish to thank Joseph Klaits, Director of the Jennings Randolph Fellows Program, and his predecessor Michael Lund; Sally Blair, who was Program Officer; Richard Solomon, the Institute's President; Charles Nelson, Executive Vice-President; and Barbara Cullicott and Kerry O'Donnell. My research assistants, Dan O'Connor and Jim Walsh, were enormously helpful. Several of the Fellows, and especially Fen Hampson, provided valuable advice.

I am also grateful for the advice and encouragement I received from my long-term friend and frequent collaborator, Bill Zartman. The anonymous reviewers, together with Steven Burg, Stephen Low and Susan Woodward, who read parts of earlier versions of the manuscript, provided valuable inputs. The Paul S. Nitze School of Advanced International Studies was also helpful in numerous ways. For help in getting the book published I am indebted to Asher Arian, my good friend since the time that we were both at Tel Aviv University. I also wish to thank Alison Howson, who accepted the book on behalf of Palgrave and lent her encouragement and assistance. I am grateful also to Kwaku Nuamah, who prepared the index. Finally, many thanks to Keith Povey for his skilful copy-editing and his patience.

SAADIA TOUVAL

Bosnia and Herzegovina, Post-Dayton 1995

Yugoslavia 1991

1
Introduction

Did any good come out of the efforts to mediate the conflicts in former Yugoslavia? The short answer is 'Yes, but...'. Mediation brought about agreements that halted the fighting in Slovenia, Croatia and Bosnia.[1] Yet these successes were overshadowed by the tragedies that diplomacy failed to prevent. The negotiations took too long and the successes came too late. Between 1991 and 1995 some 200 000 people lost their lives and close to two million were uprooted from their homes.

This book examines why the negotiations and mediations were not more effective. To be sure, mediation cannot resolve all conflicts, but it is difficult to avoid asking whether more effective mediation could have reduced the magnitude of the tragedy.

Analysing the mediation efforts in former Yugoslavia is a worthwhile endeavour even if one accepts the argument that early military intervention could have stopped the war. Even when military intervention in a conflict does take place, and succeeds in forcing the combatants to obey the intervenor's commands, negotiations are still necessary to bring about an *agreed* settlement that is self-sustaining and does not depend on continued enforcement by outsiders.

Such an examination is also worthwhile because reluctance to intervene militarily in others' wars is widespread and deeply rooted, reflecting the unwillingness of third parties to sacrifice their own in order to save Yugoslavs, Rwandans, Somalis or others from mutual slaughter. This reluctance is likely to influence the international community's response to similar situations in the foreseeable future. Therefore mediation and other forms of diplomacy are likely to remain the preferred means of intervention in such conflicts. Examining what impeded the diplomatic efforts in Yugoslavia might help make mediation more effective in the future.

As stated above, the question addressed in this book is why the mediations were not more effective. Specifically, I investigate why some mediation efforts failed, and why those which did succeed took so long to do so. Could the wars have been prevented? Could the ceasefires, especially those in Croatia and Bosnia, have been achieved sooner? Was a comprehensive settlement of Yugoslavia's problems achievable?[2]

What do I mean by 'effective', 'success', 'failure' and 'settlement'? By effective mediation I mean that the mediation effort accomplished its proclaimed purpose, and did so in a timely manner before fighting exacted many casualties, caused a massive flow of refugees or produced a major change in circumstances. A successful mediation effort was one that produced an agreement between the disputants and managed to bind the parties to its terms for several years. Failure means that the mediation attempt did not produce an agreement. Finally, settlement refers to an agreement that reduced the conflict between the disputing parties (though the parties did not necessarily view it as having resolved the cause of the dispute).

Mediation in international politics

This inquiry focuses on the political problems that the mediators encountered, and only incidentally on their tactics and skills. The discussion is influenced by certain ideas suggested by theoretical writings on the mediation of international conflicts. But the book is not about theory. When referring to theoretical concepts my purpose is not to test hypotheses or theories, but merely to use the concepts as tools for a historical–political analysis.

Since there exist a number of different theoretical approaches to international mediation it is important to clarify at the outset what I mean by this term.[3] It is also important because readers may be influenced by their notions of mediation in a variety of domestic contexts, such as disputes relating to divorce, labour relations or business deals. As will become evident, in this book international mediation is viewed as part of international politics and therefore as quite different from the mediation processes that take place within a state.

I use the term mediation to denote a particular type of third-party intervention. Like most interventions in the international arena, one of its purposes is to advance the intervenor's interests, but it differs from other forms of intervention in that it is not based on the direct use of force and is not aimed at helping one side in the conflict to win. Its goal is to bring the conflict (or part of it) to a settlement on terms that are consistent with the mediator's interests and acceptable to the disputants. To occur, mediation requires the consent and cooperation of the disputants (unlike military intervention, which does not).[4] Mediation is usually considered to be a legitimate intervention in another country's affairs, in contrast to armed intervention, the legality of which is often contested. Not only does it enjoy international legitimacy, but a government's mediatory intervention usually enjoys wide domestic support.

Mediation is a political process in which there is no advance commitment by the parties to accept the mediator's ideas. It differs from arbitration, which employs judicial procedures and issues a verdict that the parties have previously agreed to accept as binding. Mediation is pursued through negotiation, but it differs from other negotiations engaged in by states in that its declared purpose is to help others to settle their differences by mutual agreement. Furthermore the purpose is not to change the disputants' behaviour towards the mediator, but their behaviour towards each other.[5]

My interpretation of international mediation is informed by the realist tradition of international relations studies.[6] Accordingly the mediation of international disputes is regarded as an integral part of international politics. The principal actors in the process are states, acting either unilaterally or jointly with others through intergovernmental organisations and *ad hoc* groupings. International organisations are the instruments of their members, and it is difficult to separate their role from the specific interests and concerns of the leading member states.

This book therefore examines the actions of governments and international organisations, rather than those of individuals, and the word mediator refers to governments and international organisations, rather than individual diplomats. The book discusses the political and systemic influences that shaped the mediation processes in former Yugoslavia. It discusses the diplomacy directed at governments and at the principal groups concerned. It does not examine mediation efforts at the local level, directed at alleviating local tensions.

Why do states engage in mediation? They do so not only for ethical and moral reasons, but also for self-interest. States use mediation as a foreign policy instrument. Resort to mediation is usually prompted by the perception that other peoples' conflicts affect one own's interests – one's welfare and security. Therefore helping disputants to settle their conflict may be one goal of a mediator, but it is not the only goal. Mediation, like negotiation, often has additional objectives, such as fostering relationships, enhancing the mediator's stature and influence and preventing competitors from achieving their aims.

Mediators in international conflicts are seldom impartial.[7] Since third parties can be affected not only by a conflict but also by the process and terms of its settlement, mediators usually try to ensure that their own interests are advanced, or at least protected. The idea that mediation is pursued for selfish motives is not novel, and is widely held among observers of international politics. This is perhaps the reason why governments that engage in mediation often deny that their motives are self-interested and tend to characterise their efforts as those of an 'honest broker'.[8]

Although mediators may be able to accept a wider range of outcomes than the disputants, mediators' concern with protecting their own interests, both external and domestic, may lead them to reject certain options. As the mediator's interests shape the parameters of acceptable outcomes, the mediator also sets the parameters of possible settlements between the disputants.

For mediation to take place it is not enough for there to be motivated third parties. Mediation also requires the disputants to accept the mediator's intervention and to cooperate with the intervenor. How can disputants' acceptance of such interference in their affairs be explained? Sometimes, when both parties wish to find a way out of their conflict they welcome mediation. This may happen when there is a stalemate, when neither party expects continued confrontation to be to its benefit. Sometimes neither party wishes to deescalate the conflict or alter its policies. More commonly, one does and the other does not.

Yet even those who wish to continue the confrontation must weigh the consequences of rebuffing would-be mediators. When engaged in a conflict, disputants are particularly sensitive to the attitudes of third parties and usually want to gain their support. If they cannot win their support, they definitely do not want to alienate them or see them aligned with the enemy. They are therefore likely to accept mediation as the lesser evil, viewing cooperation with the mediator as less risky than antagonising it by rejecting its offer to mediate.

The mediation of interstate disputes, unlike military intervention, is considered legitimate by international law. Its legitimacy was confirmed by the 1907 Hague Convention on the Pacific Settlement of International Disputes, which proclaimed that 'Powers strangers to the dispute have the right to offer good offices or mediation even during the course of hostilities. The exercise of this right can never be regarded by either of the parties in dispute as an unfriendly act.'[9]

For state authorities confronted by internal opponents challenging their legitimacy, external attempts at mediation pose difficult dilemmas. When the government itself is a party to the conflict, acceptance of outside mediation carries a bargaining disadvantage. It implies that it recognises its opponents as being equal in status, entitled to present their point of view to an outside body, regardless of the government's claim to exclusive jurisdiction over the citizens living in its sovereign territory. Placing the internal opponents of a government on an equal footing with the regime implies that the opponents' claims are no less legitimate than those of the government. Since this inevitably weakens the position of the government and strengthens that of its opponents, governments are usually reluctant to accept external mediation in domestic conflicts.

Governments that oppose external mediation can draw support from international law, which considers respect for the sovereignty of states to be a cornerstone of international order. Indeed it is enshrined in the charter of the United Nations:

> Nothing contained in the present Charter shall authorize the United Nations to intervene in matters which are essentially within the domestic jurisdiction of any state or shall require the Members to submit such matters to settlement under the present Charter; but this principle shall not prejudice the application of enforcement measures under Chapter 7.[10]

In recent years the principle of sovereignty has ceased to shield states from external intervention in domestic disputes. But unlike military intervention for humanitarian purposes, which has given rise to extensive ethical arguments and new legal justifications,[11] the mediation of domestic disputes has provoked little controversy. The probable reason is that mediation is always consensual; it cannot take place without the active cooperation of the disputing parties.

Despite their reluctance, governments often accept external mediation of internal disputes and cooperate with the mediators. Probably the best explanation of this is again the one offered above. All disputants are sensitive to the attitudes of third parties. They are eager for support, and exert themselves to prevent third parties from aligning with their enemies. Moreover, in practice conflicts are seldom kept within state boundaries. They tend to spill over into neighbouring states, attracting intervention. Therefore governments may accept offers of external mediation in the hope that this will avert more harmful types of intervention.

The functions and qualifications of mediators

The search for explanations of why the mediation effort in former Yugoslavia was not more effective can benefit from a few ideas offered by the theoretical literature on factors that facilitate or impede successful mediation. There seems to exist a broad consensus that the outcome of mediation is the combined product of numerous factors. Some of these relate to the parties, the issues in dispute, the dynamics of the conflict and the international context of the conflict. Other factors are associated with the mediator – its characteristics and activities.[12]

For our purposes it is relevant to note that the number of parties in the conflicts mediated in the former Yugoslavia varied. While some of the conflicts that the mediators tackled – the ceasefires in Slovenia and in Croatia – were bilateral, other problems were multilateral. The Bosnian problem involved three major protagonists – the Serbs, the Croats and the Muslims. The attempt to conclude a comprehensive settlement of the problems surrounding the dissolution of Yugoslavia involved six major parties – the six republics comprising Yugoslavia. Trying to bring three or six disputants to a mutually agreed settlement is more difficult than mediating between two. It is also important to note that each of the parties perceived the issues in dispute as concerning their nations' physical security, identity and right to self-determination. Such issues are notoriously difficult to resolve by mutual agreement. The timing of mediation efforts is often considered to be of critical importance. It has been observed that interventions that take place in situations of a 'mutually hurting stalemate', where the disputants recognise that their existing policies will not achieve their goals and that alternative policies may be very risky, are particularly conducive to a settlement.

But the principal focus of this book are the mediating entities. How do the identity, characteristics, goals and actions of the mediators influence the effectiveness of their peacemaking efforts?

Mediation entails a wide range of activities. Mediators help the disputants to communicate. They sometimes seek to change a party's image of the adversary or interpret the adversary's behaviour in a manner that will facilitate settlement of the dispute. Mediators can help each party to understand their adversary's concerns and the constraints to which the adversary is subjected. Mediators may also suggest how the interests of the parties might be reconciled, and what kinds of compromise or trade-off might facilitate a settlement. They can also help the parties to save face when making concessions. Disputants usually believe that it is less damaging to their reputation to accept a proposal made by a mediator, than one made by their adversary.

To succeed in their task, mediators must influence and persuade the disputants to modify their policies, and to agree to terms they have hitherto considered unacceptable. As in all negotiations, mediators pursue their persuasive efforts through clarification of the costs and benefits of alternative courses of action. In trying to persuade the parties to change their policies, mediators often need to bargain with the parties, communicating to them conditional promises and threats, and actually employing rewards and punishments. A mediator's ability to confer or withhold benefits, or to shift benefits to the adversary, is often vital to its ability to influence the disputants to change their policies and accept the mediator's proposals. Moreover powerful mediators need not wait for a hurting stalemate to occur, but can use their resources to create it.[13]

Considering the activities that mediators engage in and the resources that are often necessary for such activities, it is obvious that the identity of the mediator and its characteristics are of critical importance. The principal mediators in the conflicts in former Yugoslavia were the member governments of the European Union, the US and Russia. Most of their mediating activities were pursued collectively through international organisations – the EC/EU[14] and the UN, and their joint agency, the International Conference on the Former Yugoslavia (ICFY) – as well as through an *ad hoc* entity called the Contact Group.[15]

Two major mediation initiatives were undertaken by the US acting largely on its own. In 1994 the US mediated an end to the Croat–Muslim war in Bosnia and established the Croat–Muslim Federation. In 1995 the US was the principal mediator in the process leading up to the Dayton Accords, which ended the Bosnian wars.

Thus the mediation processes in Yugoslavia provide ample material to compare mediation by a state acting on its own with collective mediation by a group of states acting through international organisations. Each of these two types of mediation has both advantages and disadvantages. I shall try to show that the collective endeavours pursued through the EC/EU, the UN and the Contact Group were encumbered with significant disadvantages. The participating states often disagreed about the policy to be pursued, causing the disputants to doubt the credibility of the international organisations' and Contact Group's promises and threats. These weaknesses of the collective mediation efforts detracted significantly from their effectiveness.

Multiple goals, uncertain priorities

Additional problems impairing the effectiveness of peacemaking stemmed from the multiple goals pursued by the mediators. The mediations in Yugoslavia took place in the context of massive changes in the international political landscape. The collapse of the Soviet empire was greeted with relief in the West, but this relief was accompanied by anxiety that the collapse might lead to violence and political instability. The international community's response to the conflict in Yugoslavia was therefore informed by the expectation that its policies would set a precedent for management of the conflicts that were likely to arise out of the disintegration of the Soviet Union. At the same time the members of the EC were negotiating a new treaty establishing closer union and reforming their common institutions. One of the proposed changes was closer cooperation in foreign policy and security. The Europeans' response to the conflict in Yugoslavia was seen as a test for the EC's ability to develop and pursue such a common policy.

American policy on Yugoslavia was shaped in the context of a domestic debate on the US's role in the post-Cold War era. Some (often labelled 'neoisolationists') argued that it was unwise for the US to become involved in conflicts that did not directly affect its security. Others ('liberals' or 'interventionists') claimed that – for ethical reasons and because the national interest required the US to assert its role as leader of the Western alliance – the US should not remain passive in the face of such conflicts. Thus the mediation process was also tangled up with European–American disagreement about the future of their alliance, the US's role in post-Cold War Europe and the US's desire to assert its leadership in matters relating to European security.

Within this broader context of foreign policy objectives, mediating an end to the conflicts in Yugoslavia was not the first priority. When policy options or tactical moves relating to the mediations appeared to be inconsistent with the requirements imposed by the other objectives, it was the assertion of US leadership, the nurturing of EC/EU solidarity, the management of a peaceful transition in the former Soviet Union and the protection of Western relations with Turkey and the Muslim world that took precedence. As we shall see, the mediations in the former Yugoslavia often became subordinate to the pursuit of these more important goals.

The effectiveness of the peacemaking efforts was also affected by the specific goals of each mediation initiative. Common sense suggests that mediation aimed at a limited objective, such as a ceasefire, is easier and attains its goal more quickly than pursuit of a comprehensive settlement of a conflict. The mediators in Yugoslavia sometimes set themselves the limited objective of establishing a ceasefire, while on other occasions they sought the comprehensive settlement of the disputes surrounding the dissolution of Yugoslavia. Not surprisingly, ceasefires were easier to negotiate than broad political settlements. Attempts to bring about a comprehensive settlement in Yugoslavia were abandoned, and the Bosnian settlement took three and a half years to accomplish.

When mediators are faced with a choice between these two kinds of objective they are confronted with an ethical dilemma: should they direct their energy towards stopping the violence, even if it allows an unjust *status quo* to continue, or should they aim at a comprehensive political settlement on terms that meet criteria of a just peace even if it prolongs the fighting, with its attendant loss of life? Should they give priority to order, or to justice? The belief that order cannot endure unless it is perceived to be just provides little guidance to mediators faced with the necessity of according priority to one of these two objectives. Thus any discussion of the goals that mediators set for themselves and their determination of priorities needs to address the moral consequences of the mediators' choice.

Background to the conflict[16]

This book's focus on the flaws of the mediation efforts should not be taken to imply that the conflicts besetting former Yugoslavia could easily have been settled. On the contrary, the mediators faced a most formidable challenge. The challenge was great because the conflicts the mediators were trying to settle stemmed from a particularly noxious form of nationalism – a nationalism fuelled by 'inherited fear'.[17]

Yugoslavia was established at the end of the First World War from the ruins of the Ottoman and Austro-Hungarian Empires. It was a multinational state, formed and held together by a coalition of Serbs, Croats and Slovenes, its principal constituent nations. The coalition was formed not merely to express cultural solidarity, but also with the intention of addressing concrete political problems. Chief among these was Serbian irredentism – the desire of Serbian nationalists to attach the Serb-populated areas in Vojvodina and Croatia to the common homeland of Serbia – and the wish of Croatian and Sloven- ian leaders to draw on Serbia's power to protect their territories from the expansionary ambitions of Italy. Although there were always some who opposed the concept of a common Yugoslav state, the broad consensus of all the nations involved supported it. Those who favoured a common Yugoslavia formed multinational coalitions that established the state in 1918, reconstituted it in 1943 and sus- tained it for over 70 years.

The disintegration of Yugoslavia in 1991–92 and the accompany- ing wars were brought about by an upsurge in nationalist disputes among the component nations. The nationalist upsurge has been variously attributed to the decay of institutions resting upon an ill-designed federal constitution, to economic decline and the attendant social strains, and to incitement and manipulation by unscrupulous politicians. Politicians whipped up nationalist sentiments as a means of gaining power. Their success was due to the manipulation of historical grievances against and antagonism towards 'brother' Yugoslav nations that were deeply embedded in the popular culture. The nationalist hatreds thus aroused were powerful not because they were 'ancient', but because they rested on memories of recent events.

Contemporary hatreds were stoked by the Second World War experiences of the parents and grandparents of the present generation. During the war the Croat state allied itself with Nazi Germany and pursued a policy of systematic genocide against Serbs (as well as against Jews). Croats and Bosnian Muslims suffered at the hands of guerrillas – Serbian Chetniks (professing loyalty to the exiled Royal Yugoslav government) and Tito's communist partisans. Although 50 years had elapsed since these events, and the young in Yugoslavia, as everywhere, aspired to build new lives unencumbered by past legacies, memories of the Second World War weighed heavily on people. More than a million people (approximately 6.4 per cent of the population) had been killed between 1941 and 1945[18] and the lives of almost all families in Yugoslavia were marked by traumatic experiences, thus giving 'history' a very personal meaning.

It was therefore easy for politicians to tap this sentiment and win popularity by presenting themselves as defenders of the nation, and by painting other nations and their leaders as enemies. They aroused fear that the atrocities suffered during the Second World War were about to be repeated, and this fear aroused hatred. A sovereign and independent state 'belonging' to the nation was expected to protect the nation and its individual members from hostile neighbours.

Transforming the republics comprising the Yugoslav federation into nation-states was bound to be contentious. The postwar constitution referred to Yugoslavia as a federation of five nations and six republics. The five nations – Croats, Macedonians, Montenegrins, Slovenes and Serbs – had republics named after them. The sixth republic, Bosnia, was not associated with a single nation. The Muslims living there, making up approximately 44 per cent of the population, were regarded by many as Islamised Serbs and Croats, and therefore not entitled to recognition as a separate nation. It was not until the

1970s that the Bosnian Muslims won recognition as a distinct nation, rather than merely a religious community.

Among the republics, only Slovenia was relatively homogenous, its population being 87.6 per cent Slovene. Moreover 98 per cent of the Slovenes in Yugoslavia lived in Slovenia itself. All the other republics had significant national minorities, and the nations were not concentrated in the republics associated with their names. In Croatia only 78 per cent of the population were Croats; 12 per cent were Serbs and the remainder belonged to other groups. Serbia, with a population of 9.8 million, had a large Albanian minority (estimated at 1.6 million) concentrated in the Kosovo region, and a much smaller but nevertheless significant Hungarian minority in Vojvodina. Moreover only 75 per cent of Yugoslavia's Serbs lived in Serbia, the remainder being dispersed among the other republics. Macedonia's population was only 65 per cent Macedonian; Albanians were estimated to make up close to 20 per cent of its population. Montenegro was only 62 per cent Montenegrin, the others being mainly Muslims, Serbs and Albanians. In Bosnia, no nation held a majority – its population consisted of 44 per cent Muslims, 31 per cent Serbs and 17 per cent Croats.[19]

Tito's firm rule kept national tensions under control. But many observers of Yugoslav politics believed that when he passed from the scene nationalist pressures would destabilise the country, and might even lead to civil war and its disintegration. Discussion of this issue was not confined to classified government reports; it was pursued publicly by journalists and academic analysts.[20]

Even during Tito's rule, nationalist tensions did not always remain suppressed. Albanian nationalism in Kosovo was a continuous problem for the regime; the late 1960s saw expressions of discontent in the Communist Party in Serbia; and in the early 1970s it was the Croats who voiced grievances. These nationalist rumblings were quickly stifled.

After Tito's death in 1980, nationalist tensions began to multiply. These were reflected in violent clashes in Kosovo, starting in 1981 and continuing through the 1980s. Tensions between the Albanian majority and Serb minority communities there reverberated in Belgrade and fuelled the flame of Serbian nationalism. One expression of the latter that sent shock waves throughout Yugoslavia was the publication in September 1986 of the *Memorandum* of the Serbian Academy of Sciences and the Arts, which charged that the legal, political and economic structures of the Yugoslav Federal Republic established after the war (by the Communist Party, led by Tito) had been designed to divide and weaken the Serbian nation. It warned that 'virulent manifestations of chauvinism and Serbophobia in some settings' could provoke 'reactions that could be volatile, and thus dangerous as well'.[21] The government responded by banning the distribution of the document and putting Serbian nationalist spokespeople on trial.

Nationalist sentiments were being expressed in other parts of the country too. In Bosnia, starting in 1983, several groups of people, including the president of Bosnia-Herzegovina, Alija Izetbegović, were brought to trial on a variety of charges whose common denominator was the assertion of Islamic identity. In Croatia there were numerous trials of Croatian nationalists. There were also reports of Croatian and Macedonian terrorist organisations operating within Yugoslavia. In Slovenia, beginning in 1988 the Slovene Youth Organisation openly asserted separatist goals, defying the Yugoslav National Army and the authority of the federal government.[22]

Throughout this period and until 1987 the federal and republic governments, assisted by the Communist Party, cooperated to suppress public expressions of nationalism. It is therefore significant that the first political leader openly to espouse nationalism with impunity was Slobodan Milošević of Serbia. Before entering politics in 1984, Milošević held executive posts in the economic sector. At the beginning of his political career he was perceived by the West as trying to promote market-oriented reform. He publicly espoused Serbian nationalism only in the spring of 1987 while serving as chairman of the Central Committee of the Serbian Communist Party. Calling for the protection of the Serbian population of Kosovo, he became widely popular. Milošević's nationalist policy and rhetoric helped feed Croatian and Slovenian distrust of the Serbs and by the late 1980s nationalism was on the rise everywhere.

The structure of the book

This book examines the attempt to mediate the Yugoslav conflicts through a historical analysis of the principal peacemaking initiatives between 1990 and 1995. Chapter 2 discusses the first initiative – the attempts by the US and the EC in 1990 and 1991 to avert the wars by preventing the break-up of Yugoslavia. It was only with the outbreak of war, following the failure of these attempts, that third parties intruded into the domestic politics of the still existing Yugoslav states and tried to mediate between the parties. The issues surrounding the mediators' entry into the fray, and their choice of international organisations to assume the task, are explored in Chapter 3. The EC's successful brokering of the ceasefire that ended the war in Slovenia in July 1991 is the subject of Chapter 4.

Chapter 5 examines the failed attempts by the EC in 1991 and 1992 to bring about a comprehensive settlement of the conflict, involving all Yugoslav parties. Simultaneously with the search for a comprehensive settlement, efforts were made to mediate a ceasefire in Croatia. These efforts, first pursued by the EC and subsequently accomplished by Cyrus Vance and his team, acting for the UN, are discussed in Chapter 6.

The peace efforts in Bosnia are the subject of the two subsequent chapters. Chapter 7 examines the EC's attempt to prevent the Bosnian war and the subsequent unsuccessful mediations by the ICFY and the Contact Group. Chapter 8 discusses the two US mediations: the first, in 1994, helped end the war between the Muslims and Croats and established the Croat–Muslim Federation, and the second, in 1995, ended the war with the Serbs and produced the Dayton Accords.

In conclusion, Chapter 9 reviews the outcomes of the mediation efforts, and outlines some lessons to be derived from them.

2
Failed Attempts to Prevent War[1]

For many months prior to the outbreak of fighting in June 1991, the EC and the US made a concerted effort to prevent the growing tension from erupting into war. Although their efforts did not involve mediation, they are relevant to our analysis because they served as a precursor to the subsequent, more intrusive intervention through mediation. This diplomacy is also relevant because it revealed one of the weaknesses that subsequently hindered the mediations – the inability of the intervening states and the international organisations to speak in a single voice and convey a clear message to the disputing parties.

The efforts to prevent the war were hindered by a factor that is typical of preventive diplomacy – it takes place before the situation is perceived as grave and threatening. Herein lies a contradiction. It is wise to intervene early, before the contending parties deepen their commitment to policies that will lead to violent confrontation. It is rightly expected that it will be much more difficult for intervenors to persuade the disputants to alter their course and compromise their goals after an armed clash had taken place and public opinion has been mobilised. Yet early action takes place at a time when the contending parties are hopeful and confident about their ability to achieve their aims, and are therefore disinclined to listen to pleas for restraint and moderation. Another major difficulty with timing is that an initiative undertaken before a crisis has developed usually lacks the motivation generated by a grave situation, making it difficult for the intervenors to mobilise all the necessary means to prevent the war.

The most common explanation for the failure of the European and US efforts is the familiar charge of 'too little, too late'. This, however, is an erroneous diagnosis. It implies that the policy pursued was basically sound, and that earlier application of the policy would have prevented the war. As this book will show, the problem was that the policy itself was ridden with flaws. Chief among these were the reliance on economic leverage and the conduct of incoherent diplomacy. Viewed from the perspective of the Yugoslav contenders, Western[2] diplomacy appeared contradictory and lacked credibility.

Changing Western attitudes

Western policies towards Yugoslavia crystallised within the context of the Cold War. After 1948, when the Soviet Union tried to overthrow Tito by expelling Yugoslavia from the Soviet bloc, the West embraced Yugoslavia as a *de facto* ally in helping to contain Soviet expansionism. In view of this, it was important that the country's territorial integrity be preserved. Even Germany, which in 1991 became the main supporter of the secessionist claims of Croatia and Slovenia, shared this view. Chancellor Helmut Kohl gave expression to this policy in the course of a visit to Yugoslavia in the summer of 1985, when he proclaimed Germany's 'great interest in maintaining the internal and external stability of Yugoslavia. Yugoslavia's stability is an important factor of...the political balance of Europe.'[3]

When the Cold War was winding down, Yugoslavia lost the geopolitical importance it had had for the West. The strategic lens through which Yugoslavia had been viewed during the Cold War was discarded and it came to be perceived as just another communist country that needed to be encouraged to democratise and reform its economy. This policy shift is described by Warren Zimmermann in his memoir of his ambassadorship. He relates that when he assumed his post in early 1989, he and Lawrence Eagleburger, who had just been appointed as deputy secretary of state and who was one of the foremost American experts on the Balkans, shared the view 'that the traditional American approach to Yugoslavia no longer made sense'. By then 'Yugoslavia had been surpassed by both Poland and Hungary in political and economic openness. In addition, human rights had become a major element of US policy and Yugoslavia's record on that issue was not good – particularly in the province of Kosovo, where an authoritarian Serbian regime was systematically depriving the Albanian majority of its basic civil liberties.'[4]

The preservation of the country's unity and territorial integrity which had been a matter of high priority in the Cold War strategic context, now became subordinated to democratisation. Zimmermann was to deliver a new message upon his arrival in Yugoslavia: 'I was to reassert the traditional mantra of U.S. support for Yugoslavia's unity, independence, and territorial integrity. But I would add that the United States could only support unity in the context of democracy; it would strongly oppose unity imposed or preserved by force.'[5]

It was believed that democratisation, the standard medicine prescribed for most of the world's ills, would also cure Yugoslavia's afflictions: it would redress human rights, alleviate ethnic tensions and keep the country united in peace. It is unclear whether the applicability of this theory to Yugoslavia under the conditions existing in 1989–90 was seriously examined or whether it was recognised that the transition to democracy might be accompanied by instability and conflict. US policy makers may have been excessively influenced by the domestic political need to demonstrate commitment to the spread of democratisation.

Unfortunately, when applied to Yugoslavia the West's policy of promoting economic reforms, democratisation and respect for human rights did not bring the expected results. Ironically it may even have aggravated the country's problems. Western economic assistance to remedy Yugoslavia's economic and social situation, which had been deteriorating since the early 1980s, was conditional on reforms. Among these was the return of some of the powers held by the republics (placed there by Tito's 1974 constitution) to the central government. This was resisted by Croatia and Slovenia, further stimulating the already strong Croat and Slovene aspirations for independence. While these issues were being debated the economic and social conditions continued to worsen, contributing to the malaise that facilitated the propagation of nationalist hatreds. Pressure on Serbia to cease its repression of Albanians in Kosovo was exploited by Serbia's president, Slobodan Milošević, who sought to strengthen his hold on power by fanning the flames of Serbian nationalism. This in turn helped feed Croatian and Slovenian distrust of the Serbs.

When the democratisation that was spreading across Eastern Europe led to freedom to organise political parties, it was the nationalists who benefited most. The first free multiparty elections held in Croatia and in Slovenia in 1990, brought the nationalists to power. In Serbia, Milošević was reelected as president by a large popular majority. Nationalism was gaining support everywhere.[6]

The election results and an increase in nationalistically inspired violence led observers to conclude by mid 1990 that the country was about to break apart. Experts disagreed, however, about whether this would lead to war. A sign of the thinking within the US administration came with the leaking to the media in November 1990 of a CIA report predicting that the break-up would be violent.[7]

What was not yet clear was the timing – when the break-up would take place and when war was likely to erupt. A date soon emerged. On 22 December a referendum in Slovenia approved a proposal to proclaim independence within six months unless agreement was reached prior to that date on turning Yugoslavia into a loose confederation of states. Thus Yugoslavia watchers knew that unless something happened to interrupt the process, Slovenia and Croatia would proclaim their independence, and that a civil war was likely to erupt at the end of June 1991.

Since Western policies aimed at alleviating the country's problems through political and economic reforms were not producing the expected results, there was an obvious need to adjust them. Instead of pursuing policies aimed at remedying the country's ills over the long term, it became necessary to address the more immediate danger of war.

Flawed policies

The West tried to prevent the war by means of an economic strategy aimed at dissuading the principal Yugoslav actors from taking steps that might ignite a war: dissuading the Croat and Slovene leaders from proclaiming independence, and dissuading the federal government and the military from enforcing unity.

The failure of these efforts can be attributed to several factors: the unsuitability of using economic inducements to influence parties that were anxious about their physical security, disagreements among leading members of the EC, the equivocal nature of Western policies and the preoccupation of Western governments with other more pressing issues.

The realisation that Yugoslavia was moving towards disintegration and war coincided with several other developments that were regarded in the West as having momentous significance, as presenting great opportunities as well as dangers. One was the collapse of the Soviet Union's hold over Eastern Europe. While welcome, it was accompanied by apprehension that the weakening Soviet regime might try to halt the process. Particular concern was aroused by the possibility that the Soviet army might try to prevent the Baltic republics from realising their independence, and that the presence of large numbers of ethnic Russians in the Baltics and Ukraine might cause instability.

Another issue commanding attention was the reunification of Germany. The US and Germany were actively engaged in negotiations on the reunification and the withdrawal of Soviet troops. Germany's European allies were debating whether a reunited Germany might be so powerful and domineering that it would again pose a threat to its neighbours. The members of the EC were concurrently engaged in the final stages of negotiating the restructuring of their enterprise, leading to the Maastricht Treaty. Then, at the end of July 1990 the Gulf crisis erupted, continuing through to March 1991.

The significance of these events, and the opportunities and risks they posed for the West, dominated the attention of political leaders and foreign policy officials. In these circumstances the growing crisis in Yugoslavia did not receive the attention that it deserved. In trying to coordinate their policies, Western governments gave priority to developing common policies on the Soviet withdrawal, the reunification of Germany, the Gulf War and the Maastricht Treaty. Coordination of policy on Yugoslavia was subordinate to these efforts, and contingent on its not impeding the development of common policies on the other issues.

To induce the Yugoslav parties to follow its advice, the EC, and to some extent the US, offered economic rewards and punishments. If unity were preserved, democratisation extended, human rights respected and economic reforms implemented, then Yugoslavia would receive financial assistance and trading concessions. But if it disintegrated, and if it fell short of meeting the other conditions, then some or all these benefits would be withheld.

Thus between December 1990 and May 1991 the EC committed itself to providing to Yugoslavia, through a variety of programmes, a total of 3.6 billion ECU (over $4.5 billion). Furthermore, the EC promised to open negotiations on an association agreement (which would provide Yugoslavia with opportunities to expand trade and gain access to further economic benefits) if it resolved its internal disagreements, and remained a single state. Yugoslavia was warned that these benefits would not be made available and that the current assistance would be curtailed if Croatia and Slovenia seceded unilaterally, thus breaking the country apart, or if the suppression of nationalist sentiments was pursued by force and was accompanied by violations of human rights.

The obvious reason why the EC chose to bolster its admonitions with economic inducements was that these were the only instruments of leverage available to it at that time. It is also possible that to some extent EC officials were misled by the economic justifications that the Croat and Slovene leaders cited in support of their quest for independence, claiming that their countries wished to be rid of economic exploitation by Serbia and free-riding southern republics, and to build market economies that would facilitate their admission to the EC. Moreover the main item on the agenda in Western dealings with Yugoslavia during the previous few years had been the country's economic problems.

Economic statecraft had the additional advantage of not infringing upon Yugoslavia's sovereignty. Unlike mediation and other types of direct involvement in domestic bargaining between disputants, economic inducements were a stand-off weapon that could be fired from a distance without blatantly violating the prohibition on interference in the internal affairs of states. Respect for Yugoslavia's sovereignty was important not only for reasons of principle, the EC wishing to uphold a norm that was a cornerstone of international order. It was also important for the pragmatic reason of wishing to avoid action that might hasten the break-up.

Unfortunately it was an inappropriate strategy. It may even have been counter productive, continuing the earlier policy of delaying economic assistance and thus contributing to the social tensions being exploited by the extreme nationalists.

Successful deterrence and dissuasion require the projection of clear goals and credible leverage. But instead of clarity, the West signalled ambiguity, leading the Yugoslav actors to varying interpretations of Western attitudes. The ambiguity stemmed from the West's definition of goals in terms of broad values, some of which, in the context of time and place, were contradictory. The main difficulty was inherent in the simultaneous advocacy of both unity and democracy. In the context of Yugoslavia in 1990–91, these two objectives were contradictory, undermining each other. Attempts to preserve unity were accompanied by the repression of nationalist and separatist tendencies, and with violations of human rights. Democratisation opened the way to the formation of nationalist parties, and to the victory in freely held elections in Slovenia and Croatia of leaders who were calling for the secession of these two republics from Yugoslavia. Thus attempts to preserve unity were antidemocratic, and the promotion of democracy encouraged disintegration. The contradiction inherent in the West's goals gave them an air of ambiguity, making it difficult for Yugoslav leaders to predict how the West might react to their moves.

Furthermore the strategy lacked credibility. The ambiguity of Western statements and behaviour cast doubt on the credibility of both promises and threats. Moreover the various Yugoslav parties were aware of the divisions among the EC members on the question of Yugoslavia. The Croats and Slovenes were more inclined to listen to those who promised support if they seceded from Yugoslavia, than to those who threatened them with punishment. In addition, being cognisant of the complexity of intergovernmental decision-making they doubted the ability of the EC to honour its promise of aid if Yugoslavia remained united.[8]

Finally, economic punishments (or rewards) were not well attuned to the psychology of the nationalist leaders in the republics, who were now the principal actors in the conflict. Their primary preoccupation was with their nations' physical security and the psychological need to assert their national identity, rather than with economic prosperity. The gap between the EC's frame of mind and that of the Yugoslavs was reflected in the comment made by Jacques Delors, the president of the European Commission, about his meetings in Yugoslavia – he expressed disappointment that the presidents of the republics with whom he had met were concentrating on their ethnic disputes rather than their economic problems.[9]

In these circumstances, placing one's hopes on the potency of economic influence was bound to lead to disappointment.

Ambiguities

It is generally assumed that the West supported the preservation of a unified Yugoslavia until the summer of 1991. This view rests on a somewhat narrow and literal interpretation of statements that endorsed unity and does not take into account the nuances of these statements: how they were qualified, what was implied, and how the wording evolved over time. Nor does it take into account the information available to the contending Yugoslav parties about the attitudes of political elites and the debates within and among the Western nations about the policies they ought to follow. When these additional aspects of the West's message are taken into consideration, Western policies appear far more equivocal. This equivocation undermined the credibility of the West's position, and of the promises and threats aimed at influencing the behaviour of the Yugoslav parties. The uncertainties that the Western policies created led each of the contending Yugoslav parties to believe that its actions would not be punished, but rather, after a brief interval of time, would be accepted and perhaps supported by the Western governments.

US inconsistencies

Given the US's stature in world politics, the Yugoslav parties were highly attentive to US attitudes towords the growing tensions in their country. Washington seemed to be sending out three messages. Congress expressed its approval of self-determination for the Albanians, Croats and Slovenes, thus implicitly supporting the dissolution of Yugoslavia. The US administration delivered two contradictory messages: it proclaimed support for preservation of the country's unity, yet pressed the Yugoslav federal government to refrain from exercising its authority to protect it.

Several considerations helped to shape the administration's response to the growing crisis in Yugoslavia. One was the assessment that with the end of the Cold War the preservation of Yugoslavia had ceased to be a vital US interest. Secondly, senior US officials, most notably Lawrence Eagleburger (the deputy secretary of state) and Brent Scowcroft (the president's adviser on national security) doubted the US's ability to influence the course of internal developments there. They expected that active engagement in the Yugoslav crisis might require military involvement, which public opinion would not support.[10] These considerations pointed towards minimising US involvement in the crisis. At the same time, concern that the violent break-up of Yugoslavia might encourage a resort to violence in the disintegrating Soviet Union made it difficult for the US to remain uninvolved. Especially worrisome was the prospect that an attempt by the Yugoslav National Army (JNA) to prevent the secession of Croatia and Slovenia might encourage the Soviet Army to act against the secession of the Baltic states and Ukraine from the Soviet Union. Finally, inaction was impossible in view of Congress's interest in the problem.

These disparate considerations produced a diplomacy that alternated between passivity and activism. When active, it was marked by pontification on fundamental values and principles, accompanied by equivocation about the immediate issues on the agenda. The passive side was reflected in the disposition to defer to the Europeans' claim that Yugoslavia was Europe's responsibility and not that of the US. This seemed logical in view of the economic leverage that was believed to be available to the EC: over 40 per cent of Yugoslavia's trade was with the EC and less than 5 per cent with the US.[11]

Passivity was also reflected in the virtual absence of high-level contact between senior US and Yugoslav officials for much of 1990 and until June 1991, when Secretary of State James Baker visited Belgrade – one week prior to the date announced by Croatia and Slovenia for their independence to take effect. The only other high-level contact was Baker's meeting with Foreign Minister Budimir Lončar at the CSCE conference in Paris in November 1990, at which the main topic was the US plea for Yugoslav help in enlisting the support of non-aligned states for its policy on the Gulf, and not Yugoslavia's internal crisis. In 1990, when Prime Minister Ante Marković wanted to visit Washington for talks, he was discouraged from going, and the administration did not issue the desired invitation.[12]

Moreover, US diplomats in Yugoslavia by and large avoided contact with the Serb, Croat and Slovene nationalist leaders, whose impact was growing by the day. Not that the rising nationalist leaders were overlooked; their activities were a cause of increasing concern for a variety of reasons. Relations with the Serb leader, Slobodan Milošević, were strained because of US public criticism of the repression of Albanians in Kosovo, the virulent nationalist rhetoric in which he engaged and his anger at the embassy's close relations with the liberal democratic opponents of his policy. As a result the US ambassador and the Serb leader did not meet for months. The secessionist Croat and Slovene nationalist leaders were shunned because of the extreme nature of their rhetoric, and perhaps also because contact with them could have been seen as building up their stature. Zimmermann met Tudjman for the first time only in May 1990, on the morning of Tudjman's victory in the Croatian elections. Furthermore, US diplomatic representatives did not have any contact with Serb separatist leaders in Croatia.[13]

This passivity was punctuated by spurts of activity stimulated by a number of factors. One was congressional criticism of the Serbs' policies in Kosovo. Led by Senator Robert Dole, Congress took a much stronger stance on this issue than did the administration, culminating in a highly publicised visit by a congressional delegation to the troubled region at the end of August of 1990.[14] Another stimulant was the persistent concern that action by the JNA might be seen by the Soviet military as setting a precedent, encouraging it to act against the republics seeking to secede from the Soviet Union. Other events in Yugoslavia that spurred Washington into action were the escalating violence by Croat and Serb militias and the political confrontation that was paralysing the federal presidency.

These spurts of activity were marked by contradictions and inconsistencies, producing an ambiguous message that the disputants in Yugoslavia interpreted as confirming the effectiveness of their respective strategies. The main difficulty was the simultaneous advocacy of unity and democracy. The problem was that in Yugoslavia, at that moment in history, the two objectives of unity and democracy were contradictory. Democratisation led to formation of nationalist political parties, and attempts to form parties around other ideological-programmatic bases failed. Rallying to nationalist parties encouraged fragmentation and break-up. The preservation of unity would have required repression of nationalist and separatist tendencies. Thus attempts to preserve unity would have been anti-democratic and the promotion of democracy encouraged disintegration.

Besides being contradictory, the twin principles of democracy and unity marked a sharp departure from the previous US policy of unqualified support for the preservation of the Yugoslav state. This change was recognised and considered significant by all the contending factions. The Croats and Slovenes, who perceived themselves as democrats, were encouraged to hope that the US would ultimately support their quest for independence. Milošević and other Serb nationalists, who saw themselves as protectors of Yugoslavia's continued existence and unity, believed that the US was turning against them. Their perception of US policy was reflected in the tension between Milošević and the US embassy, and by the Serbian charge that the US had joined in an anti-Serb conspiracy.[15] While talk of a conspiracy served Milošević's propaganda, it is important to note that it was widely believed, its plausibility bolstered by Germany's support for the Croat and Slovene's aspirations. The events of 1991 were seen as a repetition of the dismemberment of Yugoslavia by Nazi Germany and its allies in 1941, except this time the US was joining Yugoslavia's enemies.

Those who did not believe there was a conspiracy could not ignore the ambiguities that the parallel pursuit of democracy and unity produced. A number of examples will illustrate these ambiguities. The preservation of Yugoslavia's unity was emphasised by executive branch officials when they met Slovene and Croat representatives who were in the US to lobby for their cause, but that message was weakened by the sympathy for their cause encountered among influential members of Congress, most importantly from Senator Dole. According to Zimmermann, Congressional support for the Albanian, Croatian and Slovenian claims 'often contributed to confusing American policy rather than clarifying it'; more than that, 'Congress made the implementation of a consistent strategy toward Yugoslavia nearly impossible'.[16]

The US promotion of democratisation in Yugoslavia was further demonstrated by its repeated criticisms of repression in Kosovo, and the imposition of economic sanctions to try to influence Yugoslav policies on this issue. In November 1990, despite the administration's objections, Congress passed the 'Nickles Amendment' to the Foreign Aid Bill, which barred US loans and credits to Yugoslavia unless directed to a republic 'which has held fair and free elections and which is not engaged in systematic abuse of human rights'. The sanctions were to take effect in six months, unless the president decided that aid needed to be continued.[17]

The imposition of sanctions was consistent with the policy of making economic assistance to Eastern Europe conditional on reforms and respect for human rights. Yet, as already mentioned, in the Yugoslav case it underlined the change in US attitude: the US no longer regarded the stability and integrity of Yugoslavia as an important US interest. Moreover in the context of the times the sanctions may have been interpreted by some Croat and Slovene nationalists as indicating a weakening of support for Prime Minister Marković, who was pursuing reforms while striving to preserve the unity of the country, and who had hitherto been supported by the West. The wording of the amendment, and the assertion by some officials that assistance would be considered on a case-by-case basis, apparently encouraged some Croat and Slovene leaders to believe that the seceding republics might be granted *de facto* recognition. This hope was bolstered by the Croat-American lobby which apparently advised Zagreb that the administration's support for Yugoslav unity would not endure.[18] Parallel to pressures for democratisation, the Administration continued to express its support for preserving Yugoslavia's unity. However a joint Croat–Slovene announcement in February that both intended to secede unless Yugoslavia became a 'community of sovereign republics' (which meant a break-up by another name) prompted the administration to reiterate its support for unity.[19]

This support however, was hedged, by warnings against enforcing it. These warnings were directed mainly at the JNA, an important institution that was committed to preserving the country's unity, although it was increasingly influenced by Serbian nationalism. As well as fearing that action by the JNA to prevent Croatia and Slovenia from seceding might escalate into a major civil war, Washington was concerned that such action might strengthen the position of some of Gorbachev's opponents in Moscow who favoured action by the Soviet army to halt the dissolution of the Soviet Union. Thus as early as 10 December, the US ambassador was dispatched to meet the Yugoslav minister of defence, General Veljko Kadijević, to urge that the army avoid involvement in domestic politics. Similar admonitions and warnings were conveyed both privately and publicly by Zimmermann to Kadijević in January, when it appeared that the JNA might try to prevent Croatia from smuggling arms and establishing its own armed force, in violation of Yugoslav laws. A secret visit in March by Kadijević to the Soviet Union to seek Soviet Army support for his intended action further stimulated concern about the possible impact of JNA behaviour on developments in the

Soviet Union, prompting Washington to send another warning to Kadijević.[20]

On 6 May, the administration announced that because of continued abuse of human rights it was cutting off financial assistance to Yugoslavia, as required by the Nickels Amendment of November 1990. By then the situation had deteriorated further. Violent clashes between Serbs and Croats increased, accompanied by an escalation of threatening rhetoric. Furthermore a new political problem emerged when the Serbian representative in the eight-member collective presidency of the federation, along with his allies, prevented the Croat representative, Stipe Mesić, from assuming the post of president, to which he was entitled according to normal practice and the rules under which the presidency operated.

Recognising the uselessness of sanctions against a federal government that was rapidly losing its capacity to act, two weeks after imposing the sanctions the administration reversed its position. On 20 May, President Bush phoned Marković, and informed him that aid would be resumed, and that the US would continue to support the existence of a unified Yugoslav state.

The contradictions of US policy were also trumpeted in a lengthy policy statement issued by the State Department spokesperson, Margaret Tutwiler: 'United States policy toward Yugoslavia is based on support for the interrelated objectives of democracy, dialogue, human rights, market reform, and unity', but the US would oppose the 'use of force or intimidation to settle political differences, change external or internal borders, block democratic change or impose a non-democratic unity'. According to the statement, in this case 'unity' referred to 'the territorial integrity of Yugoslavia within its present borders' and the US 'would not encourage or reward secession'. But it added that 'unity, to be preserved, must be put on a new, democratic, mutually agreed basis'. The statement also expressed support for the Croat leader Mesić's assumption of the presidency of Yugoslavia (blocked by the Serbs), criticised the leadership of the Serbian Republic for the way it conducted elections in Serbia and for violating the human rights of the Albanian population in Kosovo, and expressed 'some concern' about human rights violations in Croatia.[21]

While the principles embodied in the statement were admirable, their policy implications were equivocal. Opposition to the use of force or intimidation to change borders or 'impose a non-democratic unity' was not a sufficiently clear expression of support for unity to deter Croatia and Slovenia from proceeding with their preparations to secede and become independent at the end of June. Indeed, given the criticism of Serbian policies included in the statement, it is possible that the Croat and Slovene leaders interpreted the statement to mean that the US would oppose the use of force aimed at preventing them from seizing independence.

As the various Yugoslav factions were seemingly preparing to act as they had proclaimed they would, regardless of the US statement, the US embarked on a last-minute effort to prevent the war. On 21 June, four days before Croatian and Slovenian independence was scheduled to take effect, Secretary of State James Baker went to Belgrade to talk to Yugoslav leaders. He travelled directly from the Conference on Security and Cooperation in Europe (CSCE, now OSCE) meeting in Berlin, where Yugoslavia had been discussed. Baker held nine meetings during his visit. He met first with the federal prime minister and the foreign minister, then with the presidents of the six republics and an Albanian leader from Kosovo, concluding his visit with another meeting with the prime minister. The meetings with the leaders of the republics were occasions on which the visitor and the host lectured each other, anxious to recite their points before their time expired.[22]

The main purpose of the visit appears to have been to delay the Slovene and Croat assertions of independence, and thus prevent the imminent outbreak of war. A major effort was made to persuade the Slovene leader, Milan Kučan, to postpone the proclamation of Slovenia's independence, in the expectation that if Slovenia put off taking this step, Croatia would follow suit. Baker thought that Kučan had acceded to his request for Slovenia to confine its move to a declaratory level and refrain from seizing the border posts, which were under federal control, and was reportedly surprised and disappointed when Kučan denied that he had made such a promise.[23]

It has been claimed that Milošević misinterpreted Baker's reference to unity and democracy and took it as a 'green light' for the use of force to prevent a break-up.[24] This is highly unlikely. The background to the visit was a sharply deteriorating Serbia–US relationship, with the US rebuking the Serb leadership for violating the human rights of Albanians in Kosovo, and charging that Serbia was the main obstacle to a peaceful resolution of the crisis. The meeting itself was stormy and contentious, with Baker repeating US criticisms of Serbian policies and accusing Milošević of being the main source of the crisis. Moreover Baker conveyed a warning to the military leadership, through the federal prime minister, not to use force. He is reported to have said to Marković, 'If you force us to choose between unity and democracy, we will always choose democracy.'[25]

The US efforts proved ineffective. The assertion of opposition both to secession and to the enforcement of unity sounded like an equivocation, not a statement of policy. Hence it is not surprising that the Slovenes and Croats were not deterred from proclaiming independence, and the JNA from trying to quash it by force.

European ambiguities

West European policies towards the deepening crisis in Yugoslavia stemmed in part from common concerns about security and stability in Europe. Some were particularly concerned because of their geographical proximity. Germany, Italy and Austria (the latter not yet a member of the EC) feared that their well-being would be affected if war erupted and triggered an outpouring of refugees.

The EC member countries were motivated to act not only by their concern about the impact of a war in Yugoslavia, but also by their ambition to strengthen the EC's capacity for collective action on foreign and security policy. They hoped that joint action through the EC would provide an impetus for the launching of the new European institutions. Replacing the loose mechanism of European political cooperation with a better coordinated common foreign and security policy was a major item on the EC agenda at that time.

They were also aware of the differences between their attitudes towards the Yugoslav problem, and each government expected to utilise the common institutions to constrain the others from pursuing what it regarded as wrong-headed policies. Britain and France wanted to constrain Germany, partly because they were apprehensive about the course that the reunified Germany might pursue, but also because they saw Germany's involvement in Yugoslavia as tactless, as the perfect example of a bull in a china shop. Germany, on the other hand, considered Britain and France as remote and lacking sufficient understanding of Balkan nationalist movements.

Their divergent attitudes stemmed largely from cultural–historical preconceptions in their respective societies. German and Austrian officials were socialised in versions of history that put much of the blame for Balkan instability during the past 100 years, as well as the First World War (and its disastrous consequences for the Austrian and German Empires), on Serb nationalism. The establishment of Yugoslavia in 1918 was closely associated with unjust peace settlements imposed on Austria and Germany at the end of that war. Nor did Italian historical accounts paint a favourable picture of the establishment of Yugoslavia. Territorial conflicts with Yugoslavia after both world wars had contributed to an unfavourable image of that country in Italian eyes.

These historical–cultural preconceptions were reenforced by the political and ideological climate prevailing at the time (1989–91). Engrossed with the process of reunification, which they perceived as an act of self-determination, some German political groups accepted the Croat and Slovene argument that these two nations' desire to secede from Yugoslavia was also an act of self-determination, no less justified than the unification of the two German states. Support for Slovene and Croat aspirations was particularly strong among sections of the Catholic public and in parts of the media, especially the *Frankfurter Allgemeine Zeitung*. Support was also strong among left-leaning groups that were critical of human rights violations by Serbian authorities in Kosovo. The presence of a large number of *gastarbeiter* Croats in Germany helped to build sympathy for the Croats' national aspirations.[26]

In Britain and France the attitude was very different, favouring the preservation of Yugoslavia. Yugoslavia was remembered as a valiant ally in the Second World War, and Serbia as an ally in the first. Indicative of the French attitude was the official government statement welcoming Prime Minister Marković's visit to Paris on 23 May 1991. It was laced with a pro-unity historical allusion, tracing the friendship between the two nations to 'the Napoleonic era and the creation of the Illyrian provinces' – suggesting perhaps a link between the legacy of the French administration, and the nineteenth-century expressions of southern Slav solidarity known as the 'Illyrian Movement'. The statement further stated that it was up to the Yugoslavs alone, through a process of a political dialogue 'shielded from internal provocations and external interventions, to determine the future of their state. It is this unitary state ... that Europe awaits as a partner'.[27] The reference to 'external interventions', though ambiguous, was assumed to be directed at German and Austrian supporters of Croat and Slovene self-determination.

Wishing to present a common stance, the member states were able to agree to a platform expressing generally accepted international norms. They called for the preservation of Yugoslavia's integrity, and supported democratisation, constitutional reforms and respect for human rights.

These general principles did not convey to the disputing Yugoslav parties a clear sense of how the EC would react in certain contingencies. The ambiguity of the EC's stance was reinforced by discrepancies between the collective European policies emanating from the European institutions, and the policies of individual states conveyed in bilateral contacts.

Nevertheless a gradual shift in emphasis is discernible. In 1990 and early 1991 EC statements strongly emphasised the preservation of Yugoslavia's integrity, but in the spring and early summer of 1991 they placed increasing emphasis on political and constitutional changes being arrived at by negotiation and mutual agreement, and calls for the preservation of Yugoslavia's unity became less frequent.

The evolution of the EC's policy can be traced through the wording of its statements and the diplomatic activity pursued on its behalf. A declaration by the EEC–Yugoslavia Cooperation Council, meeting in Brussels on 18 December 1990, welcomed 'the progress Yugoslavia has made ... towards a pluralist, Parliamentary democracy ... and towards a market economy'. It expressed the wish that these objectives be pursued with 'full respect for human rights and the preservation of the unity and territorial integrity of Yugoslavia'. It further expressed 'its confidence that the continuation of this process' would lead to negotiations on an association agreement between the EC and Yugoslavia.[28]

The date of this statement is significant – it was issued four days prior to the Slovenian referendum on secession from Yugoslavia. If one of the objectives of the statement was to persuade Slovenes to reject secession, it was a dismal failure. Over 90 per cent of Slovenian voters chose independence, mandating that unless agreement to transform Yugoslavia into a loose confederation was reached within six months, Slovenia would declare its independence.

As tension in Yugoslavia continued to mount the EC foreign ministers, at their meeting on 4 February 1991, called on the Yugoslav authorities to maintain the unity and territorial integrity of the country, and to avoid the use of force. They also said that the EC was following the process 'leading Yugoslavian society towards a democratic arrangement, satisfactory to the whole of Yugoslavia', and expressed their hope that the discussions within the country would lead to a 'new Yugoslavia on the bases of freedom and democracy'.[29]

Doubts about the EC's support for the unity of Yugoslavia were raised, however, when EC officials and representatives of the member states began to confer with representatives of the republics. For example European Commissioner Abel Matutes met in February with the Slovene Prime Minister Alojz Peterle, and German Foreign Minister Hans-Dietrich Genscher met in March with Slovene President Milan Kučan and Foreign Minister Dimitrij Rupel.[30]

During a visit to Belgrade on 4 April the Troika – the current president of the Council of Ministers (Luxembourg's Foreign Minister Jacques Poos), his predecessor (Italian Foreign Minister Gianni De Michelis) and his successor (Dutch Foreign Minister Hans van den Broek) – tried to allay these doubts and reaffirm the EC's support for preservation of the country's unity. The Troika made their point by meeting only federal officials and refraining from direct contact with leaders of the republics.[31]

Throughout this period the twin conditions of maintenance of unity and the introduction of democratic reforms were emphasised as preconditions for an EC–Yugoslavia association agreement. But in May this position was modified. When EC representatives Jacques Santer and Jacques Delors visited Belgrade they met not only federal officials but also the presidents of the republics. Moreover, the EC no longer explicitly listed the preservation of Yugoslavia's unity among the preconditions for opening negotiations on association, though this was implicit in the longer and more detailed list of preconditions that was now put forth: respect for the constitution, human rights and minorities, negotiations for new structures, and continued economic reforms. Similar conditions were reiterated in early June at a meeting of the EC foreign ministers in Dresden, and in a letter from Santer to Marković.[32]

As tensions and violent incidents in Yugoslavia increased, and as the military authorities threatened to intervene against the secessionists, the EC became more emphatic in stating its opposition to the use of force. Balancing this position the EC also expressed its opposition to secession by unilateral acts, and reiterated its support for a mutually agreed solution to the crisis. A final attempt to deter secession by unilateral acts was made on 23 June, two days before Croatia and Slovenia proclaimed their independence, with the EC foreign ministers agreeing not to acknowledge unilateral statements of independence, and declaring that they would refuse any contact with the secessionists. The chairman of the Council of Ministers, Jacques Poos, qualified these statements by adding that 'the Twelve [EC members at the time] do not state that they will never recognise a Yugoslavian Republic wanting to leave the federation, but that this decision "must be the result of negotiation and internal agreement".'[33]

The Yugoslav factions closely followed the changing nuances of the EC statements and interpreted them as reflecting internal disagreements over the EC's policy towards Yugoslavia. Vasil Tupurkovski, Macedonia's representative in the Yugoslav presidency, who indefatigably tried to reconcile the antagonistic factions, warned Santer and Delors that Europe was sending mixed signals to the different parties, and that this was resulting in divergent reactions and exacerbating the crisis.[34] The Yugoslav parties' awareness of the divisions among the EC members was sharpened by actions and statements by the European Parliament and member governments. The strongest support for the preservation of Yugoslav unity came from French Prime Minister Edith Cresson, who proclaimed on 23 May, as mentioned already, that 'Yugoslavia cannot be part of Europe unless she remains united'.[35] The opposite point of view was reflected in a resolution adopted by the European Parliament on 13 March, accepting 'that the constituent republics and autonomous provinces of Yugoslavia must have the right freely to determine their own future'.[36] More significant were public signals from Germany. In a letter in February to Prime Minister Marković, Chancellor Kohl expressed concern about the crisis and called for political dialogue and respect for human rights, but made no mention of the need to preserve Yugoslavia's unity.[37] In May, Norbert Gansell, a prominent member of the main parliamentary opposition party, the Social-Democratic Party (SPD), proposed that the party call on the EC to change its policy, suggesting support for Croatian and Slovene independence and calling on Croatia to grant autonomy to the Serbian minority.[38] Croat leaders were particularly encouraged by the motion supporting their cause adopted at the foreign affairs committee meeting of a governing coalition member party, the Christian-Social Union (CSU), on 1 June, and by the warm reception accorded at the end of May to visiting President Franjo Tudjman by the Italian president and prime minister, as well as the pope.[39] They were also encouraged by Gianni De Michelis, the Italian foreign minister and member of the EC Troika, who sent them a message in the middle of June contradicting the formal EC calls for the preservation of unity and saying that the EC would provide assistance and open its doors to a 'changed Yugoslavia of sovereign republics'.[40]

Given these divergent voices, the EC's efforts to prevent the war were bound to fail. Being aware of the complexities of multilateral decision-making within the EC, the various Yugoslav parties doubted the ability of the EC to honour its promise to reward the preservation of unity with financial aid.[41] More than that, confident of German support and cognisant of Germany's weight within the EC, Croat and Slovene leaders could not believe that the EC would carry out its threat to sever contact with them if they proclaimed independence.

Multiple failures

The most obvious reason for the failure of the West's efforts to prevent the war were the equivocations of its diplomacy. As already noted above, proclaiming support for both democracy and unity was confusing because in the circumstances prevailing in Yugoslavia in 1990–91 the two principles were contradictory. The shifts in US policy, alternating between activity and passivity, and the different attitudes conveyed by the administration and Congress, combined to suggest ambiguity rather than resolve. The discrepancies between the position adopted by the EC and what the Yugoslav parties heard from the member states reenforced the image of equivocation. The EC's failure to develop an effective common policy did not stem from weaknesses particular to the EC. Such weaknesses are inherent in intergovernmental organisations whose attempts to pursue a common policy towards a conflict are often frustrated by bilateral interactions between the members of the organisation and the parties concerned.

Besides being undermined by equivocation, the efforts to prevent the war were handicapped by their reliance on economic induce-ments. Economic inducements were chosen because they were easier to apply than military measures. Moreover the West might have been misled by the economic justifications that Croat and Slovene leaders cited in support of their quest for independence. Croat and Slovene nationalists claimed that their countries needed to be independent in order to rid themselves of economic exploitation by Serbia, and because they wished to build market economies that would facilitate their admission to the EC.[42] Furthermore the main item on the agenda in Western dealings with Yugoslavia during the previous few years had been the country's economic problems.

But the tactic of economic inducements was not well attuned to the psychology of the Yugoslav actors at that time. In 1990 and 1991 Yugoslavs were dominated by fear for their physical safety on account of being members of one or other ethnic group, by their desire for national autonomy (not to be subject to rule by another nation) and by an ambition to set right real or imaginary wrongs inflicted on their nation in recent history. The economic rewards and punishments proffered by the international community were unsuited to the cir-cumstances, and had little if any impact on the calculations and behaviour of the Yugoslav actors.

In addition Western diplomacy was hampered by inopportune timing. It is easier to influence leaders to change their policies before they become too deeply committed to them, than after they have staked their reputation on the pursuit of such policies. In the autumn of 1990, when intensive efforts to prevent the war began, the leaders of the contending political movements were already committed to courses of action that were bound to lead to violent confrontation. Their respective commitments were especially firm because they had risen to prominence on the nationalist platform that they had helped to formulate and articulate. Their political identity, the *raison d'être* of their political movements, were justified by the nationalist goals they espoused.

Thus the effort to prevent the war was launched at a highly inaus-picious moment. The effort had not started early enough, before the adversaries became too deeply committed to their goals, nor had it come at a moment of a hurting stalemate, when the adversaries might have been motivated to rethink their policies and be amenable to outside influence. Worse than that, they started at a time when each party had high expectations that it would prevail. Each believed in the justice of its cause, that its goals were consistent with international norms and with the interests of at least some of the major powers.

Those who wanted to preserve Yugoslavia, Serbs as well as members of other nations, communists as well as non-communists, believed that international law and norms were on their side. They viewed the dispute with the advocates of Croat and Slovene independence as falling within the internal jurisdiction of the state, and believed that the federal government was entitled to use force to prevent secession. They trusted the ability of the army to do so. If the federal government failed to act, or if Croat and Slovene independence could not be prevented, they expected that most of the Serb-populated areas of Croatia would remain within Yugoslavia. If self-determination was to decide the future of Yugoslavia, then it should apply to the Serbs no less than to the Croats and Slovenes (but not to the Albanians, a logic that was hard to follow). They expected that their military power would secure the realisation of such an outcome. They were aware that the international climate was not supportive, but they expected that attitudes in the West would change in their favour once they demonstrated their resolve, and once the US, Britain and France realised that Croat and Slovene separatism was being encouraged by Germany, just as it had been in 1941, and was aimed at expanding Germany's political and economic influence.

The Croats and Slovenes, together with the advocates of independence in Macedonia, also believed that their objectives were supported by international norms. Self-determination was a recognised right. The collapse of communism would make it impossible for the federal government – installed by the defunct Communist Party – to sustain itself. Free elections would open the way to self-determination. Although during the Cold War the West had had an interest in the continued existence of Yugoslavia, the end of the Cold War was believed to have brought a change in the West's attitude. Supportive statements by important political groups in Germany, Austria and Italy, and by the European Parliament and members of the US Congress were seen as indicative of this change in attitude, which would help transform the policies of Western governments. The West was becoming aware that unity could be sustained only through the suppression of human rights and democratic freedom, and therefore would not allow the Serbs to use force to prevent Croatia and Slovenia from achieving independence.[43]

To prevent the war the Western intervenors should have quashed the parties' hopes and reversed their expectations. But the West's equivocation undermined its efforts. Moreover, as already mentioned, Western governments were disinclined to resort to military force. It is only on rare occasions that political leaders feel strongly enough about an impending war in another country to call on their people to make sacrifices in order to prevent such a war, as people are more likely to accept the need for sacrifices when the events in question pose a direct threat to their own society. But efforts to thwart such dangers are not called preventive diplomacy; they address national defence. Preventive diplomacy is practiced in situations that pose no threat to national security, or only a remote and indirect one. It addresses situations in which *other* people *may* be threatened by war. It is usually difficult, if not impossible, for nations to commit themselves to making the necessary sacrifices to prevent such a war from erupting. But without such a commitment, their diplomacy may be to no avail.

It might cause some surprise that the Western intervenors did not try to mediate among the Yugoslav parties. An opportunity to mediate presented itself in the negotiations on constitutional reform conducted among the republics' leaders. But the Western governments held back from any significant involvement in these talks, and indeed the EC disclaimed on several occasions that it was making any attempt to intervene in the constitutional debate or mediate in the conflict. It was only on 23 June, two days before Croatia and Slovenia proclaimed their independence, that the EC offered to help the federal government and the republics to draw up a new constitution.[44]

The West avoided mediation because such involvement would have been interpreted by the parties as implicit acceptance of the Croatian and Slovenian republics' desire to be treated as sovereign states, equal in status to the federal government of Yugoslavia. The Croat and Slovene leaders had in fact indicated their interest in mediation by the EC, and one of their principal supporters, Austrian Foreign Minister Alois Mock, advocated it. But the federal government, the Serb leadership and the military opposed it.[45]

In these circumstances, any attempt to mediate between the parties would have exposed the EC to the criticism that it was violating the normative and legal injunction against interference in the internal affairs of a sovereign state. To be sure, the EC was engaged for months in an effort to influence the internal politics of Yugoslavia. But it did so indirectly, from a distance. Mediation would have required intensive involvement in the political manoeuvring inside Yugoslavia. The EC and the US were reluctant to become involved in this way. Mediation would have drawn the intervenors into much deeper participation in Yugoslavia's internal politics, leading them into commitments they were not prepared to assume. After the war erupted, this attitude began to change.

3
The Entry of Mediators

Slovenia and Croatia proclaimed themselves independent sovereign states on 25 June 1991. Two days later, on 27 June, the federal government ordered the JNA (Yugoslav National Army) to restore federal authority over the border and customs control posts in Slovenia, which had been taken over by the Slovenian government. This operation quickly escalated into a war between the JNA and Slovenian forces.

When the fighting in Slovenia erupted on 27 June, the European Council happened to be meeting in Luxembourg, and immediately decided to dispatch the Troika to Yugoslavia.[1] The timing of this initiative was obviously not influenced by a consideration that the moment was ripe for mediation. It was determined by the member states' belief that they could not ignore the outbreak of fighting and had to react to it. What better way for states with divergent sympathies to react than to protect their solidarity by assuming the role of peacemaker?

The Troika's visit was significant because it transformed the EC's role from a stand-off dissuader to an intrusive mediator. Before the Slovene and Croat proclamations of independence and the outbreak of war, external third parties had tried to influence developments from the outside, advising the federal institutions of the presidency and the government, and to a lesser extent the leaders of the republics as well, on how they ought to behave in order to prevent violence and war. Having failed to dissuade or deter the various Yugoslav actors from actions that they had correctly foreseen as leading to war, they now turned to mediation. As mediators, they engaged in negotiations with the disputants about possible compromises between the disputants' respective positions. The mediators also bargained with the disputants, promising rewards or threatening punishment, in an effort to persuade them to accept a compromise.

The EC's assumption of the mediator's role is significant for a number of reasons. First, it is significant that the Western powers chose to mediate through the EC, due in part to its presumed ability to influence the behaviour of the Yugoslav parties thanks to its economic leverage. Another, perhaps more weighty reason for the choice was the EC states' desire to avail themselves of the opportunity to assert their role in managing the continent's security problems, complemented by the US reluctance to become involved and its distrust of the UN and the OSCE. Second, the EC's role is significant because it helped to prevent unilateral intervention by member states, and helped to keep their divergent attitudes towards the Yugoslav problem from erupting into a quarrel that might harm the EC. Third, it is significant for its impact on the future of Yugoslavia. The mediator's treatment of the Croatian and Slovenian governments as equal in standing to the federal authorities facilitated the seceding republics' achievement of international recognition and accelerated the disintegration of the Yugoslav state.

This chapter first discusses the Western powers' preference for the EC as the vehicle of intervention. Next it describes the entry of an additional mediator – the UN. It then explains the Yugoslavs' acceptance of external mediation and concludes with a few comments on the impact of the mediation.

The EC becomes principal mediator

For three months – from 27 June to mid October, when the UN sent a representative to the region – the EC was the sole acknowledged mediator in the conflict. Although the EC's assumption of the mediator's role can be seen as a logical extension of the role it had been playing since the autumn of 1990, the channelling of mediation through the EC had not been agreed beforehand.

The interested governments had considered other mediation vehicles. For the time being UN involvement had been ruled out. Croatia and Slovenia had called for a meeting of the UN Security Council soon after the outbreak of fighting, Austria had been an early advocate of UN involvement, and the possibility of sending a UN peacekeeping force to Yugoslavia had been discussed at the G-7 meeting[2] in July. But the Yugoslav federal government had opposed UN involvement on the ground that the issue was an internal matter and therefore outside UN jurisdiction. This had also been the view of the Soviet Union and China, which did not want to create a precedent for international intervention in their internal problems. The non-aligned states had taken a similar position. The secretary-general, Javier Pérez de Cuéllar had been of the opinion that there was no ground for a Security Council meeting because the issue was an internal Yugoslav matter.[3] Finally, the US had opposed referring the matter to the Security Council. According to Secretary of State James Baker, the US's 'greatest problem with involving the United Nations was that it would broaden the number of actors involved. The EC was having its own problems maintaining a coherent policy; adding the United Nations to the mix would only complicate matters.'[4] No less important had been the unwillingness to grant the Soviet Union a role in the crisis.

Some of the interested governments had initially preferred the Conference for Security and Cooperation in Europe (CSCE) over the EC. As the Cold War was winding down, the members of the CSCE had been engaged in transforming it from a forum for managing East–West tensions into a pan-European security organisation. The CSCE had been much less active in mediating among the disputing parties in Yugoslavia than the EC; its role had been limited mainly to monitoring conditions in the area. An initial attempt to utilise it for mediation was made at the CSCE foreign ministers meeting in Berlin on 19 June. Only after very difficult negotiations were the foreign ministers there able to agree on a statement expressing support for Yugoslavia's territorial integrity, and calling for reforms and a peaceful resolution of the crisis.

Once the fighting had begun the prime movers for utilising the CSCE had been Austria and Germany. Foreign Minister Hans-Dietrich Genscher had proposed on 27 June that the CSCE emergency mechanism be activated. Austria, which was not yet a member of the EC, had also called on 27 and 28 June for action through two newly created CSCE mechanisms – the Crisis Prevention Center in Vienna and the Committee of Senior Officials in Prague. After some debate, these two bodies had produced formal statements on 1 and 3 July respectively.[5]

There had been a number of reasons for Germany's initial preference for the CSCE. One had been that Germany was serving as
current chair of the CSCE, and hoped to be able to steer the organisation's actions in the direction that German policy makers deemed
desirable. It appears that Genscher had been somewhat uneasy about
the EC and 'worried that historically rooted "old thinking"' among
some of Germany's partners there 'might blind them as to the true
responsibility for what was happening in Yugoslavia'.[6] In addition,
Genscher had wanted the US to be actively involved. Since the US
was a member of the CSCE, but not the EC, the former had appeared
an appropriate vehicle for international action. Furthermore the
Soviet Union had preferred the CSCE, of which it was a member,
and with Soviet troops not having yet completed their withdrawal
from East Germany the German government was being careful to
avoid antagonising the Soviets. But at the urging of other members
of the EC and the US, Germany had quickly joined those in favour of
working through the EC.

It is noteworthy that despite the CSCE members' efforts to turn the
organisation from a forum for managing Cold War tensions into a
continent-wide security organisation, the West had chosen to pursue
its diplomacy through the EC, which had no formal security functions.[7] There had been several reasons for the US and West Europeans' rejection of the CSCE. One had been its lack of effective
organisational machinery. Its decision-making process was cumbersome, requiring the consensus of 34 members (decisions could be
taken without the consent of the 35th, the one directly involved).
Even so the participation of Yugoslavia and the Soviet Union in the
organisation had been seen as a potential impediment to effective
action. An indication of the obstacles likely to be encountered had
been provided by the refusal of the Yugoslav federal government to
invite the 'Good Offices Mission' that the CSCE had proposed to send
to Yugoslavia.[8] Furthermore the CSCE had lacked economic or military resources that might be utilised to wield influence.

The EC, in contrast, had appeared to possess the machinery and
mechanisms for joint action. It had extensive experience in dealing
with Yugoslavia, and maintained many contacts at both the political
and the bureaucratic level. Its decision-making process, however
complicated, was far more effective than that of the CSCE. Finally,
the members had been eager to utilise the opportunity to develop

mechanisms for a joint foreign policy and assert the international role of a more cohesive European Union, due to be launched with the signature of the Maastricht Treaty in December. To avoid antagonising the Soviet Union and other European states that were not members of the EC, and implying that the CSCE might serve as a regional arrangement for dealing with international peace and security, the West had agreed to define the EC's activities with respect to Yugoslavia as being conducted under CSCE auspices.

The US had played an active part in persuading the European governments to address the crisis through the EC. One reason was, that being pessimistic about the prospect of stopping the fighting, the US had preferred the EC, of which it was not a member, to the CSCE, in which by virtue of its membership it could not avoid assuming a major role. In addition, some US officials had believed that 'hooking' the EC onto the Yugoslav problem would teach its members to moderate their ambitions. The US had been especially irritated by the Europeans' efforts to add to the EC's range of activities a defence and security dimension, thus reducing Europe's dependence on the US. According to former Secretary of State James Baker, this mood had reflected 'an undercurrent in Washington, often felt but seldom spoken, that it was time to make the Europeans step up to the plate and show that they could act as a unified power.'[9]

Since mediation in internal conflicts constitutes an infringement of sovereignty and weakens the government's position relative to that of its opponents, it might have been assumed that Yugoslavia would have rejected the EC's intervention. Yugoslavia's acceptance of EC mediation is therefore puzzling.

An explanation of the Yugoslav responses to the mediation initiatives must begin by noting that the parties in question cannot be adequately described as 'government' and 'secessionists'. Nor can their responses be dichotomised as 'acceptance' and 'rejection'. The central authority of the Yugoslav state was fragmented, and so were its opponents. Their attitudes were complex and changing, depending very much on the situation and on who the proposed mediator was. The principal criterion determining their preference was their expectation of how a particular mediator might affect their prospects.

The central authority consisted of three main actors: the presidency, the cabinet ('the federal executive council') and the military establishment. The presidency was for the most part divided, with

the Croatian and Slovenian representatives usually welcoming mediation, the Serb and Montenegrin usually opposing it and the others
displaying less consistent attitudes. The cabinet generally accepted
the EC's and CSCE's initiatives. Accordingly, in deference to the EC's
insistence on playing a key role, the cabinet opposed UN involvement until September, when at the urging of the EC the foreign
minister, Budimir Lončar, appealed to the UN. The military establishment was the most coherent and consistent in its opposition to
external intervention including mediation, as it expected that this
would restrict its freedom of action.

The Croat and Slovene leaderships generally favoured external
involvement. Despite the EC's prior public support for the preservation of Yugoslavia, the Croats and Slovenes welcomed its intervention, expecting that by assuming the role of mediator the EC would
have to tone down its support for unity. Moreover they expected that
the internationalisation of the conflict would help constrain the
JNA's freedom of action, and thus improve their chance of achieving
independence. They also hoped that cooperation with the EC would
help win the support of European governments and public opinion
for their cause. But certain responses varied. The Slovenes refused to
attend the first meeting with the EC Troika on 28 June, ostensibly
because it was held in Belgrade, but more importantly because the
mediators wanted them to suspend for three months the independence they had just proclaimed. The Croats had initially favoured UN
involvement, but in deference to the EC they toned down their calls
for UN intervention and channelled their diplomacy through the EC.
In tandem with the EC they changed their stance again in September,
calling for UN involvement.

The Serbs, although generally opposed to external involvement,
preferred the UN to the EC. They hoped that Germany's influence
would not be felt in the Security Council, and expected the Soviet
Union (later Russia) to show sympathy for their cause. Later they
developed an interest in UN peacekeeping, hoping that UN forces
would help to safeguard their hold over the areas that they controlled
in Croatia.[10]

Overall the important point to note is the lack of any significant
obstacle to external mediation. The Yugoslav parties were divided
over how to respond, and determined their position neither on
grounds of principle, nor on the mediators' chance of helping to

achieve an agreed settlement, but according to how they expected a particular intervention to affect their cause. Even when they expected the effect to be negative, they often muted their objections because they feared that outright opposition would be more harmful than the pretence of acceptance. The mediators were almost always able to impose themselves on the parties, but as we shall see, they were frequently unable to elicit the cooperation that effective mediation required.

Enter the UN

On 25 September, three months after the war had started, the UN was activated as an additional instrument for international involvement. The UN was brought into the Yugoslav conflict not because the interested governments wanted its assistance in mediation, but for a variety of other reasons.

The common basis for the agreement by France, Germany and other EC governments to place the Yugoslav conflict on the Security Council's agenda was the perception that a peacekeeping force was necessary to ensure the observance of a ceasefire in Croatia. The EC at first tried to organise such a force under the auspices of the Western European Union (WEU), but having failed in this attempt the UN was a logical fallback. The UN would legitimise the dispatch of troops, it had the experience of organising such action and it was likely to spread the burden among a wider circle of states. Moreover the Soviet Union was on the verge of collapse and was in no position to oppose the West and veto the matter. France was especially insistent on the need for Security Council involvement, and finally won Germany's consent during President Mitterrand's meeting with Chancellor Kohl in Bonn on 19 September. A formal decision by the EC Council of Ministers was taken on the same day.[11]

For France, the involvement of the Security Council was also a means to limit Germany's influence and increase its own. Germany was using its weight in the EC to promote policies that favoured Croatia and Slovenia and was pressing its European partners to recognise the two states. By shifting the locus of collective efforts to the Security Council, where France was a member and Germany was not, France's influence on policy would increase and Germany's would diminish somewhat.

Despite the consensus on the need for a peacekeeping force, enthusiasm for engaging the UN was not universal. While going along with its European allies, the US was apparently not eager for UN involvement, perhaps in part because it was inevitable that this would impose on the US greater political responsibilities and financial burdens.

Potentially more damaging to the EC's plan for UN involvement were the continued objections by China, India and a few other states. Concerned that UN involvement in the Yugoslav conflict might serve as a precedent, they insisted on strict adherence to the UN charter's prohibition on intervention in the internal affairs of states (Article 2, Section 7).

To neutralise these objections, at the last moment the Western powers persuaded Foreign Minister Lončar formally to notify the president of the Security Council that Yugoslavia would welcome the convening of the Council. At a carefully staged session on 25 September, presided over by French Foreign Minister Roland Dumas, Lončar said that the concern of the Council was fully justified, and that 'the Yugoslav crisis threatens peace and security on a large scale'. He appealed for UN assistance with the EC's efforts to resolve the Yugoslav disputes, and called for an embargo on the delivery of military equipment to all parties in Yugoslavia. The Council meeting was obviously well prepared in advance, and ended with unanimous adoption of a resolution expressing support for the European efforts, calling on the parties to cooperate and abide by the ceasefire agreements they had signed, and imposing an embargo on all deliveries of weapons and military equipment to Yugoslavia.[12]

Two weeks later the secretary-general appointed Cyrus Vance, the former US secretary of state, as his special representative and asked him to travel to Yugoslavia for consultations with the parties. Starting with this first mission by Vance, the UN joined the EC in the mediation process.

The impact of mediation

The mediators affected the situation in two ways: by influencing the course and outcome of specific negotiations (this is discussed in detail in the following chapters), and by their less widely recognised contribution to the dissolution of Yugoslavia.[13]

Mediation of an internal conflict within a state usually works to the detriment of the government and in favour of its opponents. By negotiating with the government's opponents the mediators implicitly raise the opponents' status to equality with that of the government. The mediator's intervention implies that the opponents' challenge to the government's authority is recognised as legitimate. It implies that the opponents are no longer required to accept the government's interpretation of laws and are no longer subject to the government's authority. It acknowledges that the opponents are entitled to negotiate with the government as equals.

In the Yugoslav conflict it elevated the status of the Slovene and Croat republican governments from that of rebels against the legitimate state authority to one of equality with the federal government. The mediation also internationalised the conflict, establishing the Croat and Slovene republics as parties whose interests deserved to be protected by the international community. By accepting external mediation the federal authorities relinquished their right to impose law and order, and implicitly agreed that their opponents, who challenged the government's legitimacy, be accorded equal status in the dispute. The mediation process gradually led to Slovenia, Croatia and other republics being granted recognition as sovereign states, and accordingly to the dissolution of Yugoslavia.

This should not be interpreted as suggesting that the intervention of the mediators caused Yugoslavia to disintegrate. Most probably the country would have broken apart anyway. The mediators' contribution was to accelerate the process by changing the balance between the federal government and the republics, and by channelling and legitimising the dissolution process.

4
The Ceasefire in Slovenia

The mediation of the ceasefire in Slovenia was the most effective international intervention in the conflict. Within the short time of two weeks it helped stop the fighting there and achieved a provisional agreement that ended the conflict over Slovenia's secession from Yugoslavia. In view of the obstacles faced by subsequent mediation efforts, the mediators' success in this case needs to be explained.

Slovenia and Croatia proclaimed themselves independent sovereign states on 25 June 1991. Slovenia's proclamation was accompanied by the occupation of border and customs posts along its boundaries with Italy, Austria and Hungary. The Yugoslav federal government responded to these acts by ordering the military to reestablish control over the border areas. The JNA's actions were, however, more extensive than authorised by the cabinet. Nonetheless it met with well-organised and determined resistance and was forced to retreat.[1]

As soon as the fighting began the international community called on the parties to end the combat and urged the federal authorities to exercise restraint. Acting mainly through the EC, the Western European states mediated a package agreement consisting of Serb acceptance of Stipe Mesić (the Croatian representative), as president of Yugoslavia, a three-months suspension of implementing the independence proclamations of Croatia and Slovenia, a ceasefire and the return of the JNA and Slovenian forces to their barracks. This agreement paved the way for Slovenia's separation from Yugoslavia and its emergence as an independent state.

As we shall see, the EC's mediation efforts contributed significantly to the achievement of the ceasefire. However it was not the mediation alone, but its confluence with several additional factors that combined to produce the outcome. Among the critical additional factors were Slovenia's brilliant strategy, both military and diplomatic, Serbia's belief that if it acquiesced to Slovenia's departure it would be better able to pursue its goals in Croatia, and nearly unanimous international pressure to stop the JNA's operation in Slovenia.

The EC's decision to send a mission

The EC leaders were assembled at a summit meeting in Luxembourg when the fighting erupted. Uneasy about the destabilising effects of the fighting, and perceiving the situation as an opportunity to advance their plans for transforming the loose European political cooperation into a more coherent common foreign and security policy, the summit leaders were motivated to act.

The adoption of a common policy was hampered, however, by the member states' divergent attitudes towards the crisis. The leaders were not even able to issue a statement on Yugoslavia 'because of disagreements over the relative importance it should give to the potentially contradictory principles of self-determination and territorial integrity'. German Chancellor Helmut Kohl, reflecting German sympathy for the Croat and Slovenian aspiration for independence, wanted to stress the right to self-determination, whereas French President François Mitterrand, supported by several others, insisted that Yugoslavia's territorial integrity should be considered a priority. Unable to agree about the principles to guide the EC's policy on the issues at stake, the summit participants decided to focus on the immediate objective, for which there was unanimity: the need to stop the fighting. The heads of state dispatched the Troika of foreign ministers to Yugoslavia and left it to them to 'decide how to phrase their message'.[2] In other words the Troika was dispatched without detailed instructions, except to stop the war.

The Troika's first round

The mission, consisting of Jacques Poos (the Luxembourg foreign minister and current chair of the Council of Foreign Ministers),

Gianni De Michelis (the Italian foreign minister and former chair) and Hans van den Broek (the Dutch foreign minister and future chair), travelled to Belgrade and Zagreb on 28 June. It was on this occasion, as the emissaries boarded their plane, that Poos uttered his now famous words: 'This is the hour of Europe. It is not the hour of the Americans.'[3]

Yet on the substantive issues at stake in the Yugoslav conflict the members of the Troika were as divided as the governments they represented. According to one account, De Michelis told the Slovenians at the first meeting that they should wait for three months, and thereafter they could do whatever they wished; Poos was 'open' to the Slovenian viewpoint; and van den Broek was perceived by the Slovenians as 'hostile'.[4] It is therefore remarkable that the EC was able to conduct a coherent mediation process and conclude a ceasefire.

In their meetings with the federal cabinet and leaders of the republics the Troika suggested a package agreement for ending the crisis. This was based on a proposal by the federal prime minister, Ante Marković, adopted the previous day by the cabinet. It called for a ceasefire, a three-month suspension of the Croat and Slovene independence proclamations, and the installation of Stipe Mesić, the Croatian representative, as president of Yugoslavia. According to the rules of rotation of the office of president, he had been due to assume his duties in May, but had been blocked by Serbia and its allies. As a result the eight-member presidency was paralysed. The proponents of the package hoped that with the reactivation of the presidency, which had constitutional authority over the armed forces, it would be possible to rein in the army and stop its operations in Slovenia.

The mediators left Yugoslavia believing that agreement had been reached to adopt the formula. Unfortunately, the impression that the matter was settled had been gained only from the parties' oral undertakings as no documents were signed.[5]

The second round

As the fighting in Slovenia continued and nothing was done to implement any aspect of the agreement, the Troika returned two days later (30 June). They spoke first to the presidents of the republics of Serbia, Croatia and Slovenia, the three most powerful leaders in the country, and obtained from them a reaffirmation of their acceptance of the package deal.

Then, ignoring the sovereign status of the hosts and disregarding protocol, the Troika called the Yugoslav federal presidency into session. The members of this august institution grumbled, but complied. The ambassadors of the 12 EC states were also present.

The readoption of the settlement package by the presidency was hampered by the exchange of bitter accusations among the Yugoslav representatives, and by the Serbian members' doubt that the Croats and Slovenes would honour their commitments. They demanded that the EC guarantee Croatia's and Slovenia's compliance in writing, but in the end accepted an oral guarantee from Hans van den Broek on behalf of the EC. The presidency thereupon adopted a formal resolution incorporating the Troika's formula.

The Troika's manner of conducting the session was directive and didactic. As if to demonstrate to unruly children how mature democracies conducted their affairs, the Troika interrupted the proceedings precisely at midnight to mark the biannual rotation of the EC presidency. In a brief ceremony the Luxembourg foreign minister transferred his responsibilities as chair of the EC Council of Ministers to the Dutch foreign minister. Shortly thereafter Croatia's representative, Stipe Mesić, who had hitherto been prevented by the Serbian representatives from assuming the rotating position of president, was installed in office.[6]

The third round: Brioni

Implementation of the ceasefire, however, ran into continual difficulties as neither the JNA nor the Slovenian nationalists were willing to compromise. The JNA believed in its ability to defeat the Slovenians and impose the federal government's authority on the republic. The Slovenians were encouraged by their military achievements, and by the political support their struggle had received from Germany and Austria.

The EC's efforts to persuade the disputants to honour their commitments were weakened somewhat by a parallel intervention by German Foreign Minister Hans-Dietrich Genscher, acting as the current chair of the CSCE. On 1 July he met the members of the federal government and the republics' leaders in Belgrade, and the following day conferred with the Slovenian leaders in Austria. According to Libal, 'given the fact that Germany did not participate in the EC Troika, he [Genscher] doubtlessly wished to give German diplomacy a higher profile'.[7] Genscher's initiative was stimulated largely by domestic political considerations. But whatever his motives and intentions, his initiative inevitably diverted attention away from the EC's ceasefire efforts. Furthermore he reportedly told the Slovenian leaders that if the JNA's military operations continued the international community would respond by recognising Slovenia's independence.[8] Since the Slovenian goal was to win recognition, the statement led some Slovenians to believe that the quickest way to recognition was to extend the war, rather than abide by the ceasefire.

The parties' delay in honouring their ceasefire commitments was facilitated by the lack of detail in, if not the superficiality of, the ceasefire terms. For example the parties had agreed that each side would return their troops to their barracks. But since the ceasefire terms did not specify that they could keep their equipment, the Slovenes blocked the return of the federal troops to their barracks, demanding that they give up their equipment. The JNA regarded this as a violation of the ceasefire and resumed its operations against the Slovenes.[9]

As the efforts to resolve this and other disagreements and to establish the ceasefire were unsuccessful, the EC foreign ministers decided on 5 July to send the Troika on another mission to Yugoslavia. The 5 July foreign ministers' meeting was also remarkable for the statement it issued. Still unable to agree on a common goal and strategy for addressing the Yugoslav problem, beyond the limited objective of stopping violence, the statement echoed the disparate approaches of the member states. It called for a dialogue, based on respect for human rights, the rights of minorities, the right 'of peoples' to self-determination, and the norm of the territorial integrity of states. The majority did not accept Germany's call for recognition of Croatian and Slovenian independence, but implied that the EC might consider recognition if the fighting continued. The foreign ministers also decided to impose an embargo on all shipments of arms and military equipment to Yugoslavia, and to suspend the EC's financial aid to the country.[10]

The arms embargo hurt the Croats and Slovenes more than it hurt the federal government forces, but the financial sanctions were designed to restrict the resources available to the JNA. There is reason to believe that the financial sanctions were imposed at the suggestion (or at least with the agreement) of Prime Minister Marković, who was hoping they might help the cabinet impose its authority over the military. In an earlier confrontation with the JNA over its resistance to civilian control, Marković reportedly threatened the military that he would use the government's ties to international financial institutions to bring about the withdrawal of assistance to the armed forces.[11]

Having arranged for an invitation for another visit to be issued by the federal cabinet, the Troika again controlled the proceedings. Unable to persuade the Slovenes to go to Belgrade, the Troika arranged to meet the various Yugoslav parties on the island of Brioni, the site favoured by Tito for entertaining foreign dignitaries. There the Troika met separately with the various actors. It appears that the main obstacles at this stage were the Slovenians' reluctance to accept the suspension of independence and their desire for a more assertive mandate for the international monitoring of the ceasefire, and Prime Minister Marković's objection to the border regime and custom revenue clauses. It was only after it appeared that agreement had been reached that the Troika convened a plenary session, chaired by President Mesić, formally to adopt a declaration embodying its terms. In view of the continuing objections Mesić refrained from submitting the text to a vote, and instead announced its adoption 'by consensus'.[12] Significantly the document was termed a 'declaration' rather than an 'agreement'. No wonder that its subsequent implementation continued to encounter difficulties.

The declaration stated that the parties 'reaffirmed their commitment to full implementation of the European Community's proposals of June 30' and agreed to accept a monitoring mission. The modalities relating to implementing the ceasefire were detailed in an annex to the declaration. These recognised Slovenian authority over some matters, but without explicitly accepting Slovenia's independence. Its main points were as follows.

First, with respect to border controls, the issue that had triggered the JNA operation, it was specified that control of the border crossings would be in the hands of the Slovenian police, who would act in conformity with federal regulations. Custom duties would remain a federal revenue, collected by Slovenian officials and paid into a joint Slovenian–federal account. As for border security, the situation prevailing before June 25 would be reestablished, and negotiations would be completed during the three months suspension period in order 'to ensure an orderly transfer of the competencies of the JNA in this field'.

Second, with respect to air traffic control, which the Slovenes had seized at Ljubljana airport, the annex stated that there would be a single air traffic control authority for the whole of Yugoslavia, operating under federal control.

Third, with respect to the ceasefire, it was specified that this would be accompanied by the lifting of the blockade on JNA units and facilities, the JNA's unconditional return to barracks, the clearing of all roads, the return of equipment and facilities seized by the Slovenians to the JNA, the deactivation of the Slovenian territorial defence units and their return to quarters, and the release of all prisoners. All these measures were to be implemented by midnight on 8 July.

Another annex to the declaration set out guidelines for an observer mission to Slovenia, and possibly also Croatia, under CSCE auspices.[13]

The declaration was subsequently ratified by the Slovenian legislature and the federal authorities. It paved the way for the full withdrawal of JNA troops from Slovenia, and Yugoslavia's *de facto* acceptance of Slovenia's independence. This point needs to be clarified.

The declaration did not require the withdrawal of the JNA from Slovenian territory, only the return of JNA troops to their barracks, many of which were located in Slovenia. But during the debate on ratification by the federal presidency on 12 July, the Serbian representatives and General Veljko Kadijević (the minister of defence) proposed going further. Insisting that the army could not stay in Slovenia if it was not wanted there, they proposed that the JNA be withdrawn from Slovenian territory. Their proposal reflected Serbia's readiness to accept Slovenia's secession, and the JNA's transformation into an instrument of Serbian nationalism. These Serbs' priority was Croatia, which had a significant Serb population whose links to Serbia they wanted to preserve. The proposal to withdraw the JNA from Slovenia did not have the support of Prime Minister Marković, who believed that Yugoslavia would not survive if Slovenia were allowed to secede, and it was opposed by President Mesić, who feared that the JNA forces withdrawn from Slovenia would be redeployed to Croatia. Nevertheless the proposal for full withdrawal from Slovenia was adopted by the presidency on 18 July.[14] The withdrawal was completed on 26 October 1991, thus enabling Slovenia to realise its independence without further bloodshed.

The mediators' contribution

The ending of the war can be attributed in part to the mediation. But the success of the mediation cannot be understood without taking into account how certain contextual features combined with the mediation process to produce the successful outcome.

A key element facilitating the settlement was the readiness of the parties to settle the conflict on the basis of the *status quo* – that is Slovenia's *defacto* secession. Such a readiness to settle is often induced by a hurting stalemate, but no such stalemate had developed in this short war. The Slovenes had achieved their goal: they were independent in fact, and they expected that their sovereignty would soon win international recognition. The JNA had suffered a humiliating setback in the fighting, partly because it had committed only a minor force to the Slovenian war. Yet despite facing some serious problems the JNA was still capable of launching a major operation and reimposing federal authority over Slovenia. But it did not have sufficient forces to fight simultaneously in both Slovenia and Croatia. It gave priority to Croatia.

This was a political choice, reflecting the growing influence of Serbia's president, Slobodan Milošević, and the advocates of a 'Greater Serbia' in the federal army. Until 1990 a significant proportion of Yugoslav elites of all nationalities supported the preservation of a common Yugoslav state. The military was one of the bastions of Yugoslavism and believed its chief mission to be the preservation of its integrity. Much of Serbian opinion, heavily represented in the JNA officers corps, supported the Yugoslav idea. But by 1990 a competing vision of a Greater Serbia, encompassing the Serb-populated regions of Croatia and Bosnia, took hold among Serbian elites, and was apparently espoused by Milošević as well. According to this view, Serbs would be best protected in a Serbian state, rather than in a multinational Yugoslavia. The realisation of this idea would require a redrawing of the republics' boundaries so as to incorporate the major-ity of Serbs within Serbia. (Only 75 per cent of Yugoslavia's Serbs lived in Serbia, in contrast to 80 per cent of Croats and 98 per cent Slovenes in their respective republics.) By the summer of 1991 the JNA command, consisting largely of Serbs, had been converted to this view.[15]

It is widely believed that by early 1991 Milošević had given up on the attempt to keep Slovenia within Yugoslavia, and may have even told Slovenia's President Milan Kučan that Serbia would accept Slo-venia's secession. There was no Serbian population in Slovenia, and Serb–Slovene relations were not burdened by memories of conflict. Milošević and his Serbian nationalist supporters concentrated their efforts on keeping the large Serb-populated areas of Croatia and Bosnia within a single state – a rump Yugoslavia or Greater Serbia. Zimmermann relates that Milošević told him and British Ambassador Peter Hall on 12 July that 'Serbia will present no obstacles to Slo-venia's departure....Marković behaved stupidly with his halfway measures toward Slovenia. He should have put 100,000 troops into Slovenia or he should have put no troops there. We would have favored no troops. Slovenia isn't worth the life of a single Serbian soldier.'[16]

In view of the priority that Serb politicians accorded to Croatia and Bosnia, both of which had large Serbian populations, the JNA fell in-to line, agreed to withdraw its troops from Slovenia and concentrated its efforts on Croatia.

But this alone – the readiness of both sides to disengage – could not bring the war to an end. An agreement was necessary, and negoti-ations were needed to produce an agreement. But with the deep rifts between the republics and within the central federal governmental structure it was difficult for the Yugoslav actors to maintain a sys-tematic and coherent negotiating process. The EC mediation allowed such a process, and provided a focal point for the negotiations.

The formula for the agreement, as we have seen, was not produced by the mediators. It was suggested by Marković and the federal cabinet. The mediators appropriated it, modified it, shrouded some of its aspects in sufficient ambiguity to make it acceptable, and then announced it in a manner that rendered it difficult for the parties to reject.

One element of the agreement was that Serbia and its allies would accept Mesić as president, thus enabling the reactivation of the federal presidency. Although the restored presidency did not last long or fully reestablish its authority over the armed forces, its existence nevertheless helped the negotiating process because legal authority for many of the decisions was vested in the presidency. The presidency's ratification of the Brioni terms, and its decisions regarding their implementation, were essential to the successful conclusion of the negotiations.

To make the agreement acceptable to the Slovenes the mediators modified Marković's initial text, watering down the clauses relating to the suspension of independence and control over customs. Its acceptability to all the parties was facilitated by the ambiguity of its terms. Much of the wording that endowed the Brioni Declaration with the nuances and ambiguities needed to make it acceptable to all was contributed by the mediators. Thus the general principles of the declaration referred both to self-determination and to the territorial integrity of the states. The border regime clause in Annex I placed the control of border crossings in the hands of the Slovenian police, who were required to act in conformity with federal regulations. Perhaps the most interesting feature was that only indirect reference was made to the three months' suspension of the practical effects of the declaration of independence. Acceptance of the suspension is implied in the parties' reaffirmation of their commitment to the implementation of the EC's proposals of 30 June, and in Annex I, in the item on border security, which states that 'the situation prevailing before June 25th 1991 shall be reestablished'. This is balanced by the next sentence: 'within the suspension period (three months) negotiations shall be completed in order to ensure an orderly transfer of the competencies of the JNA in this field'.

The mediators further contributed by influencing the Slovenes and the federal government to change their stance. The mediators' influence derived from desire of both the Slovenes and Marković to cultivate good relations with the EC, which they regarded as important to their future. It was the Troika members' status as EC representatives that endowed them with the influence to persuade these reluctant parties to acquiesce to terms they had previously rejected.

The other means of leverage employed by the EC – financial sanctions and the arms embargo – probably did not have much effect. The few days between their imposition and the acceptance of the Brioni terms were not sufficient for them to produce an impact.

Some uncoordinated gestures by the CSCE and statements by EC member states tended to hamper the Troika's effectiveness. The German statement that recognition would be considered if the fighting continued may have helped to restrain the army. But at the same time it encouraged some Slovenes to believe that continued clashes would help speed up recognition. Slovene deference to German views helped to resolve the problem. German diplomats persuaded the Slovenians to lift the blockades on JNA installations, and stressed that their first priority ought to be getting the JNA out of Slovenia. Citing the example of Germany's treatment of the Soviet troops stationed in East Germany following reunification, they advised the Slovenes not to humiliate the JNA or make it think that it must defend its honour or reputation – on the contrary, they should help facilitate the JNA's speedy departure.[17]

The modification of Marković's original formula, the ambiguous wording and the parties' eagerness to cultivate their relations with the EC did not suffice to overcome the parties' reluctance to accept the Brioni terms. Their hands were eventually forced by van den Broek, who promulgated the terms and let the parties know that this was a 'take it or leave it' text. Van den Broek's style was described as dictatorial. The 'diktat' helped to seal the agreement.

Considering the difficulties faced by international organisations that try to mediate conflicts, the EC's success in Slovenia was remarkable. In contrast to the subsequent EC and UN mediation efforts, the EC's peacemaking in Slovenia was unencumbered by multiple objectives and the divergent interests of member states. It was sharply focused on the single goal of stopping the war. The mediation was facilitated by the flexibility that the Troika enjoyed. Unlike subsequent mediation efforts, the mediation of the Slovenian ceasefire was not constrained by detailed instructions or the enunciation of guiding principles by the EC or the UN. As we have seen, the divisions at the 27 June summit meeting prevented the formulation of a policy statement, while the 5 July Council of Ministers' decision was broad enough to allow a wide range of outcomes. The absence of constraining principles enabled the Troika to focus on stopping the war.

Besides bringing about a ceasefire, and thus saving countless lives, the mediation effort had long-term political consequences. It helped constrain the Yugoslav central institutions' use of force to stop the disintegration. Once Slovenia's secession was accepted the principle of Yugoslav unity could no longer be defended. The subsequent wars thus became struggles among competing entities for national self-determination and territorial possession.

5
The Search for
a Comprehensive Settlement

The EC invested much effort in 1991 to bring about a comprehensive political settlement, encompassing all the parties involved in the Yugoslav crisis. This initiative was pursued in parallel to the effort to stop the wars in Slovenia and Croatia through the conclusion of ceasefire agreements.

The attempt to broker a comprehensive political settlement did not merely fail, but both the process and the outcome served to undermine the EC's credibility as a peacemaker. The shrinking credibility of the mediators removed any inhibition the disputants might have felt about forcing their will on their adversaries.

It must be recognised that the task was hampered by significant obstacles. This chapter will briefly review these obstacles, but the main question to be examined is whether and how the mediation effort itself contributed to the disappointing outcome.

Among the main difficulties facing the mediators were the complexity of the issues and the strong emotions they aroused. The most volatile issue concerned the Serb-inhabited areas of Croatia and the Serbs' desire to separate these areas from Croatia and attach them to Serbia. This highlighted the contradiction between two fundamental principles – respect for the territorial integrity of states and the right to self-determination. If Croats and Slovenes in Yugoslavia were to be entitled to self-determination, should not Serbs in Croatia, Albanians in Serbia, and Serbs and Croats in Bosnia be entitled to the same right as well?

Another difficulty stemmed from the multiplicity of Yugoslav parties involved and the divisions among them. A comprehensive settlement required not only bridging the gap between two adversaries, but also devising an arrangement acceptable to all the critical actors. In early July these included the federal cabinet, the JNA and the six republics.

Furthermore the timing of the mediatory effort was highly inauspicious. The main contenders were still confident that their policies would prove effective. Given their optimistic mood, the parties were not amenable to persuasion.

These situational features placed extraordinary obstacles in the path of the mediators. But as we shall see, the mediation process fell short of what was required not only due to erroneous tactics, but also because of the inherent inadequacies of the mediating entity. The EC, because of its nature as an intergovernmental organisation, was unable to pursue a coherent mediation programme and lacked the means to influence the disputants' behaviour. The EC had first to reach agreement among its members. As already related, the member states started out with diverse, if not contradictory, attitudes towards the issues. Once agreement among the members was reached, often cast in terms of general principles, the EC's stance became rigid, depriving the mediators of the flexibility needed for effective mediation.

The EC was also unable to project itself as having a coherent policy. The member states, besides their joint communication with the Yugoslav parties, conducted through their common institutions, could not refrain from communicating with them bilaterally through direct channels, passing messages that were not always consistent with the collective stance.

These inadequacies were aggravated by the need of the EC governments to respond to additional challenges. Despite the great importance that the EC members attached to the Yugoslav crisis, the latter was subordinate to policy considerations on two other issues. First and foremost were the negotiations on transforming the European Community into the European Union. An important component of this was the institutionalisation of a common security and foreign policy. As a result, as Stanley Hoffmann observed, 'the main consideration was not the future of Yugoslavia, or even the effectiveness of the EC in this first major postwar crisis in Europe; it was the preservation of the appearance of unity among the 12 members.'[1]

The second priority was coping with the break-up of the Soviet Union. There were persistent concerns that the dissolution might be accompanied by violence. Since violence there was perceived to pose much graver risks to European peace than the violence in Yugoslavia, the EC's stance on Yugoslavia was shaped with an eye to the signals it might send to various actors in the Soviet Union.

The priorities accorded to other issues burdened the mediation effort and hindered the attempt to devise solutions to the particular disputes in Yugoslavia.

Two months of passivity

To succeed in their task, mediators need to be flexible. Although their involvement might be motivated by self-interest, mediators need to be able to accept a much wider range of solutions to the conflict than the disputants.

However the mediators in this case did not enjoy such flexibility. For approximately two months the EC was unable to pursue a comprehensive settlement because it was bogged down by disagreements about the nature of the settlement it ought to pursue. While the majority of EC members believed it desirable for some form of joint Yugoslav framework to be maintained, and hoped that this could be achieved by a revision of the country's constitution, Germany accepted the Croatian and Slovenian position that a settlement should formalise the dissolution of Yugoslavia and recognise their sovereignty and independence.

As related above, the particpants in the European summit of 27 June were unable to formulate a joint position 'because of disagreements over the relative importance it should give to the potentially contradictory principles self-determination and territorial integrity.' Kohl, reflecting German sympathy for Croat and Slovene aspirations for independence, wanted to stress the right to self-determination, whereas Mitterrand, supported by Britain, Italy and Spain, insisted that Yugoslavia's territorial integrity should be defined as a priority.[2]

Further consultations between the members enabled the Council of (Foreign) Ministers, at their meeting on 5 July, to paper over their disagreements by including in their joint statement references both to self-determination and to the territorial integrity of states. The Council's wording was ambiguous enough to suit the Yugoslav parties as well, and it was incorporated into the Brioni agreement.[3]

Little was done, however, by the EC to promote the negotiations. All that the EC foreign ministers were able to agree to was the establishment of a group of experts from the twelve member states to help them in their deliberations, and to charge Henry Wynaendts (Henri Wijnaents) – the Dutch diplomat who negotiated on behalf of the EC in respect of ceasefire issues – with finding out how the federal authorities and the republics conceived of the negotiations on the future of Yugoslavia, and what role the EC might play in assisting the process.[4]

Prodded on by the EC, and to some extent by the US, the contending Yugoslav parties assembled on 23–4 July at Lake Ohrid in Macedonia and on 20 August in Belgrade to continue their on-off discussions on constitutional reform (these had started before Slovenia and Croatia proclaimed their independence). Not surprisingly, given the parties' positions and the very limited external support for the negotiations, these meetings failed to achieve any progress.

Among the Yugoslav parties, only a minority – consisting of the civilian members of the federal cabinet, the leaders of Macedonia and the leaders of the Bosnian Muslims – wanted the constitutional talks to succeed. They sought to revise the constitution along confederal lines, and urged the EC to assist in this endeavour. Croatia and Slovenia were no longer interested in constitutional reform – their goal was independence, and they believed that international recognition rather than internal negotiations would help them to achieve their goal. Serbia and its ally Montenegro aimed at incorporating the Serb-populated areas of Croatia within a Serb-dominated Yugoslav state. This they expected to achieve by military force, so for them the constitutional talks were irrelevant.

Inherent in the latter two attitudes was a logic favouring an escalation in the use of force. The prospect of international intervention pushed the Serbs and their allies to seize as much territory as possible before international pressures forced them to stop. The Slovenes (but only briefly) and the Croats faced a more complex dilemma. They were spurred on to take military action by the statement by German officials that if the JNA continued its operations, then Germany would recognise Slovenia's and Croatia's independence. Blockading the barracks in which JNA officers and their families resided would be certain to provoke aggressive counter-measures by the JNA, which would in turn stimulate international pressure for intervention to protect the weaker Slovenes and Croats from the brutal might of the JNA. But it would also entail heavy casualties, and risked the loss of territory. The interaction of these two policies, both of which were fuelled by the growing calls for international intervention, produced a dynamic of military escalation and political radicalisation.[5]

The Serb, Croat and Slovene willingness to continue the constitutional talks, despite their lack of interest in a successful outcome, can be attributed to the desire of each to avoid being blamed by the international community and the undecided section of their domestic public for obstructing the effort.

There is a puzzling incongruity between the Serb and Croat leaders' deliberate escalation of the war in Croatia and the public image that these leaders wished to project. That image was visible in the group photographs taken at Lake Ohrid and in the joint communiqué they issued, saying that they were 'committed to negotiations and dialogue', and affirming both their opposition to the use of force and their support for 'democratic development, respect for the individual and collective rights and freedoms'.[6] It is bizarre to read Mesić's statement in the light of his acerbic description of the contentious meeting in Belgrade on 20 August: 'I told the journalists that all questions "were examined in a constructive atmosphere".'[7] The absurdity of these proceedings is highlighted by the official text:

> It was agreed that the following principles will be respected in the search for a solution:
> 1. Respect for the right of any nation to self-determination.... Any change in external and internal borders by unilateral acts and the use of force are unacceptable; if it nevertheless takes effect, it will be based exclusively on the right of nations to self-determination and carried out in a democratic procedure and legally.[8]

The last occasion at which the warring parties displayed outward agreement was at the session of the presidency on 6 September, at which the text of Mesić's address to the opening session of the Hague Peace Conference (see below) was approved unanimously.[9]

The EC's contribution to these talks was minimal. Wynaendts helped to facilitate the meetings between the Yugoslav leaders, but his main effort was devoted to achieving a ceasefire in Croatia and gaining the parties' acceptance of monitors to bolster it. Given the disputants' optimism about their prospect of achieving their maximal aims, it is doubtful that the EC would have succeeded even if it had been more actively involved. But the disagreement among the member states about the shape of the settlement that it ought to pursue, prevented it from even trying.

Convening a conference

Paradoxically the disagreements among the member states – which during July and much of August prevented the EC from actively pursuing an overall political settlement – spurred the EC leaders at the end of August to convene a peace conference. Besides its obvious purpose of resolving the Yugoslav conflict, it was also expected to help to contain the disruptive tendencies that were developing out of the disagreements about Yugoslavia among the members of the EC. Moreover, by coincidence the same ministerial meetings at which the Yugoslav crisis was discussed also produced lively debates, under a separate agenda heading, about the extent to which governments would be bound by the common foreign and security policy (CFSP), which was to be instituted with the establishment of the European Union. The conference provided a mechanism for coordinating policy on Yugoslavia without tying the coordination too closely (except perhaps in the ministers' minds) to the controversies surrounding the future CFSP.

The motivation for a renewed effort to develop a common policy developed gradually. The possibility that the EC might convene a conference was first raised publicly in the Council of Ministers' 'Declaration on Yugoslavia' of 6 August, which expressed their readiness to convene a conference 'if necessary'.[10] This was stimulated by the intensification of warfare in Croatia. Television images of the war and the suffering it was causing were having an impact on public opinion. The EC's inability to bring about a ceasefire was highly frustrating.

A major indication of the need for close policy coordination was the attempted coup against President Gorbachev in the Soviet Union. The coup accelerated the disintegration of the Soviet Union, with the Baltic republics, Ukraine and Belarus announcing their independence. This confronted the EC with the challenge of formulating a common stance towards a situation that was considered much more threatening to world peace than the war in Yugoslavia. Germany (and Denmark) strongly advocated immediate recognition of the independence of the Baltic states. The Soviet coup further influenced the European governments' attitudes towards Yugoslavia by stimulating fear that the JNA might try to overthrow the legitimate (though powerless) civilian authority in Belgrade. France and other members of the EC had thus far been successful in persuading the German government to refrain from acting unilaterally to recognise Croatian and Slovenian independence. But in the atmosphere created by the Soviet coup, calls for urgent recognition of these two republics became louder and it was not clear how long Germany could be restrained from taking unilateral action. It was in this context that the idea of a peace conference for Yugoslavia gained new momentum.[11]

The prospect of unilateral action by Germany to grant recognition, thus widening the rift in the EC and impeding the efforts to conclude the treaty transforming the community into a union with a common foreign and security policy, prompted the political leaders to convene the conference. The call for a conference reflected a tacit expectation that it would help tie Germany more firmly to joint EC policy, and help it to fend off domestic pressure for unilateral recognition.

There are differing accounts as to who initiated the move – Hans van den Broek (the Dutch current chair of the Council of Ministers), Roland Dumas (the French foreign minister), or Hans-Dietrich Genscher (the German foreign minister). It is clear, however, that all three were in favour of convening the conference.[12]

At the Council of Ministers' meeting on 27 August a preliminary decision was taken to that effect. The final decision was taken at an extraordinary foreign ministers' meeting on 3 September. The statement announcing that the conference would meet in the Hague on the 7th also outlined the principles and procedures that would guide it.[13]

Lord Peter Carrington, who had formerly served as Britain's foreign secretary and as secretary-general of NATO, was appointed to chair the conference. His considerable diplomatic and political experience included the mediation of the Rhodesia/Zimbabwe settlement. His style in helping to end that conflict was described as 'tough and controlling', and his role 'as less a mediator than an "arbitrator"'.[14]

A French proposal for the establishment of an arbitration commission was also adopted. Robert Badinter, a respected lawyer and politician who was serving as president of France's Constitutional Court, was appointed to chair the commission. Its other members were the heads of the Constitutional Courts of Belgium, Germany, Italy and Spain. The Council of Ministers further decided that issues to be submitted for arbitration would be transmitted to it by the chairman of the conference. This helped to keep the process under centralised direction.

Besides ruling on issues that divided the Yugoslav parties, the commission had the potential of serving as a face-saving mechanism for resolving differences among the members of the EC. Transferring contentious issues to a judicial panel held out the prospect of softening the sharp political edge of the EC's deliberations, and helping it to arrive at a common policy. One of the principal bones of contention was the French view that the Helsinki principles did not apply to internal borders, and that the question of whether internal boundaries might acquire the same status as international boundaries must be decided by means of an appropriate legal mechanism. Mitterrand made this point twice in the course of his press conference in Weimar on 20 September.[15]

None of the principal Yugoslav parties – Serbia, Croatia and Slovenia – wanted a conference, fearing that they would lose more than they would gain from negotiations there. This perhaps explains their pretence that the 20 August session of the constitutional negotiations in Belgrade had been held in a 'constructive atmosphere'. The Slovenes and Croats did not want the conference to derogate anything from the full sovereignty that they claimed. The Serbs and the JNA were concerned that the conference would put pressure on them to accept the internal boundaries of the Yugoslav federation as the legitimate boundaries of Croatia's new independent state. They were also wary of Germany's proposal to invite representatives of the Kosovo Albanians to attend the conference. But despite their concern that the conference might damage their cause, none refused to attend.[16]

The convening of the conference was accompanied by drama. The EC's call for a conference was linked to an ultimatum to Serbia to lift its objections to the stationing of EC ceasefire monitors in Croatia by 1 September, and a threat of sanctions if Serbia refused to do so. Tense bargaining between van den Broek and Milošević continued until the very last moment, with Milošević signing on the dotted line a few minutes after the midnight deadline.[17]

There was some disagreement as to whether the conference should commence while fighting was taking place in Croatia. This reflected the division between those (for example Delors and van den Broek) who suspected that a ceasefire would not take hold in the absence of a political settlement, and those who took the opposite view, as articulated by Carrington: 'it will certainly be impossible to make progress against a background of violence'.[18] Thus after the opening session on 7 September, Carrington invested considerable effort in trying to arrange a ceasefire. His most dramatic action on this issue was the summoning of Milošević, Tudjman and the federal government's defence minister, General Kadijević, to Tito's holiday home at Igalo, on the Montenegrin coast, on 17 September, where they concluded a ceasefire agreement. Mesić said that it was 'dictated' to them by Carrington.[19] Be that as it may, the agreement, like many that preceded and followed it, did not hold. Unable to stop the war, Carrington apparently concluded that it was better to proceed with the conference than to suspend it. In the absence of a ceasefire, the conference was considerably influenced by the concurrent fighting, and especially by the JNA's brutal assault on Vukovar and the shelling of Dubrovnik. (A ceasefire was finally brokered by Cyrus Vance in January 1992. The negotiations that produced it are discussed in Chapter 6.)

The development of common principles

The effort to protect European solidarity from the disruptive effects of the Yugoslav crisis was pursued along two parallel tracks. One was the establishment of an institutional framework – the conference – which served to restrain German unilateralism. The other was the gradual development of a consensus on the principles to guide European policy and serve as the basis of a comprehensive settlement of the Yugoslav conflict.

It will be recalled that during the spring of 1991 the EC's policy statements gradually shifted from explicit and clear support for the preservation of Yugoslav unity, to equivocation. In a last-minute attempt to deter Slovenia and Croatia from proclaiming their independence, Jacques Poos (the Luxembourg foreign minister who chaired the 23 June Council meeting) declared that the 'EC would only recognise the independence of Slovenia and Croatia "if such independence were the result of negotiations and of an internal agreement accepted by all" in Yugoslavia'.[20] But four days later at a summit meeting the EC heads of state found themselves in disagreement over whether the principle of self-determination or the territorial integrity of states should be given precedence, and were unable to formulate a joint statement on the issues in question.[21]

This disagreement grew sharper and more vocal in the following days as German public opinion came out strongly in support of Croatian and Slovenian independence. As the German political leaders' call for recognition of these two states and the meeting between Foreign Minister Genscher and Slovenia's President Kučan seemed to suggest that Germany might embark on a unilateral journey, France called for another Council of Ministers meeting with the purpose of reining in the Germans. Since some of Genscher's activities were formally undertaken in his capacity as chairman in office of the CSCE, this Council meeting also served decisively to shift the locus of European diplomacy from the CSCE to the EC, a shift actively supported by the US.[22]

Meeting on 5 July, the Council this time succeeded in formulating a joint statement. It made no reference to the German call for recognition. The statement acknowledged the 'reality that a new situation has arisen', expressed opposition to the use of force and, as mentioned already, papered over the disagreements among member states. The statement called for a peaceful solution, based on the principles of the CSCE's Helsinki Final Act, the Charter of Paris, respect for human rights, 'including rights of minorities and the right of peoples for self-determination in conformity with the Charter of the United Nations' and 'relevant norms of international law, including those relating to territorial integrity of states'.[23]

This long list of principles is particularly interesting because it marked the starting point from which the common European positions subsequently evolved. The most significant change was the omission from subsequent statements of reference to the principle of territorial integrity and of explicit affirmation of the inviolability of Yugoslavia's internal borders.

The reference to the Helsinki principles in the Council of Ministers' statement of 5 July left the Council's position on the internal boundaries ambiguous. According to David Owen, on 13 July van den Broek circulated a memorandum to the member states pointing out an inconsistency in the interpretation of the principle of self-determination, in that it was applicable to the republics but not to national minorities within the republics. In the memorandum he also expressed concern that Serbia would not accept 'an independent Croatia with 11 percent Serbs within its borders.' His conclusion pointed towards 'a voluntary redrawing of internal borders as a possible solution.' He recognised that it would be impossible to redraw borders in such a way that no national minorities would remain, but he believed it possible to devise 'better borders than the present ones' so as 'to reduce the number of national minorities in each republic.'[24]

However van den Broek's suggestion that an attempt be made to revise the internal borders was rejected by the other 11 EC governments on the grounds that this would open a Pandora's Box, and that the idea was impractical in view of the large number of ethnic pockets in the different republics.[25]

Thus a fundamental premise of the EC's stand was established – that the internal boundaries of Yugoslavia defining its republics ought to be preserved. This was reflected in the Council of Ministers' 'Declaration on Yugoslavia' of 6 August. In view of Serb military actions aimed at separating the Serb-populated areas of Croatia from the territory of the republic, as defined by Tito's Yugoslav government, the EC proclaimed that 'any change of internal and international borders by force is not acceptable'. It restated this even more forcefully in its declaration of 27 August, proclaiming its 'determination never to recognize' changes of borders brought about by force, its declaration of 3 September announcing the opening of the conference, and its 19 September statement, issued in support of Carrington's ceasefire effort.[26]

When peacemaking efforts began in July 1991 the majority of EC members thought that solution of the conflict required Yugoslavia's constitution to be reformed in a manner that would allow a large measure of autonomy to the republics, but would stop short of full sovereign statehood, thus preserving a common Yugoslav framework. The escalating war, the brutality of JNA operations and the deepening commitment of Slovenia and Croatia to independent statehood led to the gradual abandonment of this idea. The growing support for independence in Macedonia and among Muslims and Croats in Bosnia cast further doubt on the prospect of preserving Yugoslavia. The shift in opinion was reflected at the Council of Ministers' meeting on 29 July, when the participants accepted a German proposal to author-ise a group of experts to consider *all* proposals for a political settle-ment, implicitly including the previously excluded option of dissolving Yugoslavia.[27] Even France, which had been considered as pro-Serb and pro-Yugoslav, had concluded that Yugoslavia no longer existed, and Foreign Minister Roland Dumas confirmed this evalu-ation publicly in a speech to the National Assembly on 9 October.[28] Thus, when the conference convened a consensus had developed that Yugoslavia could not be salvaged, and that the mediators' task was to bring the parties to agreement on the terms for the dissolution of the Yugoslav state.

The Carrington Plan

For the first few weeks after the opening of the conference on 7 September much of the activity was concerned with establishing a ceasefire in Croatia. When this effort failed the conference reverted to its main purpose – to bring about a comprehensive settlement of the conflict. The settlement was to be based on the Carrington Plan, and the conference was essentially an effort by Carrington and his associ-ates to persuade the parties to accept the plan, rather than an attempt to mediate between the parties.

The plan incorporated the principles described above, which had been adopted during the previous two months by the Council of Ministers, along with a new element of fundamental importance. While the previously developed principles opened the possibility of acceptance of the independence of Croatia and Slovenia, they did not say so explicitly. The critical new element that was now added to these principles envisaged the recognition of those republics wishing to be independent, to be granted within the framework of a general settlement. In other words, Carrington and the EC Council of Ministers now took it for granted that Yugoslavia had ceased to exist. This was reflected not only in the plan, but also in the exclusion of the representatives of the federal government from the negoti-ations.

The attempt to obtain the parties' acceptance of the plan pro-ceeded through several stages. Its main points were outlined at a meeting chaired by Carrington and van den Broek and attended by

Milošević, Tudjman and Kadijević on 4 October. A statement read by van den Broek after the meeting suggested that these points had been accepted by the participants:

> It was agreed that the involvement of all parties concerned would be necessary to formulate a political solution on the basis of the perspective of recognition of those republics wishing it, at the end of the negotiating process conducted in good faith. The recognition would be granted in the framework of a general settlement and have the following components:
> (a) A loose association or alliance of sovereign or independent republics;
> (b) Adequate arrangements to be made for the protection of minorities, including human rights guarantees and possibly special status for certain areas;
> (c) No unilateral changes in borders.[29]

But when a more detailed version was presented at a plenary session of the conference on 18 October, Milošević told the meeting that the plan was unacceptable in its present version. Undeterred, Carrington ended the session by saying that since the plan received wide support, Serbia's reservations should not prevent the conference from discussing it.

Essentially the same provisions as those in the plan, but now formulated as a treaty, were presented to the parties at a plenary meeting on 25 October. Again Serbia rejected it, this time joined by Montenegro. A final version, adjusted to take into account some of the Serbian counterproposals, was presented on 5 November. But the revisions failed to meet the Serbian demands, and the treaty was rejected by Serbia.[30]

The treaty proposed by Carrington presented a framework for 'new relations between the republics'. These relations were to be based on several principles. The republics were to be sovereign and independent 'for those that wish it', and they were to be bound by 'comprehensive arrangements, including supervisory mechanisms for the protection of human rights and special status for certain groups and areas.' The treaty also envisaged, 'in the framework of a general settlement, recognition of the independence, within existing borders, unless otherwise agreed, of those republics wishing it.' It further listed in detail various human rights and rights of ethnic and national groups, and it outlined areas of cooperation and established institutions for cooperation in economic matters, foreign affairs and security, and legal affairs.[31]

There were several highly contentious elements in the plan, including the premise that Yugoslavia no longer existed, as implied in the reference to 'a free association of republics with an international personality'. This reflected the reality that Croatia and Slovenia had already seceded, that Macedonia had voted for independence in a referendum on 7 September, and that the Muslim and Croat members of the Bosnian assembly were about to proclaim (on 15 October) the independence of their republic. Serbia bitterly criticised the plan for starting from this premise and for glossing over the unilateral secession of Slovenia and Croatia, and argued that the plan encouraged the remaining republics to secede from the federation.

Serbia and Montenegro further objected that the plan 'de-recognised' Yugoslavia, and placed its recognition on an equal footing, within the framework of a general settlement, as the other republics. Carrington tried to accommodate this objection by adding in the November draft a reference to 'a common state of equal Republics for those Republics which wish to remain a common state', but he did not accept Milošević's call for the continuity of the Yugoslav state. Besides saving Yugoslavia (Serbia and Montenegro) from the need to apply for recognition as a 'new' state, acceptance of continuity could have given them title to Yugoslav state assets.

Milošević also proposed adding the word 'nations' to the clause on republics that wished to remain together. Adding 'nations' would have carried on the concept of a federation of nations and republics that had appeared in all Yugoslav constitutions after 1945. But Tudjman and others objected to the inclusion of the word nations since it could serve as justification for the Serbs of Croatia to secede.[32]

The second major controversy concerned the plan's designation of the areas populated by an ethnic or national minority which 'shall enjoy a special status of autonomy'. The 18 October version specified that this status would 'apply, in particular, to the Serbs living in areas of Croatia where they form a majority'.[33] But the Croats objected to this, and succeeded in persuading Carrington to delete it from subsequent versions. The controversy over the areas to which the special status would apply escalated further because the 25 October version provided for the restoration of Vojvodina and Kosovo as autonomous provinces of Serbia, a status they had enjoyed until it was abolished by Milošević in 1990. This was only hinted at in the 18 October version, but was brought out explicitly in the 25 October text.[34] Since the retention of Kosovo under Serbian control was a matter of highest priority for the Serbian nationalists, and had been skilfully exploited by Milošević in his rise to power, the inclusion of this clause was vehemently opposed by the Serbs. In an attempt to win Serbian acceptance of the plan, the reference to the former autonomous provinces was deleted from the November version.

The rejection of the plan by Serbia and Montenegro can be explained by their perception of the conference and their assessment of the alternatives open to them. They saw the conference as an international effort to present political and legal obstacles to their goal of annexing the Serb-populated areas of Croatia to Serbia. As they saw it, the Croatian *nation* could secede from Yugoslavia, but they should not be allowed to take the Serbs living in Croatia with them and separate them from their brethren remaining in Yugoslavia. The 'special status' for the Croatian Serbs offered by the plan was not attractive for two reasons. First, it acknowledged Croatian sovereignty over the Serb-populated *krajinas*. The Serbs apparently expected the JNA to be able to prevent Croatia from establishing its authority over these areas, thus opening the way for their separation from Croatia and annexation to Serbia. (As we shall see, they subsequently accepted the special status as part of the ceasefire, pending a political settlement, in the vain hope that it would be a step towards separating them from Croatia.) The second reason why the 'special status' concept was unattractive was the likelihood that there would be pressure for it to be applied to Kosovo and Vojvodina.

It seems that after the 5 November session of the conference, further amendments to the plan were considered in the hope of persuading Milošević to accept it. This may have been an opportune moment for such an attempt. As pointed out by Steven Burg and Paul Shoup,[35] at that time the Serbian leadership was reconsidering its policy on the Serb-populated *krajinas* in Croatia, as reflected in Yugoslavia's call on 9 November for the dispatch of a UN peacekeeping force to Croatia. (This is discussed in Chapter 6.) But the prospect of further negotiations with Milošević prompted Genscher to send a strongly worded letter to van den Broek 'demanding full details' of rumoured new proposals that departed from the wording agreed on by the EC.[36] It is unclear whether these ideas were not pursued because of Germany's objections and the problems associated with revising a common EC position once it had been agreed upon, or whether there were other reasons.

Croatia and the other republics accepted the plan. In Bosnia (among Croats and Muslims) and in Macedonia, support for breaking away from Yugoslavia and proclaiming independence was on the rise. The Carrington Plan was consistent with such an outcome. Croatia and Slovenia saw as their first priority the winning of formal international recognition of their independence. Acceptance of the plan seemed to offer the prospect of hastening the attainment of this goal. Croatia was reluctant to grant to the *krajina* Serbs the special autonomous status provided by the plan. Nonetheless it accepted the plan in the expectation that Serbia and Montenegro would reject it, thus rendering Croatia's acceptance of the special status inoperative.

In opposing the plan Serbia was joined by its customary ally Montenegro. The partnership between the two was almost broken when at the 18 October session Montenegro's President Momir Bulatović indicated his republic's acceptance of the plan. According to Silber and Little this was accomplished by the Italian foreign minister, Gianni de Michelis, who asked Mesić 'how Montenegro could be coaxed away from its loyalty to Belgrade'. Mesić's advice was to 'buy them'. Silber and Little quote de Michelis as saying in a meeting with Bulatović that 'I insisted that Montenegro adopt a position of its own'. He also discussed with Bulatović a multimillion dollar EC development plan, as well as a programme for cooperation between Italy and Montenegro of 'about 30 or 40 billion lire'. Bulatović was reported as being 'interested', and according to the Italian foreign minister said that 'he considered Italy [to be] Montenegro's natural channel to Europe'.[37] Bulatović's defection was short lived, and he soon reverted to supporting Milošević. One is tempted to speculate about the kinds of pressure that persuaded Bulatović to forego the generous Italian offer. The episode undoubtedly fed Serbian paranoia, which was constantly drawing a parallel with the break-up of Yugoslavia during the Second World War. Not only did Germany encourage Croatia to secede, but Italy – which had ruled Montenegro during the war – was trying to reestablish its influence over that country.

As will be recalled, the convening of the conference was coupled with the establishment of an arbitration commission. The commission, headed by the president of the French Constitutional Court, Robert Badinter, was not formally involved in the proceedings until November. On 20 November, under the influence of the Serb/Montenegrin criticism that the conference was dissolving Yugoslavia, Carrington requested the arbitrators' opinion on three legal questions submitted by Serbia.

The first was whether the Yugoslav state continued to exist, as claimed by Serbia, or whether 'the question is one of a disintegration or breaking-up of the SFRY as the result of the concurring will of a number of Republics'. The commission responded on 7 December that in view of the republics' desire for independence, expressed in referenda in Slovenia, Croatia and Macedonia, and by a parliamentary resolution in Bosnia, 'the Socialist Federal Republic of Yugoslavia is in a process of dissolution'.[38] Thus the commission provided legal justification for the premise in the Carrington Plan, presented in early October, that Yugoslavia no longer existed.

Carrington also asked the commission whether the Serbian populations in Croatia and Bosnia were entitled to self-determination. The third question was whether the internal boundaries between Serbia and Croatia and Serbia and Bosnia could be considered boundaries from the standpoint of international law. The commission responded to these questions on 11 January 1992, three weeks after the EC Council of Ministers agreed to grant recognition, within their existing borders, to those Yugoslav republics that desired to be recognised as independent states. The commission declared that 'the right to self-determination must not involve changes to existing frontiers', and that the Serb populations of Croatia and Bosnia were entitled only to the rights of minorities.[39] As for the question on the status of the boundaries, the commission decided that they 'may not be altered except by agreement', and that 'former boundaries become frontiers protected by international law'.[40]

The EC's political position was now buttressed by a judicial ruling. Yet Carrington's efforts to persuade Serbia and Montenegro to accept the plan were to no avail. At its meeting in Rome on 8 November, the EC punished their defiance by imposing economic sanctions.[41] The conference ground to a halt.

Recognition

The next stage in the drama was recognition of the republics. The controversy over the recognition still reverberates as analysts continue to disagree about whether the timing and the manner of the recognition helped or harmed the peace process.

Once the Serbs had rejected the Carrington Plan the German government intensified its pressure on the other members of the EC not to delay recognition any longer. It indicated that it was prepared to act unilaterally, and would grant recognition to Croatia and Slovenia before Christmas, without waiting for other members of the EC to do so.[42]

The issue provoked a vigorous debate. The question was not whether to recognise the individual republics as sovereign states. Rather the disagreements concerned the *timing* and the *conditions* under which recognition was to be granted.

The opponents of immediate recognition included France, Britain and the US. They were supported by UN Secretary-General Pérez de Cuéllar, and by the two individuals charged with directing the mediation efforts – Carrington and Cyrus Vance (the latter had been appointed in October by the secretary-general). They called on the EC to adhere to its existing policy, reiterated as recently as 8 November, that recognition could 'only be envisaged in the framework of an overall settlement'.[43] Their argument was twofold. First, granting recognition at that time would deprive Carrington and the Hague Conference of critical leverage, thus making it much more difficult to persuade the parties to make the concessions necessary for an agreed comprehensive settlement. It would be harder to persuade Croatia to give way on the issue of the special status for the Serb-populated areas of Croatia. Furthermore Carrington would be left with no means to pressure the Serbs. Secondly, they expressed concern that recognition might broaden the conflict. Bosnia and Macedonia would find it necessary to hasten their independence, possibly triggering war in these two republics as well. Pérez de Cuéllar, who wrote to van den Broek on 10 December urging the EC ministers to delay recognition, reported that the leaders of Bosnia and Macedonia had emphasised to Vance 'their strong fears', describing 'the possibly explosive consequences' of recognition 'as being a "potential time bomb"'.[44]

In his reply to the UN secretary-general, Genscher claimed that refusal of recognition 'must lead to further escalation of the use of force by the national Army which would construe it as a validation of its policy of conquest'.[45] German diplomats further reasoned that recognising the independence of these two states would transform the war raging in Croatia from a domestic civil war within Yugoslavia into an international one. As long as the Serbs could claim that it was a civil war, they could justify the JNA's involvement as an attempt to restore law and order. But once the international community defined the conflict as one between sovereign states, the JNA would have to withdraw from Croatian territory or risk international enforcement.[46]

The German pressure for early recognition has been attributed to domestic political considerations.[47] Political elites remained strongly supportive of the Croat and Slovene demands for self-determination. Moreover the Serbs' behaviour stirred strong and lingering emotions. These were reflected in a statement issued in March 1993 by the German Foreign Office, which concluded its justification of the German stand on recognition by saying that refraining from recognition 'would have meant capitulating to a master-race logic' (*herrenvolk* in the original German text), implying an analogy between Serbian nationalism and Nazism.[48]

The sharp disagreements over recognition confronted the EC with the challenge of preserving a solid front, and preventing the disagreements from hampering its transformation from an economic community into the European Union, with a common foreign and security policy, as provided for in the Maastricht accords being concluded at that very moment.

In an attempt to delay recognition, prevent Germany from proceeding unilaterally and construct a basis for joint European action, on 10 December France proposed to the Council of Ministers a list of criteria that the republics of the former Yugoslavia and the new states in Eastern Europe ought to meet in order to be recognised. These included respect for the UN charter and the Helsinki principles, guarantees for ethnic and national minorities, and respect for the inviolability of 'all frontiers'.[49] Furthermore, with British and French backing the UN Security Council included in a resolution adopted on 15 December a call for all states 'to refrain from any action which might contribute to increasing tension' or 'to impeding or delaying a peaceful and negotiated outcome to the conflict in Yugoslavia'.[50]

But within the EC the German position prevailed. Britain and France apparently assented to recognition as part of an informal package deal concluded at the December 1991 Maastricht European summit negotiations on the establishment of the European Union. The package provided concessions to Britain on the question of monetary union and the social chapter of the proposed European treaty; France won concessions on institutional reform; and Germany won the acquiescence of Britain and France for the EC to proceed with recognition.[51]

The summit was followed by a 12-hour session by the foreign ministers on 16–17 December. They decided to recognise all Yugoslav republics that met certain conditions, with formal recognition taking place on 15 January 1992. The EC announced that it was 'inviting all Yugoslav republics to state by December 23 whether they [wished] to be recognized as independent states', accepted the guidelines for the recognition of new states mentioned above, accepted the provisions of the draft of the Carrington Plan, especially those relating to human rights and rights of national and ethnic groups, and continued to support the continuation of the conference. 'The applications of those republics which reply positively will be submitted ... to the arbitration commission for advice before the implementation date.' In deference to Greece's objection to the recognition of Macedonia (because of apprehension that Macedonia, after becoming independent, might claim the area known as Macedonia in northern Greece), the decision also required a commitment by the applicants not to make territorial claims on a neighbouring EC state.[52]

The decision was ambiguous enough to allow for differing interpretations. France interpreted the EC decision as making recognition conditional on the advice of the arbitration commission. But Germany announced immediately, without waiting for the certification of the arbitration commission, that it was granting Croatia and Slovenia recognition, to take effect on 15 January.

Croatia's failure to comply with the EC criteria for recognition posed a potential threat to the solidarity and coherence of the EC's foreign policy. Sensing that Croatia's stance would expose German policy to criticism, Germany pressed Croatia urgently to amend its legislation, and provided legal advice that would help it to do so.[53]

Applications were submitted by Bosnia, Croatia, Macedonia and Slovenia. Serbia and Montenegro did not submit applications, holding to the view that they were part of Yugoslavia, a state long recognised by the international community. After reviewing the applications the arbitration commission made a positive judgement on those by Macedonia and Slovenia, but found that Croatia's constitutional law did not fully cover all the provisions of the draft Carrington Plan, notably those on the special status of national minorities. Subject to Croatia 'completing' a constitutional law that satisfied the draft Carrington Plan, Croatia too would meet the conditions for recognition. With respect to Bosnia the commission, referring to the opposition expressed by the Serbs, found that the will of Bosnian citizens to become independent had not been fully established, but raised the possibility that this assessment might change if independence was demanded by a referendum in which all citizens were 'called to participate'.[54]

On 15 January, the president of the Council of Ministers (the presidency had in the meantime passed to Portugal) announced that the EC and its member states had decided to proceed with the recognition of Croatia and Slovenia. The recognition of Macedonia was delayed because of objections by Greece, while that of Bosnia awaited confirmation of support for independence by means of a referendum.[55]

Considerable controversy later developed over the question of whether recognition helped to reduce the conflict or served to aggravate it.[56] Examination of this question requires it be broken down into its separate parts.

With respect to Croatia, it has been pointed out that a ceasefire finally took hold soon after the EC announced its intention to recognise the independence of the republics. This may seem significant considering the fact that innumerable ceasefire agreements had been concluded earlier, but were not honoured. The achievement of the Croatian ceasefire will be discussed in detail in the next chapter. Here it is sufficient to say that recognition had a mixed impact. It was one of the factors contributing to the ceasefire, but at the same time it contributed to a crisis that almost caused the ceasefire to collapse on 28 January 1992, when Tudjman retracted Croatia's acceptance of the Vance ceasefire plan, pronouncing it incompatible with Croatia's sovereignty.[57]

With respect to Bosnia, there is persuasive evidence that the EC decision contributed in a major way to the outbreak of the fighting.

This too will be discussed in greater detail below. For now, it needs to be pointed out that it seems that President Izetbegović was still hesitant about pressing for independence at the time of the EC's call for the submission of applications by 23 December. The EC's invitation deprived him of the time and ability to manoeuvre. It is quite possible that the Muslim–Croat coalition would have decided to proclaim independence in any event. Yet given Izetbegović's misgivings it is possible that had he not been pressed by the EC, the negotiations for an agreed solution to the conflict between the Bosnian national communities would have had a more positive outcome.[58]

Carrington had warned that recognition 'would undoubtedly mean the break-up of the conference'.[59] In fact it remained in existence until August 1992, when Carrington resigned, and the original conference was replaced by a new forum, the joint EC–UN-sponsored International Conference on the Former Yugoslavia (ICFY). After recognition was granted both conferences ceased to pursue a comprehensive settlement, and focused their attention on particular issues – Bosnia, Macedonia, the Serb-held enclaves of the *krajinas* and the status of minorities in Serbia. The attempt to negotiate an overall settlement of the Yugoslav conflict was abandoned.

The failure in perspective

It was not the granting of recognition that caused the efforts for a comprehensive settlement to fail. The failure has to be attributed to three kinds of difficulties. Some derived from the problems that the mediators were trying to resolve, and the broad political context within which the mediation took place. Others stemmed from errors in judgement and tactics. Still others stemmed from the nature of the mediating entity.

The disputants' perceptions of the issues at stake were a major obstacle. Many among the Croat, Serb and Slovene elites perceived these issues to relate not merely to recognition of their identity, but also to the security of their national community – protecting it from outside oppressors, and enabling it to develop economically and culturally. After the wars erupted, hundreds of thousands of people perceived the issue as one of personal safety and physical security. Issues that generate fear and strong emotions are usually difficult to resolve by compromise.

The number of parties that needed to be brought to agreement added to the difficulty. At first there were seven significant Yugoslav actors involved: the federal government, the JNA and the governments of the republics (Serbia and Montenegro are counted as a single actor). Even after the demise of the federal government and Serbia's taking control of the JNA, there remained five parties that needed to be brought to agreement. Formulating an agreement for five willing parties would not have been easy, but resolving the conflicts among five adversaries was a formidable challenge.

The political context in which the mediation took place greatly complicated the mediation effort. Other issues competed for the EC governments' attention and commanded priority. One cannot blame the member states for wishing to promote principles of world order that, if implemented, would help bring about a more peaceful world. Nor could they be faulted for their concern that policies directed at the Yugoslav conflicts might influence the behaviour of actors in the disintegrating Soviet Union. But one should not be surprised that general principles for world order, or policies tailored to potential crises in the Soviet Union, failed to resolve the Yugoslav conflict. Peacemaking in Yugoslavia might have been more effective if it had been given first order of priority, rather than third or fourth, coming after the need to smooth the way to Maastricht, to assert principles for world order and to send appropriate signals to actors in the Soviet Union.

Some of the EC's tactics were probably counterproductive. Proclaiming as early as 4 October that Yugoslavia no longer existed, and ignoring the federal government, may have encouraged and hastened the process of disintegration without contributing to bridge-building between the antagonists.[60]

As if the problems of the Serbs in Croatia and the future relationship between the republics were not difficult enough, the Carrington Plan expanded the agenda further by including a reference to the problems of Kosovo and Vojvodina. Broadening the agenda to include these problems made sense considering the potential for future violence, and also in terms of the logical consistency of the principles the EC enunciated. However Kosovo and Vojvodina did not merely add complex issues to the overloaded agenda. Introducing them was perceived by the Serbs as aimed at the dismemberment of their republic, thus increasing their motivation to wreck the plan rather than cooperate with it.

The most significant obstacles (besides the defiant nature of the issue in dispute) stemmed from the fact that the principal mediator was an intergovernmental entity. This by itself need not have precluded effective mediation; the EC was successful in mediating the ceasefires in Slovenia and Croatia, the latter jointly with the UN. But in this instance several of the impediments to mediation can be attributed to inherent characteristics of international organisations.

One was the difficulty of pursuing a coherent policy when the members were not in agreement. As we have seen, the member states started from different premises and promoted incompatible policies. Germany decided as early as the first week in July (if not even earlier) that Croatia and Slovenia should be supported in their quest for self-determination and independence, and that Yugoslavia should be allowed to disintegrate. On the other hand France, Britain and most other members of the EC believed that Yugoslavia was worth preserving. As a result, the initial Council of Ministers' decisions were compromises, straddling the two contradictory objectives of helping preserve Yugoslavia and managing its disintegration. It took many weeks for the Council to develop coherent policy guidelines.

The lack of coordination between national policies and EC policies further undermined effective peacemaking. The Croats and Slovenes drew encouragement from 'back-channel' messages from Germany urging them to 'go for it',[61] leading them to believe that they need not compromise. Many Serbs, aware of France's and Britain's irritation at Germany's policies, deluded themselves into believing that they were seeing was a repetition of 1914 and 1941, and expected France (and perhaps others) to align itself with Serbia to stop what they thought was German expansionism.

It took the member states many weeks to coordinate their policies. In the meantime the antagonists deepened their commitment to incompatible goals, the war escalated and public opinion became inflamed. By early September 1991, when the Hague Conference opened, it was much more difficult to mediate the conflict than it had been at the beginning of the war in June/July.

To be effective, mediators need to be flexible. They need to be open to new ideas and to invent new formulas. But the EC lacked flexibility in its peacemaking role. Once the member states had succeeded in hammering out a common platform they were reluctant to open the issues anew and risk dissension. The EC's decisions solidified into rigid principles that left little room for negotiation.

Another major obstacle to the success of the mediation effort was its unpropitious timing. A settlement requires concessions, and disputants are usually less resistant to making concessions when the pursuit of their objectives encounters difficulties. In this case the mediation process began when each of the disputants expected to achieve its goals through unilateral action. With the parties optimistic about their prospects, they were disinclined to concede. In such circumstances a mediator's ability to influence the disputants to change their stance is of crucial importance. But the EC lacked the resources to do so. The lack of a military option that would enable the EC to impose its will, as a last resort, was also obvious.

It appears that the European governments continued to believe, as they did in the months preceding the war, that the EC's economic power could be exerted to persuade the Yugoslav parties to follow the EC's political advice. This was no doubt one of the purposes of the warning that sanctions would be imposed on parties that rejected a ceasefire and failed to abide by the EC principles for a settlement.[62] It is difficult to tell whether (and if so, how much) the 27 August threat of sanctions contributed to persuading Serbia formally to assent to the stationing of ceasefire monitors in Croatia, and to attend the Hague Conference. The sanctions finally imposed against Serbia on 8 November did not move Serbia to accept the Carrington Plan. Overall, with the disputants believing that their policies helped protect vital national security interests, the EC's economic sanctions were limited in their effectiveness.

Carrington apparently believed that recognition could serve as leverage in the negotiations: that Croatia, eager for recognition, would agree to grant its Serbian minority a special status and that this might induce Serbia to cease its efforts to detach Serb-inhabited areas from Croatia.[63] But the Croats gave greater credence to Germany's promise of recognition than to Carrington's implied threat that recognition would be delayed until a satisfactory settlement was reached. As for Serbia, it assumed that recognition would be granted, and therefore it should hasten to establish *de facto* control over the *krajinas*. Thus the power to grant or withhold recognition, or more broadly to confer or deny legitimacy, did not serve as an effective means of influencing the disputants' policies.

It is impossible to know whether a different mediating entity would have been more successful in brokering a comprehensive settlement. But the EC was clearly unsuitable for the task.

6
The Ceasefire in Croatia

As we have seen, concurrently with its attempt to negotiate a comprehensive settlement the EC also tried to broker a ceasefire in Croatia. In October 1991 the mediation effort was joined by the UN. Finally, in February 1992, with the UN playing the principal mediatory role, the negotiations produced an agreement and the ceasefire took effect.

The mediation effort that led to the ceasefire can be regarded as both a failure and a success. It was a failure because it took six months to bring about the ceasefire, and in the fighting that went on in the meantime many thousands of people lost their lives and over half a million were displaced from their homes. It was a success in that a ceasefire was eventually achieved. It is impossible to tell what would have happened had there been no ceasefire in February 1992. But it seems plausible that despite the numerous violations that occurred between 1992 and 1995, and the subsequent war in 1995, fewer people were killed than would have been killed had there been no ceasefire agreement.

The mixed outcome prompts several questions. First, why did it take six months for the mediators to arrange a ceasefire? Second, how can the ultimate accomplishment of a ceasefire be explained? Fourteen ceasefire agreements were concluded during the six months of negotiations, but the first 13 were not implemented. Why was the fourteenth successful, and why did it take three months for it finally to take effect? Third, what were the effects of the mediators being international organisations? Initially the mediator was the EC, but in October the UN joined in the negotiations and assumed the principal mediatory role. What difference did the UN make? In what ways did the shift from the EC to the UN affect the outcome?

In trying to answer these questions this chapter will first briefly review the background of the negotiations – the issues in dispute and the war that erupted. This will be followed by a description of the negotiation process. Drawing on this description, the final section will offer some answers to the questions posed.

The issue

Unlike Slovenia, which was able to sever its ties with Yugoslavia with relatively few complications, Croatia's secession brought to the fore the complex issue of the status of its Serb population. There were approximately 582 000 Serbs in Croatia, constituting some 12.2 per cent of its population. While the majority of them lived throughout Croatia, close to 26 per cent were concentrated in areas adjacent to Serbia or to Bosnia-Herzegovina, the *krajinas*, where they constituted an absolute majority in eleven communes (69 per cent of the population compared with 22 per cent of Croats) and a sizable minority in other areas.[1]

As already mentioned, Croatia's secession provoked fear and insecurity among the Serbs, accompanied by a major surge in nationalist sentiments. The fire of nationalism had been flickering for a long time, but was fanned into flames by Milošević and his associates by means of rhetoric and political manipulation. The fears and the nationalism were caused not so much by the centuries-old tension between the Serb and Croat peoples, as by the more recent experience of genocide against the Serbs by the *Ustasha*-led Independent Croat State, established by Nazi Germany during the Second World War. Many Serbs had personal memories of that period, and the younger generation had heard about the massacres from their parents and grandparents. The fears stemming from these memories were exacerbated by the policies pursued by the Croat nationalists following the victory of their political party, the HDZ (Hrvatska Demokratska Zajednica – Croatian Democratic Union) in the first free elections, held in May 1990. The new legislature adopted a constitution that diminished the Serbs' legal status in Croatia from one of equality with the Croats to a national minority. This constitutional change was followed by legislation that abolished the use of the Serbian alphabet in education and public life. Worse, the newly elected authorities reinstituted names and symbols associated with the *Ustasha* regime.[2]

It was in this context that the Milošević government in Serbia encouraged the Serbian nationalists in the *krajinas* to proclaim their regions' autonomy. They drove out local officials who were loyal to the Croatian government in Zagreb, intimidated the Croat population in order to encourage them to leave, and established their own local government, tied closely to Serbia. They associated themselves with the drive to establish a Greater Serbia, and with the Serbian statement that Croatia was free to leave Yugoslavia, but that it could not take its Serb population with it. In 1995 this Serbian nationalist stance produced an unintended and ironic outcome. Croatia did indeed leave Yugoslavia and did not take the Serb population with it, but that was because some Serbs left and others were driven out.

The war

The tension between the two peoples led to numerous violent incidents in 1990 and 1991, even before Croatia's formal proclamation of independence.[3]

After the 25 June 1991 declaration of independence, fighting escalated only gradually. By mid August it was reported that the war had claimed some 300 lives, and that close to 80 000 people had fled or been expelled from their homes. By January 1992 the casualty numbers had increased significantly to 6000 dead and 23 000 wounded.[4]

Initially the main protagonists were local Serb and Croat militias, the Croatian police and Croatia's fledgling army, consisting of the Territorial Defence Force. During this initial phase the JNA, although breaking out of the control of the federal government, was still guided by its Yugoslav ethos and often intervened in a relatively neutral manner to separate the nationalist combatants. But as it lost its Yugoslav character through the defection of its non-Serb (and non-Montenegrin) personnel and became dominated by Serbian nationalists, the JNA's purpose changed from protecting the unity of Yugoslavia to effecting the separation of the Serb-populated territories from Croatia. In pursuing this goal the JNA employed brutal violence against civilians, as exemplified by the destruction and killings in Vukovar and the bombardment of Dubrovnik.

The Serbs perpetrated most of this 'ethnic cleansing', though Croats engaged in it as well. Many Croatian nationalists, including some in authority, considered it desirable that the number of Serbs in their country be reduced, expecting that areas with substantial Serb minorities would be more secure if fewer Serbs lived there. Serb nationalists, supported by the Milošević government and the JNA, believed that their goal of detaching the Serb-inhabited areas from Croatia would be facilitated by expelling the Croats living there. As a result of these policies, by December 500 000 people had been displaced from their homes.[5]

The fledgling Croatian forces were unable to match the JNA. But they achieved considerable success through a tactic of besieging and blockading JNA barracks and installations throughout Croatia. Besides the obvious goals of putting pressure on the JNA to withdraw from Croatia and capturing JNA weapons and equipment for the Croatian army, the blockades also had a political objective. The JNA was expected to respond furiously to the blockades, not only to defend its image but also to protect the approximately 30 000 personnel and their families besieged in the barracks, often deprived of food and essential supplies.[6] In turn the JNA's violent response was expected to mobilise sympathy for Croatia and increase the support for its recognition as an independent state.

The adoption of this tactic was encouraged by the statement by German leaders that if the JNA did not cease its operations the international community should recognise Croatia's (and Slovenia's) independence. On 4 September Foreign Minister Genscher was addressing the JNA when he said in a speech to the German parliament that: 'With every shot by your cannons and tanks, the hour of recognition moves closer.'[7] As already noted, recognition was expected to recast the legal and political definition of the war. It would transform the domestic civil war into an international war and turn the JNA into an invading foreign army, thus establishing legal justification for the Croatian demand for the JNA to withdraw from Croatian territory. Moreover, as a recognised independent state Croatia would be entitled to protection by the international community.

EC efforts for a ceasefire

As we saw in Chapter 4, the attempts to arrange a ceasefire began as soon as the fighting erupted. But although the parties' political and military leaders seemingly accepted the intervenors' request for a ceasefire and committed their forces to comply with the terms of the ceasefire agreement, the fighting did not stop.

When the EC convened the Hague Conference the effort to arrange a ceasefire was invigorated, as Carrington added his voice to the British and Dutch view that the continued fighting would hamper the efforts to conclude a political settlement.[8] In one more attempt to bring about a ceasefire, Carrington summoned Milošević, Tudjman and Yugoslavia's defence minister, General Veljko Kadijević, to Igalo, on Montenegro's Adriatic coast, and persuaded them to sign another agreement on 17 September. This agreement provided for a ceasefire, the return of the JNA to barracks and the demobilisation of the reserve units of the Croatian National Guard.[9] However this failed to be put into effect, so Carrington and van den Broek arranged for yet another agreement. On 4 October, the Croats committed themselves to lifting the blockade on JNA garrisons and the JNA agreed to relocate its units with the assistance of EC monitors. The continued fighting led van den Broek to convene a meeting on 18 October of the eight-member Yugoslav collective presidency, along with Milošević and Tudjman. With Carrington and the UN secretary-general's personal envoy, Cyrus Vance, also present the Yugoslav participants agreed to an 'immediate and unconditional cease-fire; immediate deblocking of all JNA barracks and installations' and 'evacuation of these JNA barracks ... directed towards evacuation out of Croatia'[10] This agreement, like the previous ones, was never implemented.

The main reason for the failure of the ceasefire agreements to take effect was that the principal parties expected to gain by continuing their military operations. Croatia expected that the continuing war might induce the international community to send a peacekeeping force to Croatia, which would help restrain the JNA and, as already mentioned, increase support for the recognition of its independence. Serbia continued its operations in order to secure control of the Serb-inhabited territories.

The customary international practice when encouraging the compliance of parties to their ceasefire commitments is to have their behaviour monitored by third-party observers, and to interpose peacekeeping forces between the combatants. From July the EC and the CSCE tried to arrange for observers to be sent to Croatia. Croatia encouraged the initiative, hoping that the presence of observers might deter the JNA from trying to quash its just proclaimed independence, or at least restrain its activities. The presence of monitors would fit well with the Croatian strategy of internationalising the conflict. The same logic, but in reverse, guided the Serbian leadership and the JNA. They wanted to minimise international intervention and retain maximum freedom of action for the JNA.

It was only with difficulty that the JNA was persuaded at the Brioni Conference to accept the stationing of monitors in Slovenia. The Brioni Declaration of 7 July and a follow-up 'Memorandum of Understanding on the Monitor Mission to Yugoslavia', concluded on 13 July, mentioned the possibility of extending the mission to Croatia, but the JNA and Milošević remained firmly opposed to this proposal.[11]

In an attempt to press Serbia and the JNA to accept monitors, the EC Council of Ministers adopted a resolution on 29 July to that effect, though at British insistence their deployment would take place only after an effective ceasefire had been established. To encourage this, the Council promised to consider requests for economic assistance from the federal government once the ceasefire was in effect and negotiations on the future of Yugoslavia had commenced.[12] But the resolution was completely out of tune with the situation, perhaps even counterproductive. Since the deployment of the monitors (to which the Serbs were opposed) was conditional on a prior ceasefire, the decision added an incentive to the Serbs and the JNA to prevent a ceasefire from taking effect. As for the Croats, they were totally against the idea of economic assistance being used to shore up the federal government and the JNA.

The EC also decided to send the Troika to Yugoslavia to obtain signed agreements on the deployment of monitors, and sent its special envoy, Henry Wynaendts, ahead to prepare the agreements. But Milošević would have none of it and firmly rejected the Troika's demands during their visit on 2–4 August.[13] The divisions among the EC governments rendered this rejection virtually risk free.

Galvanised to make a greater effort to develop a coherent policy in the aftermath of the attempted coup against Gorbachev, at a meeting on 29 August the EC took more resolute action. It finally obtained the Serbs' agreement to the stationing of monitors by presenting them with an ultimatum. As will be recalled, the ultimatum combined the demand for a ceasefire, the acceptance of monitors in Croatia and the convening of a peace conference, stating *inter alia* that 'without a comprehensive and effective cease-fire and impartial foreign monitors the situation in Yugoslavia cannot be sufficiently stabilized to allow for productive negotiations to be held'. The EC governments voiced 'their determination never to recognize changes of frontiers which have not been brought about by peaceful means and by agreement', and explicitly blamed Serbia and the JNA for the violence. Finally, they threatened sanctions, saying the EC would 'consider additional measures including international action' unless its demands were met by 1 September.[14]

Croatia expressed full support for the EC position, but Serbia's acceptance required some additional tough bargaining by Wynaendts and the Troika. According to Wynaendts, having heard Genscher raise the possibility of recognition if the JNA did not end its violent activities, and expecting Serbia to continue to defy the EC, the Croats envisaged joint action with the EC against Serbia. Tudjman, when told that Milošević was to sign the document accepting the EC terms, was 'visibly disappointed'.[15]

If Wynaendts perceived Tudjman's attitude correctly, then it seems that neither the Serbs nor the Croats were eager at that time for a ceasefire to take effect, and both expected to be able to improve their bargaining position by a combination of military and diplomatic means. In any event the arrival of the 200 monitors on 5 September, pursuant to the agreements that had just been concluded, did not bring about compliance with the ceasefire.

While pressing for acceptance of the monitors, some EC governments arrived at the view that monitors would not suffice, and that implementation of the ceasefire agreements might require assistance, perhaps even enforcement, by an outside military force. The discussions about the desirability and feasibility of such a force, as well as all other discussions relating to the EC's role in Yugoslavia, were caughtup in the debate simultaneously taking place among member states, (often at the same foreign ministers' meetings) about the proposed institutional innovation of replacing the European policy cooperation with a common foreign and security policy.[16]

Their different approaches to this project – its scope, organisation and decision-making rules – were reflected in the policies they advocated with respect to Yugoslavia. French officials believed that a robust military peacekeeping force would help calm the situation. Britain, fearful of committing its forces to an uncertain operation, insisted that an effective ceasefire should precede the deployment of peacekeeping forces. Germany argued that formal recognition of Croatian and Slovenian independence would help end the war. Inevitably the positions of these three countries were influenced by a number of factors. France's long-standing desire to make Europe less dependent militarily on the US meant that it was eager to add a security dimension to European political coordination by activating the WEU. Britain's reluctance to commit forces to Yugoslavia was influenced by the inability of its forces to end the conflict in Northern Ireland, and the prospect that once sent to Yugoslavia the forces would have to remain there for years, without an end in sight. German officials were acutely conscious of their country's inability to participate in such a force due to constitutional limitations. Pressed by domestic political considerations, they urged immediate recognition of independence.[17]

Sensing that the EC would be unable to agree on how to bring about a ceasefire and was incapable of deploying the peacekeeping force that might be required for the task, France and Germany agreed at a meeting in Bonn on 19 September between Mitterrand and Kohl to initiate an EC request to the UN Security Council to place the Yugoslav problem on its agenda. The EC governments, meeting in the Hague later that day, agreed to the initiative and adopted a formal resolution to that effect.[18]

The UN and the ceasefire

Transferring the responsibility for the ceasefire to the UN removed a contentious issue from the EC's overloaded agenda and offered the prospect of protecting the EC from further damage to its reputation. Moreover, if a military peacekeeping force was needed the UN might serve as the most appropriate vehicle for organising and deploying such a force. Sanctions, too, stood a better chance of being effective if mandated by the Security Council rather than the EC Council of Ministers. Besides, French officials may have expected that a Security

Council role in managing the crisis might help to reduce Germany's pressure for EC recognition of the republics' independence, which was being strongly felt in the EC.

But the shift to another forum still left the governments with the dilemma of how to stop the fighting in Croatia. Neither the member states nor the UN secretariat considered a UN force feasible as long as the fighting continued and unless both warring sides agreed to the UN's presence.

A change in Croat and Serb attitudes presented itself in November. Croatia was prompted to reassess its strategy as a result of its inability to prevent the fall of Vukovar. The fall of the town proved to Croatia that its forces were unable to stop the JNA if it was determined to push forward, and that international political pressure was not strong enough to stop it either. Hundreds of thousands of Croats had already been displaced from their homes, and the Serbs and the JNA controlled approximately a quarter of Croatia's territory. Besides the high cost of the war, there was the risk that the JNA might escalate its operations and bring more territories and towns under Serb control.[19]

The Serbian political leadership and the JNA were also prepared to consider a change of tactics. The Serbs were now in control of the Serb-populated areas in Croatia. Thus a major Serb objective had been attained. But the JNA had been weakened by the defection of officers and men from the other republics. Its morale was low, and there was little support for the war among the Serbian public. The chance that continuing the war would bring Croatia to its knees or make it accept the loss of territory was not promising. Diplomatically, Serbia's isolation was making itself felt, its policies were widely condemned and concern began to develop about the potential impact of sanctions.[20]

In early November Yugoslavia's Serb-dominated presidency called for a UN peacekeeping force to help establish a ceasefire, and Croatia too signalled its interest in the deployment of a UN force.[21] But deployment and ceasefire became locked in a vicious circle: a ceasefire was unlikely to hold without the presence of a peacekeeping force, yet the UN member states and the secretariat were unwilling to send a force unless 'there was a peace to keep'. In other words, the member states were unwilling to expose their soldiers to danger, and both the relevant governments and the secretariat were reluctant to assume the inherent political risks as long as the fighting continued, and until they were sure that the terms of the deployment were agreed to by the warring parties.

Defining the terms for the peacekeeping force ran into difficulty because Serbia and Croatia hoped to achieve contradictory goals through the stationing of UN forces. Croatia wanted the forces deployed along the republic's borders to shield it from Serbia, and to ensure international protection of its territorial integrity. Serbia wanted them deployed along the front lines, thus establishing a new *de facto* border, implicitly recognised by the international community, that left sizeable parts of Croatia under Serb control. This issue engaged the attention of other governments as well. Van den Broek is reported to have warned Vance to avoid repeating the Cyprus situation where, according to his view, the stationing of UN forces along the front line had rendered a settlement of that conflict more difficult.[22]

It took four more months of negotiations to overcome these problems. After holding preliminary talks with the parties in early November, Vance returned to Yugoslavia on 17 November. His talks there led to a meeting in Geneva on 23 November at which Kadijević, Milošević and Tudjman signed a ceasefire agreement (the fifteenth). The agreement specified that Croatia would immediately lift its blockade on JNA barracks and installations, the JNA would immediately begin to withdraw from Croatia, and an unconditional ceasefire – also to be obeyed by irregular units not formally under Croatian or Serb control – would come into effect the following day. At the meeting Vance also presented the parties with a plan for the peacekeeping operation ('the Vance Plan'). The plan called for the UN forces to be deployed as 'inkblots' or 'leopard spots' within the Serb-populated areas, rather than along the frontlines (as preferred by the Serbs) or Croatia's boundaries (as preferred by the Croats). According to the UN secretary-general's report to the Security Council, the plan was 'generally welcomed' by the Yugoslav participants.[23]

In fact the parties continued to disagree about the UN force, and the ceasefire to which they committed themselves was not observed. Subsequent talks, in which Vance, Carrington, Herbert Okun (Vance's deputy), Marrack Goulding (UN under-secretary-general) and Wynaendts participated, developed the details of the deployment concept, allayed some of the parties' concerns and obtained their acceptance of the UN terms. UN forces were to be stationed in three areas, designated as UN Protected Areas (UNPA). These areas were to be demilitarised and the JNA withdrawn from them. The areas were to be administered by the existing local authorities and policed by local police forces. Refugees were to be allowed to return to their former homes. To reassure the Serbs, the UN promised that 'the operation would remain in Yugoslavia until a negotiated settlement of the conflict was achieved'. To reassure the Croats, who feared that the plan might lead to permanent alienation of their territory, the UN stated that the force was merely an interim arrangement to create the necessary conditions for the negotiation of an overall settlement, and that 'it would not prejudge the outcome of such negotiations'.[24]

There were two major obstacles to implementation. One was the opposition of Serbs in Knin, led by Milan Babić, who announced that they would resist the implementation of the plan. This was overcome with the help of Milošević and the Serbian authorities, who engineered Babić's replacement by a more pliant politician, Goran Hadžić. The second obstacle was presented by Tudjman, who in February retracted his acceptance of the plan, conveyed to Vance on 1 January, saying that 'he could not accept any formula that did not provide for the immediate restoration' of Croatian authority in the UNPA, and that the local authorities would have to be accountable to the Croatian government in Zagreb. In response to Goulding's argument that the plan was an interim arrangement, pending the outcome of negotiations on an overall settlement, Tudjman stated that following international recognition of Croatia 'there were no political issues left to negotiate'.[25] Strong pressure was applied to Tudjman, not only by Vance and Carrington, but also by Genscher, until he eventually withdrew his objections and reconfirmed his previous acceptance of the plan.[26]

Finally, with the ceasefire generally respected and the parties' full and unconditional acceptance of the deployment plan, on 21 February the Security Council authorised the immediate dispatch of the UN Protection Force (UNPROFOR).[27]

Although the ensuing ceasefire was violated on numerous occasions and key provisions of the plan, such as the return of refugees, were not implemented, the arrangement helped keep relative peace until the summer of 1995, when the Croatian army launched a major offensive and occupied three of the four UNPAs. An agreement for the restoration of Eastern Slavonia, the remaining UNPA, to Croatian authority was concluded between Milošević and Tudjman in Dayton, Ohio, in November 1995. The area was transferred to Croatian control on 15 January 1998.[28]

An explanation of the outcome

The main reason for the mediators' inability to conclude the ceasefire negotiations more expeditiously was their lack of influence with the warring parties. As we have seen, the EC spoke with several voices, weakening the credibility of its formal joint position. It also lacked the means to press the parties to accept its proposals. Economic rewards and punishments were not adequate for that purpose, and its lack of a military option was obvious. Initially the UN also lacked influence. It acquired bargaining power only after the parties had proclaimed their interest in a peacekeeping force. Even then it took four more months for the negotiations to conclude. The additional delay derived in large measure from the fact that the ceasefire terms and the deployment of the peacekeeping force were perceived as having a direct bearing on the substantive issues in dispute, and were believed likely to affect the shape of their ultimate settlement.

The mediator succeeded in concluding the agreement only when both sides changed their tactics because they realised they could not gain much by military means. As related above, the disaster at Vukovar demonstrated to the Croats the risks of continuing the war. The Serbs and the JNA had attained their principal goal of controlling the territories with the largest concentration of Serbs. The Serbs were also painfully aware of the weakening of the JNA, the erosion of domestic support for the war and the international condemnation of their policies. There was no point in continuing the war. They preferred to conserve their strength and whatever political capital they had left for the coming struggle in Bosnia.

This was not a typical 'hurting stalemate'. Rather both sides believed that the Vance Plan offered them opportunities for further gains. They did not perceive these gains as a 'win-win' outcome, as each side expected to win and its adversary to lose. The principal gain for the Croats was the withdrawal of the JNA from Croatia. In addition, they hoped that the terms of the agreement, requiring the disarming of the Serbian militias and the return of the Croatian refugees, would help them to loosen the Serb grip on the disputed territories. Milošević apparently hoped that the 'special status' would enable the Serbs to consolidate their control over the territories, and perhaps legitimise it through a referendum held under UN auspices.[29]

In fact neither Croatia's nor Serbia's expectation of gaining control of the disputed territories through the ceasefire terms was realised. The ceasefire did, however, enable Croatia to build an army. The UNPAs came to an end in 1995 once the Croatian army was strong enough to conquer the territories.

In many respects the brokering of the ceasefire resembled the standard theoretical model of mediation: keep the adversaries engaged in negotiations even in the absence of progress until propitious circumstances emerge, then present the parties with a general formula, negotiate the details and persuade them to agree to the terms. In this case, as often happens, the mediator and other third parties helped to create the propitious circumstances. The EC and its individual governments were sharply critical of the Serbs and the JNA. It was obvious that Croatia would soon be recognised. Economic sanctions were being imposed on Serbia, and there was a possibility that they would be expanded and their implementation made more effective. The arms embargo slowed Croatia's attempt to build an army that would be capable of matching the JNA.

Once Serbia and Croatia became disposed to end the fighting, the next task was to negotiate the terms. The terms of the ceasefire had long been on the table. They emerged from months of discussions by Wynaendts and other EC negotiators, as well as from Vance and Okun's preliminary explorations with the parties. This still left many details of implementation to be agreed to: the lifting of the blockade on JNA barracks, the JNA's withdrawal from Croatia, the actual cessation of firing by both regular and irregular forces, and the arrangements for the delivery of humanitarian assistance. Negotiation of the details and implementation of the ceasefire was done mainly by Wynaendts, Dirk van Houten (head of the EC monitoring mission), Vance and Okun. But fighting continued. In a further step towards the implementation of the ceasefire, the parties concluded another Implementing Accord on 2 January 1992. On 5 January, the UN secretary-general was able to report that the unblocking of JNA barracks and the withdrawal of JNA units from Croatia 'had been essentially completed'.[30] Following the latest agreement, notwithstanding 'sporadic violations', the ceasefire had been 'generally observed'.[31]

The concept of UNPAs did not arise from a vacuum. It emerged from the discussions on the Carrington Plan provision for 'special status' to be conferred on Serb-inhabited areas, and Milošević's emphasis that this was an issue of high priority.[32] The initial version of the concept was relatively brief, leaving many details open, and the principles were vague. Details were added and ambiguities cleared in the course of subsequent negotiations. Yet the more the ambiguities were removed, the more difficult it became for the parties, and especially Croatia, to accept the terms. The 'ink blots' and 'leopard spots' metaphors turned out to be poor analogies to what was to happen on the ground. In reality UNPROFOR had to be deployed along the lines that separated the Serbs inside the UNPAs from the Croats outside, eager to establish control over the territories. Moreover Croatia's objections to the independence from Zagreb of the local authorities in the UNPAs provoked a crisis. But Tudjman, under to strong pressure from Germany, which was eager for a ceasefire to be established, was unable to withdraw his agreement to the UNPA concept.[33]

For a brief moment the international community spoke in one voice. This time the coherent collective policy presented through the UN was not undermined by bilateral relationships, but supported by influential states.

Besides the key elements of timing, back-channel support, the skilful use of ambiguous formulations and their gradual transformation into explicit operative details, Vance's success depended ultimately on his ability to persuade the parties to accept his proposals. Some observers have attributed part of Vance's influence with the Serbs to his treating them with greater respect than some previous mediators, and especially to his understanding that the JNA would cooperate only if it was allowed to withdraw honourably, along with its equipment.[34] Another factor that may have helped him with the Serbs was that he did not represent the EC, which they distrusted (viewing it as dominated by Germany), but served the UN, in which Yugoslavia, as a leader of the non-aligned states, used to carry considerable influence.

Most important in making Vance a persuasive negotiator was the parties' perception that he spoke not only for the UN but also for the

US.[35] All parties were eager for US support and none was willing to risk antagonising it. The fact that Vance was a former secretary of state, and that his principal advisor, Herbert Okun, was also a former US government official, helped to create this impression. (It was only later, in the course of Vance's attempt to broker a settlement in Bosnia, that his disagreements with the US government developed and his effectiveness was undermined.)

Finally, Vance had bargaining power. He benefited from the fact that both the Serbs and the Croats now desired a ceasefire and wanted a peacekeeping force to help stabilise it. The member states' and UN Secretariat's refusal to agree to the deployment of a force until a stable ceasefire took effect greatly enhanced Vance's leverage.

There has been much speculation about the effect that recognition of independence had on the ceasefire negotiations. For example Genscher claims that recognition brought peace to Croatia and Slovenia. James Gow, an academic analyst, believes that recognition made the 'crucial difference' because once it was granted the Serbs realised that their interests would now be better served at the negotiating table. Mihailo Crnobrnja, former Yugoslav ambassador to the EC, suggests that recognition had contradictory effects, making an overall settlement more distant but a ceasefire more likely. According to his reasoning, recognition meant that the Croats no longer had a reason to go on fighting and were thus more amenable to a ceasefire.[36]

The analysis presented here suggests that recognition had only a minor effect on the Serbs' considerations. It was not so much that they were deterred by the potential complications of having the JNA's fighting in Croatia become illegal with the granting of recognition, rather it was the need to conserve the JNA's resources for the coming war in Bosnia, and the possibility of attaining most of their objectives through the establishment of the UNPAs, that led the Serbs to accept the ceasefire. Recognition probably weighed more heavily on Croatia. As we have seen, it emboldened Tudjman to try to renege on his agreement to the UNPAs. But at the same time, since the territories in question were generally recognised as belonging to Croatia, the risks of agreeing to this temporary arrangement were diminished. If this assessment of the contradictory effects of recognition is correct, then the overall impact of recognition on the success of the ceasefire was not significant.

Certain features of collective mediation through international organisations that have often hindered their efforts did not prevent a successful outcome of the UN's ceasefire negotiations. There were few if any differences among the member states about the ceasefire and the need to shore it up with the presence of peacekeepers. The identity of views among the member states enabled them to give wide latitude to the UN secretary-general and his special envoy in negotiating the terms. And the member states did not send inconsistent messages to the parties, but instead supported the mediator, thus making the negotiating process relatively coherent.

While some mediations by international organisations are hampered by the mediator's lack of bargaining power, on this occasion the UN team was well positioned to impose its terms. Its bargaining power stemmed from the parties' desire for a ceasefire and for the deployment peacekeepers. Furthermore, in contrast to the EC's image in autumn 1991, the UN's credibility on this issue was not doubted. The UN's ability to organise and deploy peacekeeping forces had been demonstrated on numerous occasions, the potential contributors were lined up and waiting and Vance's role seemed to indicate that the US stood behind the UN's effort.

7
Collective Mediation in Bosnia, 1992–94[1]

It took three and a half years of incessant diplomatic effort to stop the Bosnian wars. During the first three years, these efforts were pursued jointly by a number of European states, with growing US involvement and some Russian participation, acting through intergovernmental entities – the EC/EU, the UN and the Contact Group. These collective mediation attempts failed to produce a settlement. The fighting ended only in November 1995 with the conclusion of the US-mediated Dayton Accords. The ending of the war will be discussed in the next chapter. This chapter will examine the unsuccessful efforts pursued between 1992 and 1994.

As we shall see, the failures of the 1992–94 period can be attributed in large measure to the fact that the mediation efforts, were collective. They were hampered by disagreements among the participating governments and international organisations, and by inadequate leverage. It was obvious that achieving a settlement would require pressuring the disputants to accept terms that fell short of their ambitions, and a willingness on the part of the mediating states to commit troops and other resources to implement the terms. But domestic and foreign policy considerations imposed different preferences on which parties should be pressed and by what means, and what commitments could be made regarding implementation. Attempts to coordinate the mediating governments and organisations took almost as much effort as mediating between the three warring parties. US policies contributed in a major way to this failure. Although the US kept its distance from the mediations until 1994, its impact on the diplomacy was very considerable. Because of its standing as the sole remaining superpower and its presumed influence, it was a major element in everybody's calculations. Its formal detachment undermined the credibility of the mediating entities, and its haphazard interventions and silences contributed to the incoherence of the mediation efforts. We shall consider the US role in the next chapter.

This chapter starts with a discussion of the issues and parties involved in the Bosnian conflicts. It then turns to an examination of the EC's attempt to prevent the war through the Cutileiro Plan. This is followed by a discussion of the 1992 London Conference, which enunciated the principles to which a settlement would have to adhere, and established a peacemaking entity, the International Conference on the Former Yugoslavia (ICFY), which was charged with negotiating a settlement on this basis. The next section examines the negotiations over the three peace plans presented by the ICFY, and over another plan offered by a new entity, the Contact Group, representing five major powers. The concluding section discusses some common elements that contributed to the failure of these peace efforts.

Parties and issues

The negotiations aimed at ending the Bosnian wars were more complex than those on the wars in Slovenia and Croatia. The conflict in Bosnia was between three major parties, rather than two. The mediators were thus confronted with the need to negotiate with three actors (and more – because of the internal divisions within each camp). Any settlement had to be accepted by all three. This was obviously a more challenging task than that faced in the negotiations on Slovenia and Croatia.

Three major national groups live in Bosnia. Before the war the Muslims numbered approximately 1 906 000 (43.7 per cent of the population), Serbs 1 369 000 (31.4 per cent) and Croats 7 56 000 (17.3 per cent). An additional 240 000 people (5.5 per cent) defined themselves as Yugoslavs.[2] The war drew much attention to the history of the relationship between its national communities, with some emphasising the solidarity and mutual tolerance among them, and others the conflicts and violence.

From the 1980s, as nationalism surged in other parts of Yugoslavia, it gained momentum in Bosnia as well. As elsewhere in Yugoslavia, the arousal of nationalist passions in Bosnia can be attributed in large measure to those political leaders who exploited people's fears and memories of historical atrocities in order to attract support. All three communities nurtured memories of being victimised by their neighbours. The Serbs associated the Muslims with the Turks, against whom they had struggled and rebelled on numerous occasions for five centuries. The Muslims remembered their version of history. Thus a senior Muslim official referred to the atrocities of the ongoing war as 'the tenth Serbian genocide against the Muslims'.[3]

Memories of the Second World War contributed most significantly to mobilising support for the nationalists. During that war Bosnia had been incorporated into the Independent State of Croatia, which was allied with Nazi Germany and had engaged in the mass killing of Serbs not only in Croatia proper, but in Bosnia as well. A section of the Muslim population had collaborated with the Croatian regime and its persecution of Serbs. Because of its topography, which is favourable to guerilla warfare, Bosnia had been a major battleground between the Germans and their allies on the one hand, and the anti-Nazi guerilla movements on the other. For their part the Muslims and Croats remembered the cruelty of the Serbian Chetniks, as well as Tito's partisans, who had often targeted whole villages on account of the nationality of their inhabitants, without discriminating between supporters of the regime and the docile populace. Muslims feared the Croats as well, because of the Ustashe regime's policy of coercive Croatisation.[4]

The Muslims' desire to assert their identity was inspired not only by war-time memories but also in reaction to the Croats' and Serbs' view of them as either 'Islamised Croats' or 'Islamised Serbs'. The constitution of postwar Yugoslavia as a federation of five nations and six republics had stimulated the Muslims' quest for recognition. Each of the five nations – Serbs, Croats, Slovenes, Montenegrins and Macedonians – had had their own republics. Bosnia, the sixth republic, had not 'belonged' to any nation. But in a gesture to equate the Bosnian Muslims' constitutional status with that of the Serbs and Croats, in 1971 the Tito government had allowed the Bosnian Muslims (but not the Muslims in Serbia) to define themselves as a nation, rather than a religious community.[5]

As Yugoslavia began to disintegrate three nationalist camps emerged in Bosnia. In the first free Bosnian elections, held in

November 1990, each of the communities gave overwhelming support to the party claiming to represent its national aspirations. The
Communists (named League of Communists – Socialist Democratic
Party), and other parties that sought to attract supporters from all
three nations, together won only 16 per cent of the legislative seats.
Most Muslims voted for the Party of Democratic Action (the SDA, led
by Alija Izetbegović), which advocated a centralised Bosnian state.
Muslims, being the largest community, could expect to have a dominant influence in a centralised state. The majority of Serbs voted for
the Serbian Democratic Party (the SDS, led by Radovan Karadžić),
which demanded that the Serb-inhabited regions of Bosnia either
remain within Yugoslavia or form a separate political entity. Besides
reflecting popular fears, a separate entity could also serve the Serbs'
strategic objective of retaining a contiguous territorial link between
Serbia (through the Serb-populated areas of Bosnia) and the Serb-
inhabited *krajinas* in Croatia. The Croats, represented by the Bosnian
branch of Tudjman's Croatian Democratic Union (the HDZ, led by
Mate Boban), wanted union with Croatia, or at least broad autonomy.
But in 1991 and early 1992 they gave precedence to bringing about
Bosnia's secession from Yugoslavia, which the leadership in Zagreb
considered necessary for completing the dissolution of Yugoslavia.[6]

During the communist regime and until October 1991 Bosnia was
governed by consensus among the three communities. But as Yugoslavia began to disintegrate the consensus principle was abandoned.
Muslims and Croats joined together in the legislature in October
1991 and in a referendum in February 1992 to produce majorities in
favour of Bosnia's independence and secession from Yugoslavia.[7]

Their mutual antagonism notwithstanding, the parties also joined
in coalitions of two against one when the issues and circumstances
seemed appropriate. The Muslim–Croat coalition was the most dur-
able and had the greatest impact. As just mentioned, it led Bosnia to
proclaim its independence. In the summer of 1992 the Muslim-led
government of Bosnia entered into an alliance with Croatia,
although this soon fell apart as tensions between them escalated to
full-scale war. And as we shall see in the next chapter, in 1994 the
Muslims and Croats formed a federation (which in 2001 still exists
more on paper than in fact). At various times Muslims and Croats
collaborated militarily, most successfully in 1995. But other coalitions also emerged from time to time. Serb and Croat leaders met

on numerous occasions, both before Bosnia's independence and during the war, to discuss the partitioning of Bosnia between them.[8] In 1991 Serb and Muslim leaders discussed a plan for keeping Bosnia in the Yugoslav federation.[9] Even during their brutal war there were a few occasions when Serbs and Muslims cooperated militarily against the Croats.

As these observations indicate, the mediators faced a formidable task. Their inability to bring about a settlement needs to be attributed in large measure to the complexity of the relationships between the parties and the bitterness generated by the war. But our concern here is with the question of how the policies of the mediators contributed to their failure.

Preventive diplomacy: the Cutileiro Plan

The first attempt to fail was the Cutileiro Plan, named after the Portuguese diplomat who mediated between the parties on behalf of the EC. The plan was accepted by the three Bosnian parties on 18 March 1992, but the Muslims and Croats withdrew their acceptance a few days later. How did Cutileiro obtain the parties' acceptance, and why did the Muslims and Croats renege on their agreement?

Tensions between Muslims, Croats and Serbs in Bosnia had been mounting throughout the autumn of 1991. The situation became urgent when on 17 December the EC invited the six republics of Yugoslavia to submit their applications for recognition by 23 December. No doubt the EC would have granted the Bosnians an extension and considered their application even after the deadline, had they requested it. But having proclaimed their aspiration for independence the Muslim leadership, headed by Izetbegović, felt obliged to take advantage of the opportunity. Besides the natural attraction of sovereignty and independence, the Muslims probably expected that the process prescribed by the EC would protect them from the intention of Serbia and Croatia to partition the country between them. According to some accounts Izetbegović had some misgivings, but apply he did.[10]

After submitting its application at the EC's prompting, a hitch developed. As will be recalled (see Chapter 5), the Badinter Arbitration Commission ruled on 11 January 1992 that Bosnia did not fully meet the EC's criteria for recognition, but that this assessment could be reviewed if 'a referendum of all citizens' were carried out 'under international supervision'.[11] Most Serbs boycotted the referendum, held at the end of February. As a result only 64.4 per cent of eligible voters participated, with 99.7 per cent of them voting for independence.[12] Violent clashes between Serbs and Muslims erupted the following day, 1 March, in Sarajevo, and gradually spread to other parts of the country as Croat, Muslim and Serb militias fought each other.

Realising that the descent into civil war was accelerating, Carrington appointed José Cutileiro to head the effort to resolve the conflict between the three groups. Portugal had assumed the rotating presidency of the EC on 1 January, and Cutileiro's selection was expected to facilitate efficient coordination with the presidency.

During February and March Cutileiro held several rounds of talks in Lisbon and Sarajevo with the leaders of the political parties representing the Muslims, the Serbs and the Croats. An agreement that was concluded in Lisbon on 23 February was accompanied by the hope that it would help defuse the tensions related to the forthcoming referendum, due to be held on the 29th. But an important section of Muslim public opinion opposed its terms, and on the 25th Izetbegović withdrew his consent to the agreement. Thereupon Cutileiro renewed the negotiations, and on 18 March in Sarajevo obtained the three parties' agreement to a 'Statement of Principles for New Constitutional Arrangements for Bosnia and Hercegovina'. The latter stated that Bosnia-Herzegovina 'would be a state, composed of three constituent units, based on national principles and taking into account economic, geographic and other criteria'. Sovereignty was declared to reside 'in the citizens of the Muslim, Serb and Croat nations and other nations and nationalities'. The central government was vested with authority in specified fields, and residual authority in the institutions of the constituent units. The legislature would consist of two chambers, one of which would be the Chamber of Constituent Units, 'in which each of the constituent units would have an equal number of representatives'. Decisions in certain important areas would require a majority of four fifths of the members of the Chamber. This latter provision was aimed at ensuring that each of the constituent nations would have the power to veto decisions in such areas. The constituent units would be allowed to establish relations with other republics, provided that these relations were 'consistent with the independence and integrity' of Bosnia. A working group was to be established 'to define the territory of the constituent units based on national principles...and other criteria'.[13]

According to Carrington, it was generally understood that the proposed settlement envisaged the establishment of multiple 'cantons', each identified with one of the three nations, and did not propose to divide Bosnia into three territorial entities.[14] It is significant to note that this understanding was not explicitly included in the wording of the plan. Indeed several aspects of the agreement were left vague, probably in the hope that even an incomplete agreement might help to prevent the imminent outbreak of fighting.

Still the plan added fuel to the explosive issue of the territorial definition of the constituent units. It increased tensions among the intermingled communities at the local level, as Serbs, Croats and Muslims sought to establish their 'title' to particular areas. These tensions soon led to 'ethnic cleansing', aimed at reducing or eliminating the presence of inhabitants belonging to rival communities.

The agreed principles also meant that decisions would have to be reached by a consensus of the three nations. This was an important issue for the Serbs, who felt that the recent decisions of the Bosnian legislature concerning independence had violated the long-established consensus principle. Other aspects, including the division of powers between the central government and the constituent units, and the right of the units to establish relations with neighbouring states, were Serb and Croat gains that were difficult for the Muslims to accept.[15]

A few days after they agreed to the 18 March Statement of Principles, the Muslims and Croats withdrew their agreement. This raises the question of why the Muslims and Croats initially accepted the plan.

The Croats were ambivalent about the principles. Most Croats did not favour the confirmation of the political and territorial integrity of the Bosnian state. But if there was to be a Bosnian state, the principles promised to minimise the authority of the central government and provide protection to the Croatian community. The Muslims agreed to the principles only reluctantly. Izetbegović's acceptance may have been motivated by his concern that rejection of Cutileiro's compromise document could delay international recognition of Bosnia's independence. If so, why did they withdraw their acceptance?

Although this time the Bosnian Croats were the first to withdraw from the agreement, ostensibly because they objected to the map outlining the delimitation of the cantons,[16] the moving force behind the repudiation of the agreements were the Muslims. For Croatia, which determined the Bosnian Croats' policy, the first priority at that moment was to bring about Bosnia's secession from Yugoslavia. To that end, it was crucial to maintain the alliance with the Muslims.

As for Izetbegović, he accepted the plan only reluctantly, having misgivings that it might open the way to partition. He was encouraged to withdraw his consent by the impression he gained that the Cutileiro Plan did not enjoy the support of all EC governments. German officials considered it 'a disaster'.[17]

More importantly, he believed that the US did not support the plan. Although Izetbegović was told by Eagleburger during a visit to Washington in mid February that the US would back an EC-mediated settlement,[18] he doubted that this was really so. One reason for his doubt was Zimmermann's much quoted query as to why he had agreed to principles of which he was so critical. Another was the US distaste for arrangements based on an ethnic principle, and US criticism of the Europeans' endorsement of ethnic cantonisation. Furthermore the Muslims were aware of US opposition to partition and of the US's distrust of its European allies, who, it was suspected, might not resist such an outcome. The Muslims also knew that the US was pressing the EC governments to recognise Bosnia's independence regardless of whether or not agreement was reached on the constitutional principles. In these circumstances, Carrington's argument that the Cutileiro Plan represented the best terms they were likely to get, fell on deaf ears. Instead they believed that the US would support them if they tried to win a more favourable settlement.[19]

The US reservations were based on a number of factors, including doubt about whether the cantonal arrangement could be implemented and concern that explicit acceptance of nationality as a criterion for territorial delimitation would set a dangerous precedent and increase the risk of conflict elsewhere. Regret about allowing the EC to play the central role in the crisis and the desire to reassert US leadership were additional factors.

Izetbegović's assessment was correct. On 7 April Bosnia's independence was recognised.

Carrington and Cutileiro did not accept the revocation, and tried to engage the parties in new negotiations on the basis of the plan. But after recognition had been granted they no longer had any means of influencing Izetbegović. The Muslims, though suffering terribly from Serb and Croat attacks, apparently hoped that the international community would intervene militarily on their behalf. Their hope was fed by the condemnation of Serb policies by Western political leaders, the West's withdrawal of its ambassadors from Yugoslavia, the UN Security Council resolution imposing sanctions on Yugoslavia,[20] and media calls for stronger action against the Serbs. In these circumstances Carrington and Cutileiro were unable to persuade the Muslims to reconsider their stand. Their efforts ended in early June 1992, when Izetbegović reiterated the Muslims' refusal to continue talks, and said that they would resume their participation in the negotiations 'only if the basis for discussions was changed'.[21]

The recognition issue illustrates two important points. First, it is a reminder of the limited leverage possessed by the mediators when seeking to prevent the outbreak of war in Bosnia, and the dilemmas of exercising it. Recognition was the most significant instrument at the mediators' disposal. By its very essence the possible granting of recognition was perceived as a 'carrot' by the Muslims and Croats, and a 'stick' by the Serbs, and the withholding of recognition just the reverse – a punishment of the Muslims and Croats and a reward for the Serbs. The promise of recognition helped win the Muslims' acceptance of the Cutileiro Plan. Withholding recognition after the Muslims reneged on their acceptance would have been perceived as a reward for the Serbs, a gesture that nobody thought they deserved. Secondly, it again illustrates the damage caused by the Western powers' failure to coordinate their policies. While the Europeans focused their peacemaking efforts on mediation, the US gave priority to recognition. The Europeans were trying to bring the contending parties to agreement, and sought to use recognition as a lever to this end. The US did not participate in these efforts, and was pursuing a different course. Apparently expecting that international recognition of Bosnia's sovereignty and territorial integrity would deter the Serbs from using force (and probably also in deference to sentiments in Turkey and the Islamic world), the US was pressing its allies to grant

Bosnia speedy recognition, regardless of where the mediation stood. Recognition failed to deter the Serbs, and it is impossible to tell whether the negotiations would have succeeded if the mediators could have used recognition as a lever. But the West's inability to coordinate and pursue a coherent policy did not help the peacemaking efforts.

The London Conference, August 1992: establishing a new mediating agency

Background

Immediately after the European and US recognition of Bosnia's independence, fighting escalated when Serb forces launched heavy attacks on Muslim areas. Attracting most attention was the plight of Sarajevo, which was besieged and bombarded by the Serbs. The intense fighting and the suffering it caused, especially to the Muslims, highlighted the ineffectiveness of the international response. It also led to sharp criticism of the governments, the EC and the UN by the media and opinion leaders for their failure to protect the Muslims from the Serbian onslaught.

The embarrassment and frustration experienced by the governments and international organisations that were trying to end the conflict in Yugoslavia was accompanied by growing disagreement among them about how to address the situation. An important disagreement concerned the deployment of peacekeeping forces in Bosnia. The US took the lead in trying to get the Security Council to approve the dispatch of a peacekeeping force to Bosnia, and to supplement its humanitarian functions with a mandate allowing enforcement of Security Council decisions. But because of its concern about domestic criticism the US was reluctant to contribute its own ground troops to peacekeeping operations. This caused the British and some other European governments to worry about the magnitude of the effort required of them and its open-ended nature, prompting them to try to restrain US activism.[22]

Strong opposition to the dispatch of a peacekeeping force came from UN Secretary-General Boutros Boutros-Ghali, who was concerned about the organisation's meagre resources, and what in his view was an overemphasis on the Yugoslav conflict at the expense of other humanitarian disasters. There was also disagreement between Carrington and Boutros-Ghali about the role UN forces ought to play: whether their task should be strictly limited to peacekeeping, or whether they might be utilised by diplomats in support of peace-making. This erupted into the open when Boutros-Ghali objected to the agreement that Carrington had concluded with the Bosnian Serbs, without consulting the secretary-general, on placing Serbian heavy weapons in the custody of UNPROFOR.[23]

There were other divisions among the Western governments that hampered the pursuit of a coordinated policy. They disagreed about whether the Security Council ought to impose mandatory sanctions against Yugoslavia (Serbia and Montenegro), and whether Croatia should be sanctioned because of its army's involvement in the fighting in Bosnia. They were, however, able to agree to withdraw their ambassadors from Belgrade.[24]

The disagreements and frustrations of the job led Carrington – who had considered quitting since the December 1991 EC recognition decision, despite his urging for a delay – finally to tender his resignation.[25]

The London Conference

Aiming to develop a more coherent international response, the EC (with Britain in the rotating chair) and the UN convened an International Conference on the Former Yugoslavia (ICFY) in London on 26 and 27 August 1992. The conference was attended by some 30 delegations, representing governments and international organisations, and the various Yugoslav parties.

The delegates at the conference approved a number of documents that had been prepared in advance. Among them was a decision for the conference to remain in being until a final settlement had been reached, its work being carried out by a steering committee, co-chaired by representatives of the presidency of the EC and the secretary-general of the UN. The steering committee, based in Geneva, included representatives of the EC, the CSCE, the Organization of the Islamic Conference (OIC), the five permanent members of the Security Council, and states neighbouring Yugoslavia. The co-chairmen were Cyrus Vance (former US secretary of state), representing the UN, and Lord David Owen (former British foreign secretary), representing the EC. Thorvald Stoltenberg (former Norwegian foreign

minister) replaced Vance in 1993, and Carl Bildt (former prime minister of Sweden) replaced Owen in 1995. The co-chairs were assisted
by six working groups that dealt with various aspects of the Yugoslav
problem, including one on Bosnia. The latter was headed by Martti
Ahtisaari, who had previously headed the UN's work on Namibia,
and who after his service with the ICFY became president of Fin-
land.[26]

Altogether the steering committee and its staff embodied an
impressive concentration of talent and experience. It was not a lack
of skills that prevented it from settling the Bosnian conflicts, but it
should have been obvious, as Carrington predicted in a newspaper
interview, that 'the problems are not going to go away by finding a
new forum. One has to recognize that a new forum other than the EC
would be much more unwieldy'.[27] The ICFY was put in charge of
peacemaking, peacekeeping and preventive diplomacy in all of the
states of former Yugoslavia. Its tasks included promoting 'a cessation
of hostilities and a constitutional settlement' in Bosnia, implementing sanctions, implementing the ceasefire arrangements in Croatia,
and developing confidence and security-building and verification
measures. It dealt with humanitarian issues, the protection of ethnic
and national communities and minorities, including in Kosovo, and
the recognition of Macedonia's independence, which was being
blocked by Greece. It also dealt with economic issues and the succes-
sion issues arising from the emergence of new states throughout
former Yugoslavia.[28]

Also approved at the conference were statements of principles to
serve as a basis for settling the conflicts in former Yugoslavia.

As we have seen in previous chapters, concern about potential
instability in Eastern Europe and the former Soviet Union, and the
conclusions that leaders and movements there might draw from
Western policies on former Yugoslavia, persuaded Western governments to subordinate their national policies to the need to affirm
principles that might help stabilise the situation in the former Soviet
domain. While these concerns persisted, another worry entered into
policy consideration: the impact of the Bosnian conflict on the Islamic world. The suffering of the Muslim community inclined public
opinion and governments to view them as victims and sympathise
with their cause. Not far under the surface there also developed a
political concern that Western policies in Bosnia might influence the

struggle between moderates and radical fundamentalists in the Islamic world. An important element in US thinking was Turkey, an essential ally in the struggle against Saddam Hussein and in the competition for influence in Central Asia.[29] An additional concern, which was reflected in the words of a German diplomat but was common to all Western nations, was the need to 'prevent the emergence of a festering Islamic problem on European soil'.[30] In Lord Owen's view, if ethnic cleansing were tolerated and its victims were not helped to return to their homes, 'then we Europeans would pay a terrible price. The Islamic world, rightly, would accuse us of racism against the Bosnian Muslims and hold it against us for centuries to come.'[31] These considerations influenced governments to support the Muslims' position, insisting on the preservation of Bosnia's political and territorial integrity and opposing partition.

Still, US and German officials suspected that Carrington, and perhaps others, might not be firm enough in their commitment to Bosnia's integrity. The statements of principles were thus intended to commit the governments and to provide mediators with binding guidelines from which they should not deviate.

The documents adopted in London reiterated many of the principles that had been enunciated earlier by the EC, the CSCE and the UN. Among these principles were non-recognition of advantages gained by force, and respect for the independence, sovereignty and territorial integrity of all states in the region. Specifically with respect to Bosnia, the statements also called for the recognition of Bosnia-Herzegovina by all its neighbours, respect for the integrity of existing frontiers, and the right of people who had been forcibly expelled from their homes to return.[32] The delegates at the conference adopted these principles by consensus.

The participants included a delegation from Yugoslavia (now consisting of Serbia and Montenegro), and there was open friction between Milošević (at that time president of Serbia) and the heads of the Yugoslav delegation: the federal President Dobrica Ćosić and federal Prime Minister Milan Panić. Ćosić's support was significant because he was a writer whose novels extolled nationalist themes, and he was also one of the principal authors of the 1986 Memorandum of the Serbian Academy of the Sciences and Arts – the Serb nationalist manifesto. The quarrels between the Yugoslav representatives in London, and subsequent clashes between the two and

Milošević, cost both men their jobs – Milošević engineered Panić's replacement in January 1993 and Ćosić's removal in May.[33]

As we shall see, several of the proposals developed by mediators between 1992 and 1995 aroused controversy on account of their insufficient adherence to the London principles.

The ICFY faced numerous dilemmas during its mediation attempt in Bosnia. One concerned the advisability of pressing for a ceasefire. By the time the ICFY started its work the Serbs had established control over two thirds of Bosnian territory. Being committed to achieving a just settlement, consistent with the London principles, the ICFY decided not to press for a ceasefire because the ceasefire lines might become frozen. If the front lines stabilised it might become more difficult to roll back the Serbs' territorial gains and preserve Bosnia's territorial integrity. Faced by potential contradiction between putting an early end to the war and thus reducing the number of casualties, and the pursuit of a just settlement, as prescribed by the London principles, the ICFY gave precedence to justice over the saving of lives. Owen explained this choice on the ground that it was unlikely that the parties would stop shooting without at least an agreed outline of a possible settlement.[34]

Another problem stemmed from the Muslims' concern that mediation would weaken their position, because it implied that the Bosnian Serbs and Croats were parties equal in status to the internationally recognised Bosnian government (which the Muslims controlled). According to Owen, the ICFY was scrupulous in treating Bosnian government officials as representatives of an independent state, but nevertheless viewed all three parties as indispensable for a settlement. The problem was addressed in London by not making the Bosnian Serbs and Croats full participants in the conference. The commitments that they were made to sign were accordingly witnessed by Douglas Hogg (the minister of state in the British Foreign Office) rather than the co-chairs of the conference. But the status of the parties was a persistent issue that frequently affected the negotiations.[35]

Besides the question of status, there was the substantive question of who to negotiate with. It was established very early that the Bosnian Croats were completely subservient to the government of Croatia. Although Mate Boban and other Bosnian Croat officials participated in the negotiations, it was clear that President Tudjman was the ultimate authority for their side. The matter was less simple with respect to the Bosnian Serbs. Milošević claimed that he did not control or represent them. The negotiators assumed that he was saying this for tactical reasons. In practice, it was he who decided for them on many issues. Yet on occasion it seemed that the Bosnian Serbs were able to defy Milošević's authority, perhaps taking advantage of some of his domestic difficulties in dealing with the military, or in protecting himself from criticism by the ultranationalists, headed by Vojislav Šešelj.

Throughout the negotiations the mediators were handicapped by their lack of leverage. Although acutely aware of the problem, Owen either fell into the trap of wishful thinking or merely pretended that the problem was soluble. In November 1992 he told the Security Council that

> the overriding question is how the international community makes any of these fine words and principles stick in the absence of superior military force on the ground or in the air. Our answer as Co-Chairmen is, we know, an unspectacular one – but nevertheless a true one. The principles of the international community will stick through steady, persistent pressure applied day in and day out to any intransigent party that fails to negotiate constructively.[36]

Since the economic and military resources needed to apply such pressure were controlled by governments and not by the ICFY, the mediators were not perceived as credible bargainers. Their credibility was also frequently undermined by the inability of the international community to speak with one voice.

Taken together, these difficulties were formidable and contributed to the ICFY's failure to broker a settlement.

The ICFY plans

Between 1992 and 1994 the ICFY proposed three successive plans: the Vance–Owen Plan; the *Invincible* (named after a British naval vessel) Plan (also called the Owen–Stoltenberg Plan) and the European Union Plan. The key components of these plans were a constitution, territorial arrangements, human rights provisions and implementation terms.[37] More will be said about each plan below. This section outlines some common features and highlights a number of significant differences between them.

Two alternative concepts were reflected in the plans. One concept, embodied in the Vance–Owen Plan, was of a unified state, though subdivided into 10 provinces with considerable autonomy. Each of the constituent nations would be dominant in three provinces. Sarajevo, the tenth province, would not identified with any national group. The other concept was of a federal or confederal union of three autonomous republics, each identified with one of the constituent nations, established on contiguous territory (or in the case of the Muslim state – a minimum of territorial fragmentation). The *Invincible* and EU plans corresponded to this second concept. All the plans called for refugees to be allowed to return to their original homes, and for an international role in the protection of human rights.

Another difference between the two concepts was in the distribution of powers between the central government and the component units. Under the Vance–Owen Plan considerable powers were to be retained by the central government. Accordingly the central government alone would be responsible for foreign affairs. It would also control the military, while the provincial governments would control the local police. Under the other two plans, the powers of the central government were limited. They included the formal conducting of foreign affairs, but the constituent republics would be allowed to establish their own ties with neighbouring countries. The *Invincible* Plan even provided for the right to secede from the common state.

The distribution of territory was a highly contentious issue in all three plans. In the negotiations on the Vance–Owen Plan the debate focused on specific localities. For the other two plans, additional issues emerged. One concerned access: how to arrange for the Muslim republic to have access to the Adriatic sea and the Sava river, and how to enable the Serb republic to link its eastern and western parts in the area near Brčko. The other issue was the quantity of territory to be allocated to each republic. Under the *Invincible* Plan the Muslims were to get 30 per cent of Bosnia's territory. Under the EU Plan the three parties agreed that the Muslims would receive 33.3 per cent, the Croats 17.5 per cent and the Serbs approximately 49 per cent. (This territorial ratio, agreed between the three parties in December 1993, was subsequently incorporated into the 1995 Dayton Accords.) Since at that point the Serbs controlled nearly 70 per cent of Bosnian territory, implementation depended on the Serbs withdrawing from the excess area under their rule.

The plans also differed in respect of the provisions for their implementation. The Vance–Owen Plan required the most extensive and intrusive international implementation role. The international community would be involved in the separation of forces, disarmament, the demilitarisation of Sarajevo, the restoration of infrastructure, protecting freedom of movement throughout Bosnia, and monitoring its borders with neighbouring states.[38] These tasks would require many thousands of military and civilian personnel.

Implementation of the *Invincible* and EU plans would be much simpler. Being less ambitious about reconstituting Bosnia and reintegrating its components, and allowing each republic a large measure of freedom to run its own affairs, international involvement would be essentially limited to two major tasks: the military tasks of separating the forces and implementing disarmament and arms control, and the civilian task of monitoring respect for human rights. Implementation would still require international involvement, but this would be more limited and less intrusive than that envisaged in the Vance–Owen Plan.[39]

It is interesting to note that the complexities and burdens of implementation had only a limited effect on the attitude of the governments that would be called upon to carry the burden. The relative simplicity of the *Invincible* and EU Union plans was not a weighty argument in their favour. What concerned governments much more were political considerations. The US attitude was influenced by the administration's belief that the public would not support the deployment of troops. It was also influenced by whether the plans would be perceived as fair to the Muslims, the main victims of the war. European attitudes were influenced by the degree of US political support and commitment.

The ICFY invested its most extensive effort in the Vance–Owen Plan. It was first presented to the parties in a tentative outline version in October 1992, and was subsequently revised and developed in greater detail. The plan was negotiated with each party separately, as well as at meetings at which two or three parties participated. On each occasion, some aspects of the plan were adjusted and revised. In the preliminary phase between 18 September and early November, ICFY representatives held some 40 formal meetings with the parties and an equal number of informal ones.[40] In the months that followed there were scores of additional negotiating sessions. As a result the Vance–Owen Plan was in a constant state of flux, and did not crystallise into a final version. The process led the parties to believe that whatever was discussed, or even agreed, was open to revision, encouraging them to try to change the terms in their favour.[41]

The negotiations on the other two plans were also intensive but of shorter duration, lasting approximately two months each. These plans also underwent many changes in the course of the negotiations. But as they were simpler the negotiations were more focused. Perhaps made wiser by the experience of negotiating the Vance–Owen Plan, the mediators were less willing to stretch the process through innumerable revisions and adjustments.

Although all three plans failed, their development and the processes leading to their ultimate abandonment were different.

The Vance–Owen Plan

The parties' reactions to the Vance–Owen Plan varied. The most consistent were the Croats, who rapidly accepted the various parts and versions presented to them. Their acceptance has been attributed by Szasz to the proposed territorial distribution, which was particularly favourable to them.[42] But their attitude was probably also influenced by their wider strategy, which assigned the highest priority to gaining control of the Serb-populated parts of Croatia and protecting Croatia's relations with Germany and the US. They could leave it to the Serbs to do the work for them of opposing the Muslims' attempt to gain approval for a constitution with a strong central government.

The Muslims' reaction vacillated between acceptance and rejection. According to Owen, Foreign Minister Haris Silajdžić was initially (in October) enthusiastic in his support for the plan. But the Muslims' attitude subsequently changed and they took a strong stand against it, criticising the wide powers allocated to the provinces at the expense of the central government, and claiming that the plan represented a step towards the ethnic partitioning of the country. In their formal position, Muslim officials embraced the new Western doctrine outlawing ethnic nationalism and proclaiming that the ethnic national state was 'out' and the civil state was 'in'. Seventy-five years earlier, Balkan elites had given their enthusiastic support to the Wilsonian principle of national self-determination. In the early 1990s most of the Balkans still adhered to this old doctrine and lagged behind in adjusting to the new ideology. But in deference to the US and Muslim officials' aversion to 'ethnic cantonisation', early drafts of the Vance–Owen proposals for the structure of provincial governments even avoided refering to the three national communities by their names, and instead labelled them as parties 'A', 'B' and 'C'.[43]

Despite their objections, on 30 January the Muslims joined the Croats and Serbs in accepting the part of the plan outlining the constitutional principles. On 25 March they finally signed the full document. It was believed that they acceded not because they were persuaded that this was a solution they could embrace, but because they wanted the onus of rejection and failure to fall on the Serbs.[44]

The Serbs opposed the plan, though they initially tried to avoid responsibility for rejecting it. Under pressure from Milošević, on 30 January 1993 Karadžić nevertheless joined Izetbegović and Boban in signing the document outlining the constitutional framework.[45] But on 25 March, when Boban and Izetbegović finally signed the full set of documents comprising the plan, Karadžić refused to approve the territorial map and the agreement on interim arrangements.[46] The Serbs wanted the provinces allocated to them to be linked so that their territory would be contiguous. This was important to them mainly because it would allow them to maintain communication with the Serb-populated *krajina*s in Croatia. Their objections also stemmed from the fact that the provincial boundaries required them to give up much of the territory that had come under their control.[47]

Efforts to obtain the Bosnian Serbs' agreement continued for the following two months. Under the threat of sanctions being tightened if the Serbs refused but eased if they accepted, Milošević was persuaded to accept the plan. But his attempt to obtain the Bosnian Serbs' agreement failed. In the end, on 6 May, the Bosnian Serb assembly rejected the plan and its vote was confirmed in a referendum held under the auspices of the Bosnian Serb authorities in the areas under their control.[48]

Lord Owen has attributed much of the responsibility for the failure of the plan to the US.[49] The latter's policies did indeed contribute significantly to the failure, but this should not obscure the part played by other factors.

First, the proposals seemed to be open to endless revisions and adjustments. To be sure, it is in the nature of mediation that proposals crystallise through discussion with the parties. It is standard procedure to work on the basis of a draft, which is amended and revised as the negotiations progress. But the process extended over too long a period, without sufficient pressure for closure. It is commonly understood by mediators that negotiations require deadlines, even crises, to move them forward. This element was missing and the negotiations dragged on for seven months. By the time that the mediators finally indicated to the parties that the time had come to choose between acceptance and rejection, their credibility had already been seriously eroded.

Secondly, the ICFY lacked sufficient leverage to influence the parties to make the concessions necessary for an agreement, and ultimately to make the Serbs relinquish their claim for a territorially contiguous entity, and to withdraw from much of the territory they now controlled. Initially the parties may have believed that the co-chairmen – a former US secretary of state and a former British foreign secretary – were influential personalities whose goodwill had to be cultivated. But when the breach between Vance and the new Clinton administration became apparent, that image dissipated and the chairmen's ability to influence the parties weakened.[50]

When trying to influence the parties the ICFY was almost totally dependent on governments. It tried to get governments that had close relations with the respective parties to influence them – France, Russia and Greece in the case of the Serbs, and the US in the case of the Muslims.[51] During Milošević's visit to Paris on 11 March 1993 France promised that it would endeavour to ease the sanctions against Yugoslavia.[52] But persuading Milošević did not suffice, because he was unable to deliver the Bosnian Serbs. Furthermore the US was half-hearted in its persuasion of the Muslims.

Thirdly, there were deficiencies in the plan itself. It was much too complex and required a massive international effort to have it implemented. The mediators proposed the plan without being certain beforehand that the troops and administrative machinery required for its implementation would be available. This shortcoming was inherent in the very structure of the ICFY. It was an international committee well equipped to design solutions on paper, but lacking means of its own to implement them. This detracted from the mediators' credibility.

As for the US, it bore much responsibility for the plan's failure. The US did not merely withhold its support for the plan, but actually undermined it by publicly stating that it was unfair to the Muslims and calling for the lifting of the arms embargo, which was hindering the Muslims' efforts to equip their army. No wonder the Muslims held back, expecting the US to provide them with military assistance, or to have the Vance–Owen Plan revised in their favour. By the time the US finally used its influence with the Muslims and persuaded them to accept the plan, five months had gone by.[53]

The US also contributed to the plan's failure by the unwillingness of both the Bush and the Clinton administrations to send ground troops to Bosnia. This too indicated a lack of support. It also weakened the Europeans' commitment to providing the resources necessary for implementation. When in February 1994 the Clinton administration informed its European allies that under certain conditions US troops might be available for the implementation of a settlement, a debate developed over whether the troops would be under UN command, as France preferred, or NATO command, as the US insisted.[54] This was not a trivial matter; it was important for redefining the US–European relationship after the Cold War. But the impact of this debate on the mediation of the Bosnian conflict was highly detrimental because it demonstrated that the major powers had other priorities.

The US contribution to the failure of the Vance–Owen Plan stemmed from the fact that its attitude had a determining effect on the policies of all the other actors. It is uncertain whether strong US support would have made the Vance–Owen Plan a success, but its criticisms doomed it to failure.

The *Invincible* Plan

The Serb rejection of the Vance–Owen Plan, and the unwillingness of the major powers to impose it, led the ICFY to abandon the concept of a decentralised state and replace it with the concept of a federation of three republics. The new concept took greater account of the existing situation – the *de facto* existence of three states, and the international community's unwillingness to use force to reshape this reality and impose the design in the Vance–Owen Plan.

Switching to the new concept was not easy for the mediators. Besides the obvious difficulty of bowing to necessity and abandoning a concept they believed in, the mediators were also concerned that espousing the three-state federation concept would make them vulnerable to the charge of being unfaithful to the London principles. Federation could be interpreted as a step towards partition, an outcome disallowed by the London Conference. The new concept was therefore presented as a Serb–Croat plan, and not an ICFY initiative. Despite this disclaimer there is little doubt that the co-chairmen played a key role in this initiative, and the new proposal was called by some the Owen–Stoltenberg Plan.[55]

The three-state federation was not a new concept; it was embodied in the Cutileiro Plan. As will be recalled, the Muslims had rejected the tripartite federation concept in 1992, refusing to negotiate with Cutileiro and Carrington on this basis. Thus the mediators faced the problem of persuading the Muslims to come to the negotiating table. Devoid of material resources to use as leverage, the ICFY employed balancing tactics. The balancing was applied to two relationships.

One was the Serb–Croat relationship. In contrast to the earlier discouragement of Serb–Croat contact, this time the ICFY assisted the Serb–Croat negotiations. The negotiations, under the ICFY's blessing, were an implied reminder of a potential Serb–Croat coalition.

The second relationship the ICFY played on was among the various factions within the Muslim camp. In the summer of 1993 the Muslim leadership was divided. Some, such as Fikret Abdić, the leader of the Bihać Muslims, considered that the federal concept was an acceptable basis for negotiations and favoured the idea of a Muslim state within such a framework. Others, such as the vice-president of Bosnia, Ejup Ganić, and the military, opposed a three-state federation, believing that a unitary Bosnian state would be more favourable for their community because it was the largest of the three Bosnian nations. Izetbegović and Foreign Minister Haris Silajdžić seemed undecided. In an attempt to put pressure on Izetbegović, the ICFY and the EC Troika invited the nine-member Bosnian presidency (a body whose existence was merely formal and had never played any role) to meetings in Geneva and Brussels. Abdić was the only Muslim member of the presidency to attend; Izetbegović and Ganić did not go.[56]

It is difficult to tell whether these manoeuvres helped to persuade Izetbegović to engage in negotiations on the new plan, but they illustrate the limited leverage available to the ICFY mediators.

The new plan now became the subject of intense negotiations. Its principles were accepted by the parties in August, but many details remained to be finalised.[57] The most important were the territorial arrangements for access to the Adriatic and the overall quantity of territory to be allocated to the Muslim republic. The Serbs and Croats initially offered the Muslims 24 per cent, but the mediators persuaded them to increase it to 30 per cent.[58]

On 20 September on the British naval vessel the *Invincible*, in the Adriatic, the mediators convened what was supposed to be the final meeting of the three parties to sign the agreement. But Izetbegović refused to sign, referring the issue for final decision to the Bosnian (Muslim) parliament. On 29 September the parliament rejected the territorial arrangements, while ostensibly approving the other parts of the plan.[59]

Again, there is no single factor to explain the plan's failure. Probably the most important reason for its rejection was the strong opposition of the Muslim military command, who thought that the Muslims could obtain a more favourable territorial arrangement if the war continued. They drew encouragement from the success of the Muslim forces in the war against the Croats in central Bosnia, and from the US's and Islamic countries' continued advocacy of the lifting of the arms embargo. The US did not exactly come out against the plan, but its support was lukewarm and after the vote, it expressed approval of the Muslims' rejection of it. Some EC members, notably Germany and the Netherlands, also let their criticism be known. Van den Broek, now the EC commissioner for external affairs, 'accused the Co-Chairmen publicly of a "strategy of capitulation" and "legitimized aggression"'.[60]

Given the opposition of some of his associates and the military command, and recognising that the international community was not strongly supportive of the plan, Izetbegović did not press the assembly to give its approval, thus dooming the plan to failure.

The EU Plan

The Muslims' rejection of the *Invincible* Plan soon led to a new initiative, the EU Plan. This initiative differed from earlier ones in that the EU governments were directly involved, rather than indirectly involved through the ICFY. It was launched on 7 November 1993 through a joint letter to the EU by Klaus Kinkel and Alain Juppé, the German and French foreign ministers. Significantly, their initiative coincided with the inauguration of the EU's Common Foreign and Security Policy on 1 November 1993.[61]

The involvement of the EU governments stemmed mainly from the dissatisfaction of some of them, most notably those of Germany and the Netherlands, with the *Invincible* Plan, which was viewed as inconsistent with the London principles and as offering to the Muslims less territory than they deserved.[62] Germany was persuaded to drop its objection about the principles and to join in the offering of new proposals, which resembled the *Invincible* Plan's concept of a union of three republics. The new initiative proposed action by the EU to obtain from the Serbs 3 per cent more territory for the Muslims, thus increasing the Muslim share to 33 per cent. In addition, the Serbs were to make concessions to the Croats in the *krajina*. In return the EU would arrange for the UN sanctions against Yugoslavia to be eased.[63]

The EU governments now became active negotiators alongside the ICFY. Intense negotiations eventually led to an agreement between the Croats, Muslims and Serbs in Brussels on 21 December, allocating to the Muslims 33.5 per cent, the Serbs 49 per cent, and the Croats 17.5 per cent of the territory.[64]

But the parties' agreement to the percentages did not resolve the question of which areas would be transferred to the Muslims. The continued negotiations over territorial issues then became entangled with the question, raised by the Muslims, of how their access to the Adriatic would be assured in the event of the union of three republics dissolving.[65]

In mid-January 1994 the negotiations for a settlement based on the EU Plan were discontinued. The plan failed not because it was formally rejected by one of the disputants, but because it was abandoned by its sponsors.[66] This must be attributed to the continued disagreements between the US and its European allies. The US had complained that it was not consulted on the EU Plan. It had been particularly opposed to the easing of the sanctions, as promised by the EU to Yugoslavia.[67] Furthermore the US had launched a diplomatic initiative that was uncoordinated with that of the EU: it was working to resurrect the Muslim–Croat alliance. By January 1994 Germany had become actively involved in this US-sponsored project, and disengaged from the initiative it had pursued in partnership with France. The Muslims too had lost interest in the EU Plan and focused on what appeared to them to be a more advantageous course that might result in greater US support and improved military prospects in their war against the Serbs.[68]

Not for the first time the US had acted as a magnet. Even if it had not intended to undermine the EU Plan its new initiative had led to the plan's demise.

The Contact Group

It had long been obvious that settlement of the Bosnian conflict required active US involvement. Russian cooperation was also deemed desirable due to Russia's presumed influence over the Serbs. Sensing that the US preferred direct intergovernmental cooperation among a few key actors, as distinct from coordinating policies through the ICFY, in April 1994 Owen proposed the establishment of a Contact Group. He believed such a framework to be desirable because the existing institutions were unsuitable: neither the US nor Russia were members of the EU; NATO was inappropriate because Russia was not a member and because France felt uncomfortable with it; and the UN seemed too cumbersome. The proposal that the Contact Group be limited to the US, Russia, Britain, France and Germany aroused some resentment on the part of other EU members, Turkey and the UN Secretariat, but had practical logic. The US, besides its vast material and diplomatic resources, had developed a close relationship with the Muslims. The Russians were believed to be influential with the Serbs. Germany carried influence with the Croats. Britain and France had large numbers of troops on the ground in Bosnia, and were permanent members of the Security Council. Last but not least, these five governments were the most heavily involved, and it was important that their activities be better coordinated.[69]

The Contact Group had an additional potential advantage. It was expected to carry weight because its decisions committed governments that had the capability to reward or punish the disputants. Thus its pronouncements would be perceived as more credible than those of the ICFY, the EU and the UN, all of which lacked resources of their own and depended on governments to support them.

The hope placed on the new mediating agency was not fully realised. Its decision-making process was cumbersome and necessitated many compromises, which impaired the coherence and effectiveness of its diplomacy. Moreover, the division of labour between the Contact Group and the ICFY was not entirely clear, as the ICFY continued to negotiate with the disputants, alongside collective negotiations by the five and bilateral contact between each of the five governments and the disputants.[70]

The Contact Group's first meeting at the ministerial level, on 13 May 1994, resulted in agreement to work simultaneously towards a ceasefire and a settlement. The Contact Group's interest in a ceasefire was a new element, since hitherto mediators had believed it preferable to achieve a settlement they could defend as being a just one, rather than a ceasefire that might be criticised as freezing the frontlines, thus enabling the Serbs to hold onto their conquests. The Contact Group's efforts failed to produce an agreement because the Serbs wanted the ceasefire to be of indefinite duration, while the Muslims wanted it to be limited to four months.[71]

The Contact Group also agreed to link the suspension of sanctions against Yugoslavia with Serb acceptance of Contact Group proposals. Over the next few weeks the Contact Group worked on a new territorial map to present to the parties, but it was unable to agree on what to do if the Serbs rejected it.[72]

The territorial map retained the percentages that had been agreed to by the parties in December 1993 – 49 per cent for the Serbs, 33.3 per cent for the Muslims and 17.7 per cent for the Croats. Its main significance was a change in the boundaries proposed in the EU Plan. It allocated to the Muslims more territory in eastern Bosnia. It also eliminated the Serbian corridor at Brčko, proposing instead that the two segments of Serb territory and two segments of Muslim–Croat Federation territory meet there at a common point. Flyover highways and railway lines would be constructed at this point to link the eastern and western parts of the Serb republic, and connect the federation's Posavina region with the main body of the federation.

The proposal submitted by the Contact Group to the parties on 6 July 1994 comprised only the map, which was considered to be the key to any agreement. Hence the proposal did not include matters relating to the constitution. According to Carl Bildt, no constitutional proposals were submitted to the parties because the Contact Group members were unable to agree on its terms. The Contact Group requested the parties to respond by 19 July and indicated that this was a take it or leave it proposal, and not a draft open to revisions.[73]

The Muslim–Croat Federation accepted the plan. But the Bosnian Serbs' response, shrouded in much drama and theatre, was not the unconditional acceptance that was demanded of them. Rather they said that the map could serve 'in considerable measure, as a basis for further negotiations'. Furthermore the Serbs argued that their response to the map depended on the nature of the constitution.[74]

In the weeks that followed the Contact Group and the ICFY made further efforts to persuade the Serbs to accept the map, and refused to consider changing it. Milošević, who wanted relief from the sanctions, supported their efforts by imposing sanctions against the Bosnian Serbs: Yugoslavia cut supplies to them, and closed the border with the Republika Srpska. But to no avail; the Bosnian Serbs refused to comply.[75]

The Contact Group's failure can be attributed in part to the territorial demands made on the Serbs. Denying the Serbs the Brčko corridor had far-reaching strategic implications because it cut off the Serbs in Western Bosnia and the *krajina* from Yugoslavia, placing their links to Yugoslavia at the mercy of the Croats and Muslims. Given the sharp criticism that Milošević faced from other nationalist politicians such as Vojislav Šešelj, and the misgivings of the military, the Bosnian Serbs believed that Milošević would not be able to force them to yield.

The divisions within the Contact Group did not help its persuasive efforts. True, its threats were more credible than those of the ICFY, which did not have the economic or military capability to punish defiance. But it was widely known that the Contact Group governments disagreed on what measures to take if the territorial map were rejected. Concluding that the Contact Group was unlikely to use force to impose its plan, the Bosnian Serbs refused to accept it.

Some common elements

As we have seen, the plans differed, the negotiation processes differed and the disputants' reactions to the plans differed. Two of the settlement proposals were rejected by the Muslims (Cutileiro and *Invincible*), two by the Bosnian Serbs (Vance–Owen and the Contact Group) and one was abandoned by its sponsors (the EU Plan). These and other differences notwithstanding, the failed mediations shared some common elements.

Timing

The timing of settlement efforts is widely considered to have a major influence on their outcome. If the disputants see themselves as being locked into a hurting stalemate, this is believed to be particularly conducive to successful mediation.[76]

It seems significant, therefore, that none of the plans was offered in a situation of hurting stalemate. The Cutileiro efforts were made before the war, when all the parties were hopeful of realising their goals. The plans offered during the war were presented when the Serbs and Croats were satisfied with their gains, and did not feel stalemated. Milošević was eager to have the sanctions against Yugoslavia lifted, but was unable to make the Bosnian Serbs accept plans that they opposed. The Muslims accepted the Vance–Owen and Contact Group Plans not because they could see no better way out or wanted either plan to be implemented, but because they thought they could rely on the Serbs to reject the plans, which would improve the prospect of having the arms embargo lifted and enable them (the Muslims) to launch a military offensive. Thus it appears that the failure of the mediation efforts can be explained in part by their inauspicious timing.

When a hurting stalemate does not exist, mediators sometimes try to create one. But no serious strategy for engineering a stalemate emerged during the course of these five mediation efforts. The lift and strike policy advocated by the US did not amount to a scheme for creating a stalemate. US proposals, as well as NATO air strikes against the Serbs, were unrelated to the diplomatic process. It was only in 1995 that such a strategy emerged.

The disputants' perception of their options

The mediation efforts ultimately failed because the Serbs and Muslims believed that they had better options than to concede.

The Muslims expected that the US would help them to overcome the consequences of repudiating the Cutileiro Plan, and that it would obtain for them better terms than those offered by the Vance–Owen and *Invincible* proposals. They were also receiving military assistance and building an army (the UN embargo notwithstanding), which they expected would enable them to achieve their goals. The Serbs thought they were strong enough to overcome the mild punishments likely to be applied against them for rejecting the Vance–Owen and Contact Group Plans. They believed that market forces, the lure of financial gains, would undermine the economic sanctions imposed on them. They did not expect that a major military effort would be mounted against them. Thus holding onto their gains would not entail unbearable costs or high risks. As both Muslims and Serbs continued to believe in the success of their policies there was no reason for them to concede.

Influence

Mediators of international conflicts need to be able to influence the disputants to change their policies and accept compromises. The collective entities mediating between 1992 and 1994 – the EU, the ICFY and the Contact Group – had few resources to enable them to exert an influence. The ICFY tried to play on Muslim internal politics, promoting Fikret Abdić in an attempt to influence Izetbegović. But it lacked economic and military resources to use as sticks and carrots in support of mediation. The ICFY's and EU's influence on the disputants was further undermined when it became apparent that they did not enjoy US support, and that they were unable to harness the economic and military resources of the major states to back their diplomacy. Furthermore the disputants were well aware of the disagreements among the members of the collective entities pursuing the mediation, and were able to play on their divisions and weaken the mediators' cohesion and influence.

These weaknesses are inherent in collective mediation, and are difficult to overcome.

Ethical dilemmas

The discussion of why the mediation efforts were not successful did not address the question of whether better outcomes were possible. They probably were, but I shall not speculate about alternative scenarios, except for one that raises an ethical question.

As recounted above, the mediators did not assign a high priority to achieving a ceasefire. Former President Jimmy Carter negotiated a ceasefire in December 1994, and may have received the quiet consent of the White House and other mediators to do so. True, the international community called on the parties on innumerable occasions to end the hostilities, and UNPROFOR negotiated many local ceasefires. But the ICFY and the governments and organisations sponsoring the mediation efforts did not to try to arrange a general truce. In their view a ceasefire would have frozen the *status quo* and thus would have exposed them to the charge that they were accepting *defacto* partitioning and ethnic cleansing.[77]

Ultimately, in October 1995, after the Croat and Muslim armies succeeded in forcing the Serbs to retreat and give up much of the territory they had conquered, the mediator arranged a ceasefire (more on that in the next chapter). This raises the question of whether it would have been preferable for the mediators to have focused on a ceasefire earlier. If successful, a ceasefire would have saved tens of thousands of lives. A major effort to negotiate a ceasefire need not have given the appearance that the international community accepted conquests and ethnic cleansing, because once a ceasefire had been achieved the mediating governments and organisations could have continued to press for a just and fair settlement.

Such a ceasefire would have required adjustments to the front lines to simplify and stabilise them. It would also have required peacekeeping forces to be deployed as buffers between the warring parties. But implementation would have been relatively simple. It would not have required risky commitments that public opinion in the West might have been loath to approve.

This course of action was excluded from consideration not only because it was considered unfair to the Muslims, but also out of concern that it might send a signal to other groups – especially in Eastern Europe and the former Soviet Union – that resort to violence might pay. We cannot know whether the international community's stance on Bosnia really prevented such activities from taking place.

This is not to question the necessity of promoting norms that hold the promise of creating a more orderly and peaceful world. The question is one of mediators' priorities and sequencing: should the mediating governments and organisations have given priority to saving lives by stopping the war, or to demonstrating commitment to principles? What comes first?

8
US Policy and the Making of the Dayton Accords[1]

It is arguable how much US policies undermined the Bosnian settlement efforts between 1992 and 1994. But its key role in the making of the Dayton Accords is undisputed.

The Dayton agreements stand out for their accomplishments, in sharp contrast to the earlier efforts to settle the Bosnian conflicts, which had all failed. For the first time all the relevant parties signed an agreement to end the war in Bosnia and the fighting stopped. Although the implementation of important aspects of the ambitious design concluded at Dayton has run into difficulties, people have been able to turn to the reconstruction of their lives. Besides the agreements on Bosnia, an agreement for the peaceful transfer of Eastern Slavonia to Croatian administration was concluded at Dayton, and has subsequently been implemented.

How can the successful outcome of the Dayton mediation be explained? The achievement can be attributed to the combined effect of numerous factors. The discussion that follows emphasises two key elements: the role of the US as leader of the peacemaking drive, and the use of military force in support of mediation.

US policy in 1995 was markedly different from that pursued during the previous five years. The attempt to explain Dayton will therefore begin by outlining the important changes in US policy that led to the Dayton Accords.

Although formally the mediation in 1995 was conducted by the Contact Group, in fact the diplomatic process was directed and managed by the US. The latter's partners in the Contact Group participated in the negotiations, but were prevented from interfering with the tight US control over the process.

This mediation initiative was led by a single state. This contrasts sharply with the previous mediation attempts, almost all of which were conducted by collective intergovernmental entities. Previous chapters have discussed the difficulties encountered by collective mediation conducted through international organisations. These tend to be encumbered by the compromises and ambiguities inherent in multilateral decisionmaking, and by the lack of military and economic resources of their own to use as levers in the negotiations. Decisionmaking within states is also affected by the multiplicity of participants in the process. But within states there exists an ultimate authority that can make decisions when officials disagree, enabling the process to produce more coherent policies than is the case with intergovernmental organisations. Moreover the mediator in this case was a great power whose promises and threats were perceived as much more credible than those of the EU, the UN, the ICFY and the Contact Group.

Obviously a settlement does not depend on the mediator alone. Studies of mediation have pointed out that disputants are more willing to make the compromises necessary for an agreement when they see themselves as locked into a mutually hurting stalemate. Hurting stalemates often develop from interactions between the adversaries, but when the adversaries do not perceive themselves as facing such a stalemate, mediators have been known to manipulate the situation so as to create such a perception.[2]

In this case the mediator went beyond the role of 'mediator as manipulator', which is quite common in international mediation efforts, and played the key role in defeating the Bosnian Serbs militarily. It did so both directly, by leading the NATO bombing campaign that devastated the Bosnian Serb army and facilitated the Muslim and Croat victories, and indirectly by enabling and manipulating the actions of the Croat and Muslim forces. Since mediation is generally understood to be a non-violent method of conflict settlement, the US policy of combining mediation with military punishment seems to be a borderline case between mediation and military intervention, best described as 'coercive mediation'.

The evolution of US policies, 1990–95

The Dayton Accords were made possible by three major US policy transformations: the US accepted the division of Bosnia into nationally (ethnically) defined entities, a principle it had previously opposed; it agreed to send US ground forces to Bosnia, an involvement that US policy makers had tried to avoid; and it took the lead in the diplomacy of peacemaking, instead of sniping from the sidelines. Appreciation of these changes requires a brief review of their background.

US policy with respect to the situation in Yugoslavia can be characterised as one of relative passivity between 1990 and 1992 (notwithstanding the secretary of state's visit to Belgrade in June 1991)[3] and gradually increasing involvement thereafter.[4]

Stepping aside

In 1990, when experts warned that the violent break-up of Yugoslavia was imminent, the initial US inclination was to take the lead in developing a joint policy with its allies to deal with the situation. This idea was quickly abandoned when the European allies objected to a US proposal to discuss the issue at the NATO Council meeting in November 1990.[5]

The US abandoned its attempt to take on the leadership for several reasons. The most immediate was the desire to avoid overburdening US-European relations, which were strained at that time due to disagreements over policy towards Iraq. Building support for the coming war in the Gulf was considered more important and more urgent than arguing about the developing crisis in Yugoslavia. Yet the US's relative passivity with respect to Yugoslavia continued even after the Gulf War. This was due in part to its preoccupation with the collapse of the Soviet Union, and in large measure because of its doubt that war in Yugoslavia could be prevented without the commitment of substantial US military forces to such an endeavour, a commitment that the American public was unlikely to support. The US reluctance to act was rationalised by the argument that after the end of the Cold War, events in Yugoslavia no longer affected important US interests. The reluctance to engage was further influenced by the European allies' claim that Yugoslavia was a European problem and was best left to the EC to take care of. US officials could not but see this claim in the context of the ongoing political battle over the desire of some European countries (notably France) to assert a European defence identity and reduce the US role on the Continent. This led to 'an undercurrent in Washington... that it was time to make the Europeans step up to the plate and show that they could act as a unified power'.[6]

The recognition of Bosnian independence

The US temporarily shed its passivity in early 1992, when according to David Gompert it 'pressured the EC to recognize Bosnia in exchange for US recognition of Slovenia and Croatia'.[7]

A number of factors contributed to this surge of activism and the push for recognition of Bosnian independence. According to Baker, the decision to press for recognition stemmed in large measure from the assumption that not to recognise Bosnia at that time 'would invite Serbian and Croatian adventurism'.[8] Officials argued also that recognition would 'internationalize the problem and deter the Serbs from meddling'.[9] The latter argument is remarkable because it reversed the position that the US had taken only two months before, when it had disputed Germany's argument that recognising Croatia and Slovenia would deter aggression. Offering US recognition of Croatia and Slovenia in return for the EC governments' recognition of Bosnia may have helped persuade reluctant European governments to do so. But it also served as a convenient opportunity for the US to get into step with the European allies (and a large number of other states) on the issue of recognising Croatia and Slovenia. Most probably, an important reason behind the US initiative was the desire to avoid friction with the Islamic world, which was supporting the Bosnian Muslims' quest for independence. Especially important was the need to protect relations with Turkey. It is estimated that between two and four million of Turkey's citizens are of Bosnian descent. Pressures from this community, and more importantly from the Welfare Party, which presented itself as the defender of Islam, placed the Bosnian issue high on Turkey's political agenda. US sensitivity to the impact of the Bosnian problem on Turkey's domestic politics and US–Turkish relations was particularly acute because of the US's need to use the airbase at Incirlik for continuous operations over Iraq (even after the formal ending of the Gulf War in 1991). Turkey's importance for the US was further elevated by a plan to move oil from Central

Asia through a pipeline that would have its outlet on Turkey's Medi-
terranean coast.[10] Finally, the recognition was facilitated by the
peaceful disintegration of the Soviet Union at the end of 1991. This
removed the concern that recognition of the breakaway Yugoslav
republics might prompt a violent chain of events in the Soviet
Union, endangering the security of the Soviet nuclear arsenal.

As mentioned in the previous chapter, recognition contributed to
the demise of the Cutileiro Plan. US criticism of the plan, and especially the ethnic/national criteria that served to delimit the proposed
cantons, reflected US support for the concept of a unitary Bosnian
state. This had a fateful consequence in that it encouraged the Muslim leadership to oppose cantonisation and federation. Moreover,
although US representatives repeatedly told Muslim leaders that the
US would not intervene militarily in Bosnia,[11] the US advocacy of
deterring the Serbs by recognising Bosnia and thus placing it under
the protection of international law, fed the Muslims' hopes that the
US would come to their assistance. It was this hope that encouraged
their resistance effort, and enabled the Muslim political entity to
ward off the onslaughts of the Serbs and the Croats and to survive.
It was also at the heart of their bitter disappointment and the feeling
that the West had betrayed them.

For the next two years the US continued to adhere to the tenet that
Bosnia should be a unitary state. Its commitment to this principle
was reflected in its lack of support for the Vance–Owen Plan, the
Invincible Plan and the EU Plan, all of which were based on the
principle of a decentralised Bosnian state, consisting of nationally
(ethnically) based autonomous units.

Compromising unity: the Croat-Muslim federation

A major change in US policy was indicated in early 1994 by its
mediation of an agreement between the Muslim-led Bosnian state
and Croatia to establish a Croat–Muslim federation in Bosnia. The
agreement had important strategic consequences. It also reflected
two significant changes in the US approach to the mediation of a
settlement in Bosnia.

First, it indicated that the US was now willing to become involved
and to commit itself deeply and publicly. This was the first time that
the US had taken the initiative in mediating (with German help) an
important agreement. Another move that signified the US's readiness

for active involvement in mediation was its attempt to help settle the conflict over the status of the Serb-inhabited *krajinas* in Croatia. Concurrently with the conclusion of the federation agreement, the US initiated the 'Z-4' (Zagreb four) process – a joint effort with Russia, the EU and the ICFY to mediate that conflict.[12] Second, it signalled that the US had in effect abandoned its support for the principle of a unitary Bosnian state.

It appears that these changes in US policy developed in response to the military situation in Bosnia. They did not stem from a strategic design for a settlement, but rather were the necessary political under-pinning of a military alliance aimed at reversing the Serbs' advantage on the battlefield. The Croat–Muslim war, which had been going on for many months, was escalating, and with the Bosnian Croats losing ground to the Muslims the regular army of the Republic of Croatia was increasing its support of the Bosnian Croats. Croatia's interven-tion posed a military danger to the Muslims, who were fighting a two-front war against both Croats and Serbs. It also threatened to cut off the supplies and clandestine arms shipments that the Muslims were receiving through Croatia (with the silent approval of the US and its allies). The Muslim–Croat war also raised the prospect of renewed Croat–Serb cooperation aimed at the partitioning of Bos-nia.[13]

The federation agreement relieved the threat to the survival of the Bosnian state, and opened the possibility of reversing the regional balance of power. It facilitated the conclusion of a ceasefire that effectively ended the Croat–Muslim war, thus allowing the Muslim army to concentrate its efforts on the Serbs. It also enabled the supply of weapons to the landlocked Muslims through Croatia.

Both the Croats and the Muslims were reluctant to enter into the agreement. The Bosnian Croats, under the leadership of the Bosnian branch of the HDZ (the ruling party in Croatia), had proclaimed the establishment of the Republic of Herceg-Bosna in July 1992. This proclamation reflected the reality that the Croat-populated areas of Bosnia were being ruled as part of Croatia. In its effort to persuade Croatia to accept the agreement and force the Bosnian Croats to comply, the US indicated to Croatia that it was fighting the wrong war. It was offered a choice of either aligning with the Muslims and receiving US support for the regaining of Croatian territories con-trolled by the Serbs, or becoming subject to international sanctions for violating the sovereignty and territorial integrity of the internationally recognised Bosnian state. In return for giving up their secession, the Bosnian Croats would be awarded federal status and Croatia was promised membership of the Council of Europe and NATO's Partnership for Peace.

The Muslims' concerns were twofold. The US federation initiative indicated that the US had abandoned its support of the unitary state. The Muslims also objected to the linking of Bosnia to Croatia through the confederal relationship that was incorporated into the agreement, fearing that confederation would restrict Bosnia's independence. They reportedly signed the agreement only after Vice-President Gore warned them that refusal might lead to the weakening of US support for their cause.[14]

In the following months the US continued to mediate between Bosnia and Croatia, nurturing their fragile relationship. Although the Muslim–Croat war in Bosnia had effectively come to an end, tension remained high and led to occasional armed confrontations, especially in the divided town of Mostar. The federation was shored-up by the conclusion of another agreement at Dayton. (But this too failed to resolve the difficulties. Renewed negotiations resulted in the conclusion of yet another agreement in November 1998.)

As for the US, its sponsorship of the federation marked the end of its support for a unitary Bosnian state. Once the US accepted the Bosnian Croats' claim for the status of a constituent nation in a Bosnian state, it became difficult to deny parallel rights to the Serbs.

Growing involvement, 1994–95

The US became associated with the overall mediation efforts within a regular institutional framework only with the establishment of the Contact Group in April 1994. Hitherto the international mediation process had been conducted through the steering committee of the International Conference on the Former Yugoslavia (ICFY), established in August 1992. As we saw in Chapter 7, one of the main problems encountered by the ICFY was that while the US kept its distance from the ICFY's activities it was deeply enmeshed in the situation, working in parallel with but at cross-purposes to the ICFY mediators. To rectify this situation and improve coordination among the governments most actively involved, the five-nation Contact

Group was established, consisting of the representatives of Britain, France, Germany, Russia and the US.

One area in which the US was trying to lead its allies even before the establishment of the Contact Group, and in contrast to its lack of leadership in the mediation efforts, was in the development of a military policy. The US pressed its allies to support the lifting of the arms embargo and to authorise NATO air strikes against the Serbs. This was essentially a continuation of the 'lift and strike' concept proposed by the US in 1993 in the early days of the Clinton administration. The US justification for lifting the embargo was that it would improve the Muslims' ability to defend themselves and would create 'a level playing field'. The proposal was opposed by the British, French and other governments on the ground that the consequent infusion of arms would escalate the conflict, not calm it down. They also argued that such action would lead to increased tension with Russia, and perhaps prompt it to increase its support for the Serbs. The US advocacy of NATO air strikes against the Serbs also encountered opposition because it was likely to trigger Serb action against United Nations Protection Force (UNPROFOR) troops in Bosnia.

At the core of the allies' opposition was concern for the safety of their own forces, and resentment that the US was advocating measures that would jeopardise that safety while at the same time refusing to send its own ground troops to Bosnia. A demonstration of some of the risks that UNPROFOR would face on the ground, and a foretaste of things to come (the humiliation of the hundreds of UNPROFOR soldiers chained as 'human shields' in May 1995) was provided when the Serbs took UNPROFOR troops hostage in response to two limited air strikes in April 1994.[15]

Ensuring the safety of their soldiers was of particular concern to the British and French governments, which had provided the largest contingents of ground forces. These governments were subject to stinging criticism for their failure to provide adequate protection to Muslim civilians. At the same time they were pressed to approve punitive air strikes against the Serbs, making their troops sitting ducks for Serb retaliation. Pressed by public opinion on the one hand and the US on the other, the British and French governments considered withdrawing their forces. But this would create other risks. Without the British and French troops the UNPROFOR mission would be unsustainable and would have to be terminated. This would probably trigger an escalation of the war, endangering the survival of the Bosnian state. Moreover, it was probable that the withdrawing UNPROFOR troops would be subject to attack, as the warring parties would try to seize the departing troops' weapons and equipment.

In trying to win the allies' support for air strikes President Clinton made a public commitment that subsequently contributed to further changes in US policy. Clinton promised in December 1994 that if the air strikes resulted in the necessity to withdraw the UNPROFOR troops, the US would send a substantial force of its own ground troops to Bosnia to help extricate the peacekeepers and ensure their safe withdrawal.[16]

The US takes over

A major change in US policy occurred in the summer of 1995. In contrast to its earlier policy of leaving the diplomatic search for a solution to the ICFY and the Contact Group, the US now took control of the negotiations, and developed a strategy for ending the war and reaching a comprehensive settlement.

It appears that the US took on this task in response to the escalation of military activity and its concern about the potential consequences – especially the US's ability to maintain its leadership of the Western alliance and the political risks to the president's standing at home. Hence President Clinton was forced to focus on these issues and to produce a coherent strategy for a combined military–diplomatic effort to end the war.

In the spring of 1995, as soon as weather conditions permitted, fighting began to escalate in many parts of Bosnia. The fighting soon led to two major crises in Western capitals, confronting the US administration with 'a moment of truth'. The first crisis erupted at the end of May, after NATO bombed Serb targets in punishment for the Serbs' shelling of Sarajevo and their refusal to remove heavy weapons from the exclusion zone around the city. The Serbs responded by taking 370 UNPROFOR soldiers hostage. Many of the hostages, shackled to presumed bombing targets, were shown on television, forcing NATO to stop its air strikes. This humiliation led Britain and France to reinforce the peacekeeping force with a well-equipped and trained rapid reaction force.

The incident increased the pressure for UNPROFOR to be withdrawn. It led to bitter criticism of the US for pushing its reluctant NATO allies to approve air strikes, thus endangering the allies' ground troops, while refusing to expose US forces to similar risks. It was clear that the moment was drawing closer for demands to be made on the US to fulfil its promise to send its own ground troops to Bosnia to protect the allies' withdrawal.[17]

The second crisis occurred in July, when the Bosnian Serb army attacked and conquered the Muslim enclave of Srebrenica in defiance of the UN injunction that this was a UN-protected safe area. Shortly thereafter, they occupied the safe area of Žepa as well. The embarrassment at UNPROFOR having refrained from putting up resistance to this violation of safe areas soon gave way to horror and guilt when it became known that large numbers of Muslims, perhaps thousands, had been killed by the Serbs soon after they occupied Srebrenica.[18]

These crises indicated to the US administration that it was unlikely that the US could avoid sending ground troops to Bosnia. Worse, it appeared that the troops might have to be sent during the forthcoming presidential election campaign. It has been reported that the administration perceived itself as forced to choose between two options: either to send troops to help extricate the allies at a moment dictated by circumstances beyond US control, an operation almost certain to exact significant casualties, or to send them to implement a settlement, where the risk of casualties might be lower, especially if the settlement was mutually agreed upon through negotiations. The second choice was obviously the more attractive. Since the Contact Group and the ICFY were unlikely to produce a settlement, the US took over the negotiations in an attempt to bring the parties to agreement as soon as possible. A detailed plan to accomplish this was prepared by National Security Council staff under the direction of Anthony Lake, and was adopted after a series of intense meetings, some of which were chaired by the president.[19]

This analysis suggests the need to supplement commonly held notions about mediators' motives and the timing of their intervention. Students of mediation have noted that third parties intervene to mediate international conflicts when the others' conflict threatens to harm them. However the threat that prompted the US mediation initiative did not stem directly from the conflict. The war and the accompanying atrocities had an impact on the public's sense of morality and stimulated the urge to do something to end the outrage. But American elites and public opinion did not perceive the war in Bosnia as posing a threat to US security or economic interests. The urgent US interest in taking over the peacemaking effort was self-generated through the rhetorical dynamics of exhorting the allies, which led to the commitment to help them in an emergency. It was this commitment, and the necessity to prove to the allies that the US was still an effective leader, rather than the war itself, that prompted the initiative. As for the timing of the initiative – it was not chosen because of any consideration that the moment was propitious, that the conflict was 'ripe' and the parties were ready to settle. Rather the timing was determined by the needs of the intervenor, not the needs of the disputants.

The peacemaking efforts in Bosnia from 1992 to mid 1995 were characterised by ICFY-led diplomacy that was not backed by force, and by a US advocacy of force that was unrelated to a diplomatic strategy. This had now changed. A new diplomatic–military strategy emerged.

The success of this initiative was seen as depending on softening the Bosnian Serbs' position, and especially on getting them to withdraw from areas that the Contact Group states had agreed to allocate to the Muslims. Both diplomatic and military measures were employed to induce the Bosnian Serbs to concede.

Part of the diplomatic initiative was aimed at Yugoslavia, which was eager for relief from the damaging effect of economic sanctions. The easing of sanctions depended on Yugoslavia cooperating with the UN embargo on the Bosnian Serbs, to which Milošević had shown a willingness to comply, provided he obtained a commitment that sanctions would be lifted. Sensing an opportunity to obtain Yugoslav cooperation, which would result in isolating and further weakening the Bosnian Serbs, the Europeans had long advocated such a course. But they had been unable to persuade the US. As long as the US had remained opposed, no easing of sanctions had been possible and Milošević had had no incentive to cooperate. However in the spring of 1995 the US agreed to explore the possibility and entered into negotiations with Milošević. Robert Frasure, the US representative, came close to reaching an agreement with Milošević in May 1995.[20] Yugoslav assistance in influencing the Bosnian Serbs, in return for the easing of sanctions, now became an important element of the US diplomatic strategy.

The military measures consisted of a ground offensive by Croatian and Bosnian Muslim forces and air strikes under NATO auspices. The Croatian offensive – aimed at reestablishing Croatia's authority over the Serb-controlled enclaves in the UN-protected areas of Croatia (which subsequently spread into Bosnia) – and the Bosnian Muslims' operations against the Bosnian Serbs could be viewed as coinciding by chance with the new US initiative. But it seems more likely that the Croatian and Muslim campaigns were not merely opportunities that the US exploited, but that the US played a key role in planning and launching them. Their timing was not a fortuitous coincidence, but was coordinated by the three actors. Owen reports that plans for a Croat and Muslim offensive supported by NATO air strikes had been discussed as early as 1994. This had necessitated both arms and training. The West had therefore not challenged the flow of arms to the Croatian and Muslim armies, although this violated the UN embargo. The US had also arranged for a private consulting firm, staffed by retired US military officers, to help organise and train the Croatian army. In addition these US officers had reportedly played an important role in planning the Croatian military operations. The US had also invested considerable effort in trying to improve the strained relations between the Bosnian Muslim and Bosnian Croat armies, and to get them to cooperate within a joint framework of the federation army.[21]

Additional evidence supporting the interpretation that the Croatian offensive was an integral part of the US strategy and not mere coincidence comes from a note passed by Robert Frasure to Holbrooke during a meeting with Tudjman on 17 August, at which the Croatian offensive was discussed:

> Dick: We 'hired' these guys to be our junkyard dogs because we were desperate. We need to try to 'control' them. But this is no time to get squeamish about things. This is the first time the Serb wave has been reversed. That is essential for us to get stability, so we can get out.[22]

The Croatian government did not view itself as being 'hired' by the US – it was already strongly motivated on its own to reestablish control over Croatian territory being held by Serbs. But the note provides an additional indication that the Croatian and Muslim military offensives were important ingredients in the US strategy.

The bombing campaign, a subject that had aroused considerable controversy during the previous two years, was approved in principle at a NATO meeting in July. According to Daalder, who has researched the US policy-making process, 'bombing was central to Lake's [the president's national security adviser] strategy and concept, and formed the crux of his presentation in Europe'[23] (on 9–14 August). The air strikes were launched in the wake of the 28 August mortar explosion in Sarajevo, which had caused yet more civilian casualties.

Keeping in mind the multiple motives of the US initiative, the NATO bombing campaign produced two beneficial consequences. First, it helped the US reassert its leadership in Europe. This was noted by the media – as William Pfaff wrote in the *International Herald Tribune*, 'The United States today is again Europe's leader; there is no other.'[24] Second, the bombings were vital to the success of the Croatian and Muslim ground offensives. They would not have been as successful as they were without NATO bombers first destroying Serb air defences, command posts, communications links, ammunition depots, bridges, artillery and tanks.[25]

Restructuring the diplomatic–military landscape

The US initiative required the US and its allies to agree on the terms of the settlement to be offered to the disputants, and the US to take control of the negotiation process. It was also desirable to simplify the negotiation structure by authorising a single negotiator to speak for the Serbs.

Control of the negotiations

The US plan was presented to the European allies by the president's advisor on national security, Anthony Lake, and Under-Secretary of State Peter Tarnoff in the course of their visits to European capitals between 10 and 14 August. The US and the Europeans also agreed on the terms of the settlement, with the US accepting European recommendations to acknowledge the Republika Srpska.[26]

The US assumption of control over the process encountered little resistance. Britain and France welcomed the US initiative because for them too the alternative of withdrawing their troops in the face of escalating hostilities appeared much worse. Besides this immediate pressure, from a broader perspective it was widely recognised that collective diplomacy – negotiations by the ICFY on behalf of two international organisations, the UN and the EU – was proving ineffective. The US initiative promised to remove one of the principal hindrances to previous efforts – the disputants' perception that the US was not committed to the process. It also indicated the US's readiness to send ground troops to Bosnia to join its allies in implementing the eventual agreement. Moreover, allowing the US to lead and direct the process promised to produce a more cohesive and coordinated diplomacy than could be achieved by the international organisations and the Contact Group. From now on there would be one mediator – a state that possessed superior military and economic power and the ability to persuade other states as well as the international organisations to support its policies. The US would be represented by Richard Holbrooke (known for both his intellect and his forceful personality), assisted by a talented team. The credibility of the peacemaking efforts would thus be greatly enhanced.[27]

While determined to take control of the negotiations, Holbrooke and other US officials were keenly aware that the US needed the cooperation of others. In a note to the secretary of state on 23 August Holbrooke observed:

> The Contact Group presents us with a constant conundrum. We can't live with it, we can't live without it. If we don't meet with them and tell them what we are doing, they complain publicly. If we tell them, they disagree and often leak – and worse…
>
> Any temporary Euro-annoyance with less information can be managed. It must be outweighed by our need for speed and security.… But we must never forget that we will need them *all* if there is ever a settlement – the E.U. for economic assistance, our NATO allies for the new post-U.N. peacekeeping force, the U.N. for legitimizing resolutions, the Islamic Conference for additional aid, and the Russians and Greeks for their influence (however limited) on Belgrade.[28]

The US mediated between the warring parties very much on its own. It kept the Contact Group members informed, but preferred not to restrict its freedom to manoeuvre by conducting prior consultations. Nonetheless, when it came to major issues such as the organisation of the Dayton conference and preparing the draft documents relating to the implementation of the proposed settlement, it had to consult and negotiate with its partners in order to arrive at a common position.

To be sure, the US efforts to keep control of the process were not frictionless. European criticism of US policy did not stop; it merely diminished. At Dayton there were tense moments when the Europeans felt that the US promise of military assistance to the Muslims was too far-reaching, and did not take adequate account of their concerns. Russia remained sharply critical of the NATO bombing campaigns. But overall, US control of the peacemaking effort was accepted and there were no serious attempts to interfere with the process.

Simplifying the negotiating process

The international community had always assumed that Serbia's president Milošević exercised a dominant influence over the Bosnian Serbs. As discussed above, this was the reason why sanctions were imposed on Yugoslavia. With Yugoslavia hurting under the impact of economic sanctions, the Europeans and Russia had long advocated inducing Milošević to cooperate by offering to ease the sanctions if he put pressure on the Bosnian Serbs. But since easing the sanctions required US acquiescence in the Security Council, the possibility of it doing so became real only when the US began to explore the terms for such a deal in talks with Milošević in May 1995.[29] No agreement was reached at that time, but the prospect encouraged Milosević to demonstrate that he was willing to cooperate and could influence the Bosnian Serbs. Thus he helped to speed up the release of the UNPROFOR hostages in June.

In the past Milošević had maintained that he did not control the Bosnian Serbs, who according to him were independent actors. This had frustrated the foreign negotiators, who suspected that Milošević was claiming lack of control because it suited his bargaining purposes. But now, with the possibility of reduced sanctions dangling before him, he found it to his advantage to stress his authority and ability to get things done. This led him to force the Bosnian Serb leaders formally to sign a document empowering him to negotiate on their behalf.[30] This authorisation simplified the negotiating process: instead of negotiating with both Yugoslavia and the Bosnian Serbs, there would be a single negotiator speaking for both. (Similarly, it was understood that Croatia's President Tudjman would speak for both the Republic of Croatia and the Bosnian Croats.) It needs to be emphasised that it was largely the US engagement to bargain with Milošević that led him to formalise his authority to negotiate for the Bosnian Serbs.

Defeating the Serbs and redrawing the map

The Croatian and Muslim military operations had three decisive consequences. First, they weakened the Bosnian Serb forces and demoralised the Serb army, leadership and population, thus making them more amenable to accept the terms proposed by the US negotiators.

Second, the loss of the *krajinas* removed an important rationale for the Serbian control of Western Bosnia. Some of the Serbian conquests there were necessary for maintaining a land bridge and territorial contiguity with the Croatian Serbs. Once the *krajina* Serbs fled or were expelled, the need for a land bridge disappeared.

Third, the Croat and Muslim offensives resulted in significant advances by these two armies, wresting large areas from Serb forces. The new front lines produced a territorial apportionment that was closer to that in the 1994 Contact Group proposal than had been the case prior to these military operations. This was an essential condition for the successful outcome of the Dayton negotiations.

The map delimiting the territories of the two entities was one of the two basic issues that needed to be resolved (the other being the constitution). During 1992 and 1993 the territorial bargaining revolved around the percentage of territory that each of the national entities would be awarded. After protracted and difficult bargaining, on 21 December, 1993 the ICFY was able to conclude an agreement among the parties allocating the Croats 17.5 per cent, the Muslims 33.5 per cent, and the Serbs 49 per cent of the territory. These percentages, initially intended for the *Invincible* Plan, had subsequently been incorporated into the Contact Group Plan.[31]

But while the parties accepted the percentages they vehemently disagreed about which areas and localities would be under whose control. The delimitation of the Croat and Muslim cantons within their federation had been agreed upon in May 1994.[32] But the territorial distribution between the federation and the Serbs remained sharply disputed. Furthermore, since the Serbs held close to 70 per cent of the territory, resolution of the territorial dispute required significant Serb withdrawals to reduce their holding to 49 per cent. Getting the Serbs to withdraw from the excess territory they held, and to hand over those areas that the Contact Group had assigned to the Muslim–Croat Federation, loomed as a major hurdle on the horizon.

Croat and Muslim offensives during the summer solved some of these problems. The Croat and Muslim advances reduced the Serb-held territory to approximately 50 per cent, and their armies conquered many of the areas that the ICFY and Contact Group proposals required the Serbs to relinquish. The US role in this was important in facilitating the build-up of the Croat and Muslim armies, and in 'unleashing' them at the appropriate time. Holbrooke relates in great detail how he tried to guide their efforts so that their conquests would correspond to the geographical delimitations of the settlement the US was hoping to negotiate, and how he reined them in, stopping them from taking the important Serb centre of Banja Luka.[33]

These conquests did not fully settle the territorial disputes between the parties. Moreover new problems arose because the Croats conquered areas that the map-makers had allocated to the Muslims. When the ceasefire came into effect the Croats held 28 per cent of the territory (instead of the 17.5 per cent assigned to them) and the Muslims 23 per cent (instead of 33.5 per cent).[34] Nevertheless the changes on the ground made it much easier to settle the remaining territorial disputes in subsequent negotiations because the adjustments required were now much smaller. They were also easier to implement because the areas conquered by the Croats and Muslims had been immediately 'cleansed' of their Serb populations.

As mentioned at the start of this chapter, it has been noted that the success of mediation initiatives depends heavily on their being launched at a propitious moment. Such a moment is often characterised as a 'mutually hurting stalemate', the moment at which the disputants realise they cannot achieve their goals or continue much longer with their current policies. If such a stalemate does not exist, mediators sometimes contribute to the creation of one, thus improving their chance of success.

The military campaign against the Serbs did not result in a mutually hurting stalemate. The Serbs had been suffering from the economic sanctions even before the military campaign began. They had been badly damaged by their military defeats, loss of territory and the massive problem of refugees, displaced by the Croat and Muslim victories. They were stalemated only in the sense of knowing that they could not reconquer the areas they had just lost. But the cause they had been fighting for – the establishment of a Serb-governed entity in Bosnia – had been attained. The Croats felt victorious, having achieved their objectives both in Bosnia and in the *krajinas*. The Muslims had obviously been hurt most by the war, and they had long felt stalemated in their quest to reunify Bosnia. The military campaign's impact on them was to weaken this feeling of stalemate. Their military achievements in the summer fighting encouraged them to hope that their greatly improved army could win further victories.

The main contribution of the military campaign – the NATO bombing from the air and the Croat and Muslim offensives on the ground – was twofold: it endowed Western diplomacy with credibility, demonstrating to the Serbs that their defiance would be severely punished, and it redrew the front lines, thus establishing a new starting point for the territorial bargaining.

Preparing the summit

The US envisaged that the negotiations, if successful, would conclude with a summit conference at which the leaders of the disputing parties would sign a formal agreement to end the conflict. To reduce the risk of failure, it was desirable that the general framework of the settlement, as well as many details as possible, be agreed upon before the conference. The terms agreed to were formalised at two meetings with the foreign ministers of the disputing parties, in Geneva (on 8 September) and in New York (on 25–26 September). These meetings also had to be prepared in advance. Holbrooke and his team spent more than two months shuttling between the capitals and negotiating the drafts that were formally agreed to by the foreign ministers. Even this procedure did not protect the process from peril. The New York meeting almost failed, and it was only strong US pressure that induced Muhamed Sacirbey, representing the Muslim-led Bosnian government, to sign the agreement.[35]

The process leading up to the Dayton Accords, thus went through the stages followed by many negotiations: first establishing a general formula, and then filling in the detailed terms of the agreement.[36]

The US task was greatly facilitated by the fact that when the US stepped in to take over the negotiations, much of the formula was already in place. The US mediation was not a new beginning, but built upon the ideas and proposals developed by the ICFY and Contact Group negotiators over the previous three years, and the conditional tentative assent given by the disputants to some of those proposals.

A key element of the Dayton Accords was the concept of a single Bosnian state consisting of two entities – the Republika Srpska and the Muslim–Croat Federation. In practice this meant that the Bosnian state would consist of three nationally (ethnically) defined units. This concept can be traced in part to the Cutileiro Plan of March 1992, which was revived in 1993 and revised to give the Serbs a contiguous territory. It was a central element in the *Invincible* Plan and the EU Plan, and was implied in the 1994 Contact Group Plan (which, as will be recalled, did not spell out the constitutional arrangements). All these plans also proposed that Bosnia be recognised as a single state under international law. It would have common governmental institutions, with limited and defined authority, while the residual powers would be vested in the component units.

The possibility of a special relationship between each entity and a neighbouring state (Article III, 2 (a) of the Dayton Constitution), opening the way for an association between the Serbian entity (to be recognised as Republika Srpska) and Yugoslavia, was also not new. It can be traced to the confederation between Bosnia and Croatia established by the 1994 US-brokered Washington agreements. Although the confederation had not been set up, the principle of a special relationship between the federation and Croatia remained very much alive.

As mentioned already, the territorial distribution between the three national groups was also rooted in earlier plans. The percentages of territory that each would receive had first been agreed upon in December 1993. What remained in dispute were the specific areas to be given up by the Serbs. This had been dealt with in earlier plans, and tentative agreements had been reached on some areas, either through the mediators or during bilateral contact between the parties. Even the arbitration of the Brčko controversy, agreed upon at

Dayton, appears to have been discussed between Radovan Karadžić and Mate Boban (the Bosnian Serb and Bosnian Croat leaders) at their secret meeting in Graz in May 1993.[37]

In addition to benefiting from earlier negotiations between the disputants, the Dayton Accords were also facilitated by previous discussions among the Western allies on NATO's role in implementing a settlement. The planning for NATO's implementation role can be traced at least to the summer of 1993.[38]

What needed to be done at the outset of the US initiative was to reaffirm the earlier understandings, develop these through the addition of details and specifics, and formalise them in legally binding agreements. Reaffirmation of the formula was important for two reasons. One was the obvious need to highlight the principles upon which the agreement would be built, and to commit the disputants to them. The other, less obvious reason was the need to demonstrate US backing for the principles of the formula, and thus remove any doubts aroused by earlier US policies. The prior understandings about the principles would have been of little use had the impression persisted that the US did not fully endorse them. This was accomplished through the agreements concluded at the two foreign ministers' meetings.

The Geneva agreement, on 7 September, outlined basic principles for the constitution and the territorial distribution. The main points agreed to were that Bosnia and Herzegovina would 'continue its legal existence', that it would 'consist of two entities' – the federation and Republika Srpska – and that each entity would 'have the right to establish parallel special relationships with neighboring countries', consistent with Bosnia's sovereignty. Disputes between the entities would be resolved through international arbitration, rather than adjudicated by the state or its courts. There were also principles relating to human rights and displaced persons.

The territorial issues were much more difficult to negotiate than the constitutional ones, and as a result only a somewhat open-ended wording was agreed upon, that: 'The 51:49 parameter of the territorial proposal of the Contact Group is the basis for a settlement', and that the 'proposal is open to adjustment by mutual consent'.[39]

Although the agreement did not contain new ideas, significance was attached to the naming of Republika Srpska, thus granting it a certain recognition that had previously been withheld.

The meeting in New York on 25–26 September produced an outline agreement on additional constitutional principles. This was more difficult to negotiate, due to the hardening of the Muslims' position. The latter pressed for the agreement to be couched in terms that would provide stronger assurance for the existence of a common Bosnian state. The agreement proclaimed the goal of holding free and democratic elections, and 'in order to maximize the democratic effectiveness of such elections', it pledged the governments of the entities to support freedom of movement, the right of displaced persons to repossess property or be compensated for it, and to protect human rights. The elections would take place after the Organization for Security and Cooperation in Europe (OSCE) certified that free and democratic elections could properly be held. The principles also dealt with the composition and powers of the common parliament, presidency and constitutional court.[40]

With the principles for a settlement agreed among the parties, the time had come to build on them and develop a detailed agreement. This the US chose to do at a conference with the presidents of Bosnia, Croatia and Yugoslavia in attendance. The conference was to be co-chaired by the US, the EU and Russia. The convening of the conference was announced by President Clinton on 5 October.

Clinton's statement also said that the disputants had agreed that a ceasefire would take effect five days later, after gas and electricity had been restored to Sarajevo. Their agreement also called for exchanges of prisoners and required the Serb forces to allow free access to Sarajevo and Goražde. The ceasefire actually came into effect only on 14 October, after the Yugoslav army threatened to intervene. The delay was intended to allow the Croat and Muslim armies to conquer additional territory and thus improve their bargaining ability in the forthcoming negotiations.[41]

The Dayton Conference

The Dayton Conference consisted of several strands. There was the mediation of the conflict between the disputants, but the conference also had to contend with debates among US policy makers, friction and cooperation between the US and the Europeans, quarrels between Yugoslavia and the Bosnian Serbs, disputes within the Muslim delegation, and numerous dramatic displays of interpersonal dynamics. Only a small part of this complex web will be examined here.

The mediators' camps

Dayton followed several aspects of the model used for the Egyptian–Israeli Camp David talks, in 1978. No date had been set for it to end, and it was closed to the media. These features carried certain advantages for the mediators. With the heads of state of the disputing parties present (but not President Clinton) it would be difficult for the parties to delay or avoid responding to proposals. Also important was the ability to limit the delegations' contact with the media, thus reducing the risk that they would lose flexibility through too much publicity. It also allowed the mediator' to manipulate deadlines, thus putting pressure on the parties to settle. This was done effectively. It was only when Secretary of State Christopher told the delegations on 20 November, the twentieth day of the conference, that in a few hours he would announce that the conference had failed, that the parties finally resolved their remaining differences, bringing the conference to a successful conclusion.[42]

The administration prepared in advance of the conference detailed drafts of the proposed agreements. These drafts were based on intensive negotiations among members of the Contact Group, and occasionally sharp disagreements between the US and its European allies. They reflected US–European agreements on the terms of the settlement, the mechanisms for its implementation, and the agreements concluded with the disputants in Geneva and New York. The advance preparations did not fully resolve the US–European differences, which continued throughout the conference. At one tense moment on 8 November the Europeans' dissatisfaction with the US constitutional proposal even led them to announce that unless the US treated the European position more seriously, they would distribute a separate European draft to the parties.[43]

The drafts also reflected US objectives: ending the war while adhering to the principle of preserving a single Bosnian state. As we have seen, support for a unitary state, that is, a state with centralised authority and no powers for the constituent nations, had been abandoned in 1994 when the US sponsored the federation. With the Muslims now divided on this issue and uncertain about the advantages of centralised power,[44] the US administration allowed itself some latitude in accepting the existence of an autonomous Serbian entity, as long as the Serbs acknowledged being part of the Bosnian state. The drafts further reflected the insistence of the Pentagon on establishing narrow and clear limits to the military role in implementing the settlement.

The administration's conviction that the success of peacemaking required that the US tightly control and manage the process had to be balanced with the need of keeping the EU and Russia engaged. The scope of the conference required the apportionment of tasks among several teams. But these were staffed largely by US officials. Europeans headed only two negotiations. Michael Steiner, a German diplomat, managed the negotiations for shoring up the Muslim–Croat Federation. The influence Germany enjoyed in Croatia, as well as its assistance in establishing the federation in 1994, qualified it for this role. Thorvald Stoltenberg, the co-chair of the ICFY (representing the UN, but not the EU, of which Norway was not a member), was assigned to negotiating with local leaders in Eastern Slavonia about the transfer of the area to Croatian control. He shared this task with US Ambassador Peter Galbraith, and with US officials simultaneously mediating between Milošević and Tudjman in Dayton.[45] Thus although they were formally cosponsors of the conference and were represented by senior diplomats, the Europeans were allowed only a limited role at Dayton. To allay their sensitivities the US agreed to schedule a formal signing ceremony in Paris, and conferences in London, Bonn and Moscow to deal with issues relating to the implementation of the accords. The treatment they received and the bestowal of all the credit upon the American mediators provoked some irritation in Europe as European negotiators had spent three and a half years developing the formula upon which the Dayton settlement was based.

Although their role was limited the Europeans were able to influence some of the settlement terms. Having been designated to head the civilian implementation tasks (a position assumed by Carl Bildt, the ICFY co-chair) they were able to limit the responsibilities of the international police task force, preferring to expand the mandate of IFOR (the military Implementation Force), of which the US was in charge. But with the Pentagon refusing to accept broad responsibility for implementation, a situation of indeterminate responsibility between the military and civilian spheres of implementation was created. Intense negotiations between Bildt and Robert Gallucci, representing the US, failed to find a satisfactory solution.[46] Another controversy developed over the US promise to the Muslims that their consent to the Dayton settlement would be rewarded by US help in training and equipping their army. The European preference was to try to reach a more equal military balance in the region by 'building down' the Yugoslav and Bosnian Serb armies, rather than by introducing additional arms to build up the Federation's army. This dispute remained unresolved at the close of the conference.[47]

Keeping the mediation under US direction allowed for a more effective process than one requiring the consensus of a group of sovereign states. But given the multiple and global interests of a superpower and the array of organisations charged with promoting these interests, the coherence of US policy was far from perfect. Besides tending to its relations with the European allies, the administration deemed it desirable to coopt Russia into the process. It needed to avoid the impression that it was putting pressure on the Muslims, both because of the sympathy they evoked in Congress and among the public, and because of concern about reactions in the Muslim world. Thus when on 20 November the mediators at Dayton requested that President Clinton call Tudjman and Izetbegović to urge them to be more flexible, the White House objected, opposing 'any call to Izetbegović, on the grounds that the President should not appear to be pressuring the Muslims'.[48] Budgetary considerations also influenced the negotiations, imposing a more limited US role in the implementation process than the Muslims desired and the mediators advocated.[49]

The wide range of interests represented and the participation of several bureaucratic organisations in the process led to frequent differences of opinion. Among the most notable were policy disagreements during the summer before Dayton about the Croatian and Muslim offensives, and enduring differences over the easing or lifting of sanctions on Yugoslavia.[50]

But the most spirited internal confrontations concerned the role of US troops in implementing the settlement. Because of its conception of the role of the military in protecting US security interests and its concern about 'mission creep', as experienced in Somalia, the Pentagon was adamant in its insistence on a narrow definition of the IFOR mandate under which US ground troops would be sent to Bosnia.

Others too were concerned about the domestic political risks that a broad mandate might entail. To advise the Muslims – whose work at the conference, according to Holbrooke, was 'completely disorganized' – and to strengthen the coalition advocating a wider IFOR mandate, Holbrooke encouraged former Defense Department officials Richard Perle and Douglas Feith to go to Dayton. Although some of their suggestions on easing the restrictions on IFOR were adopted, in the end the Pentagon's insistence on a narrowly defined military mission prevailed, much to the dissatisfaction of Holbrooke and others who fought for extended IFOR responsibilities in implementing the agreements. The Pentagon's restrictive view also prevailed in opposing a role for US troops in Eastern Slavonia. But their objection to a major US role in training and equipping the federation's army was overruled.[51]

In the end the implementation of the Dayton Accords was divided between 'the territorial and other militarily related provisions', which were made the responsibility of IFOR, and all the other terms (for example elections, refugees, human rights), which were relegated to the civilian component of the implementation process. The tasks of the civilian component were assigned to several international organisations, thus limiting direct US responsibility and domestic political risks.

The disputants and the issues

When the conference opened the Croats regarded themselves to be in a strong bargaining position, not only against the beaten Serbs but also in relation to the mediators. This allowed them to press for the resolution of the Eastern Slavonia problem, the last Serb-ruled enclave, before proceeding to the comprehensive Bosnian settlement.

They had achieved most of their goals even before the conference. Their victorious army had established control over three of the Serb enclaves in the *krajina*. The Croatian parts of Bosnia, although part of the federation and nominally subject to the central authority of the Bosnian state, were in fact ruled from Zagreb. For them the Bosnian problem was far less urgent than that of Eastern Slavonia. According to Holbrooke, Tudjman was therefore able 'both to prevent a Bosnia agreement and to threaten another war' to take Eastern Slavonia. This provided him with leverage over Milošević, while his influence over

Izetbegović came from 'his ability to break up the Croat–Muslim Federation, whose continued survival was essential for Dayton to work'.[52] Holbrooke fails to mention that this provided Tudjman with bargaining power over the mediators as well, for it was the Western powers who had initiated the recent round of peacemaking to save themselves from damaging and costly policy alternatives.

Thus empowered, Tudjman demanded that priority be given to the restoration of Eastern Slavonia to Croatian rule. The mediators acceded and established the two-track process at Dayton and in the region mentioned above. Milošević, eager to for the sanctions to be lifted, which depended on a Bosnian settlement, gave up Eastern Slavonia with little argument. He was nevertheless able to obtain a two-year transition (rather than the one year demanded by Tudjman) and face-saving arrangements to protect his domestic political position.[53]

As for the mediating states, they viewed the realisation of their blueprint for a Bosnian state consisting of two entities as dependent on the survival of the Croat–Muslim Federation. The implementation of the federation agreement, concluded in March 1994, had run into continuous difficulties and the tension between Muslims and Croats remained high. Constant efforts by the US, as well as Germany and the EU, to induce the two parties to cooperate produced only minimal results. That is why, at the start of the conference, the working group led by Michael Steiner and Dan Serwer was charged with shoring up the federation. After much argument over the division of posts between Croats and Muslims in central government and federation institutions, the merger of the Croat and Muslim armies and the repatriation of refugees, a new federation agreement was concluded on 10 November 1995. But like the earlier agreement it was 'on paper only', waiting to be implemented.[54]

The conclusion of this agreement was hampered not only by the practical issues just mentioned, but also by the implications that the federation carried for the constitution of the new common Bosnian state. The Croats insisted on vesting the federation institutions with extensive powers, whereas the Muslims, as well as the US, wanted maximum powers to reside in the central government. Repairing the federation and making it a viable entity required empowering its institutions, but doing so was seen as setting a precedent that would allow the Serb entity similar authority.

As for the main purpose of the conference – the comprehensive settlement of the Bosnian conflicts – two major issues divided the disputants: the constitution and control of territory.

The formula laid down in the preliminary agreements served as the basis of negotiations. But the constitutional principles it prescribed were flawed because they lent themselves to contradictory interpretations, binding the parties to unity but legitimising their separation. As a result there was much debate about the powers of the central government. There was also considerable controversy over the structure of the institutions, the electoral provisions and whether to allow decision-making rules that would in effect (but without saying so explicitly) provide the Serbs and Croats with the power to veto decisions.

While the Muslims hoped that the constitutional provisions could be turned into an instrument for creating a unified state, the Serbs hoped that it would facilitate the secession of Republika Srpska from Bosnia. As a result those aspects of the constitution that referred to freedom of movement, the return of displaced persons to their former homes and the right of absentees to vote in their former places of residence became especially contested. The Muslims (and some of the mediators) expected these processes to reverse the ethnic cleansing in the Serb areas, to dilute the Serbs' autonomy and to facilitate the reunification of the country. They also hoped that the Serbs' commitment to separation would be weakened if their leaders – Radovan Karadžić and Ratko Mladić, who had been indicted for war crimes – were extradited and placed on trial in the Hague. The Serbs, on the other hand, wanted to weaken the common institutions and use non-obligatory language in the prescription of these processes.[55]

The parties attached even greater importance to the possession of territory. The territorial issue consisted of two parts. One was symbolic – the percentage of territory to be allocated to each party, which had troubled the negotiations since the Vance–Owen Plan, and which had presumably been settled but caused a last moment crisis.[56] The other was the disposition of specific areas. While the constitution appeared to open the possibility of both unity and separation, the parties believed that the prospect of either of the contradictory visions being realised would be determined by the control of strategically important territory. The most sharply contested issues were the Muslims' demand that the entire city of Sarajevo be placed under their control, that they retain Goražde in Eastern Bosnia and link it to Sarajevo by means of a wide corridor, and that Srebrenica and Žepa be restored to them. They also laid claim to the town of Brčko, possession of which would have eliminated the Posavina Corridor, which connected Serb-held western Bosnia to Serb territories in the east. From the Muslim perspective, denying the Serbs possession of contiguous territory would make it more difficult for them to maintain a separate entity and secede from Bosnia. The Serbs' demands were exactly the opposite, with the highest priority being placed on widening the Posavina Corridor at Brčko, linking their territories in western Bosnia to eastern Bosnia and Yugoslavia.[57] (The arbitrator on Brčko decided in March 1999 that the Serb entity must relinquish Brčko, which would become a neutral zone under international supervision.)[58]

Bridging gaps

When trying to bridge the gaps between the parties' positions the mediators had to contend with the personalities of the principal leaders.

Having achieved most of their goals before the conference the Croats were the most relaxed. According to Holbrooke, Tudjman landed at Dayton 'proud and haughty', wanting to show 'that he was in Dayton only to regain eastern Slavonia'. Nevertheless he was very helpful in devising, together with Milošević, a territorial formula that would satisfy the Muslims and bring the conference to a successful conclusion.[59]

Leaks to the media described the Yugoslavs as the most pliable. Milošević was extremely eager to get the sanctions on his country lifted. This depended on improving his relations with the US, which in turn depended on cooperating with the US at Dayton. It was apparently not difficult for him to cooperate because the concessions he was requested to make did not threaten his political standing or Yugoslavia's security. He went to Dayton to negotiate on behalf of the Bosnian Serbs, whose leaders he wanted to humiliate and eliminate as political players.

Milošević's eagerness to mend relations with the US resulted in him constantly seeking to prove that he was a worthy partner because he could obtain the concessions required of the Bosnian Serbs. In his eyes this was best done by monopolising the negotiations, and excluding the Bosnian Serb delegates from the process. Thus he reportedly told US diplomats who wanted to consult Nikola Koljević, the Bosnian Serb delegate, that they would be wasting their time. He showed the Bosnian Serbs the map of the territorial delimitation agreed upon only shortly before the signing ceremony. (As a result they refused to sign the agreement. The US wanted them to sign in order to preempt their repudiation of Milošević's authority. The Bosnian Serbs finally appended their signature a few days later after some more persuasion in Belgrade.) Because he was so authoritative and so eager to please the US, it was easier for the mediators to negotiate with him than with the other parties at Dayton. Negotiating with Milošević was described by US diplomats as 'one-stop shopping'. The media reported on his penchant for alcohol, and that the corridor between Goražde and Sarajevo – which Milošević had conceded to the Muslims – had been dubbed the 'Scotch Road'. In his memoirs Holbrooke tones down such reports, saying that he saw no evidence that the alcohol affected Milošević as the latter 'remembered every detail of the discussion the next morning'.[60] Perhaps he needed to be put in the right mood before submitting. What mattered to him was the expected pay-off – relief from sanctions.[61]

In sharp contrast to the Yugoslavs, the Muslims were far from flexible. The US diplomats found them frustrating to deal with. Part of the reason for this lay in Izetbegović's personality. He was reserved, not very sociable, and being a devout Muslim he never drank. Quarrels within the delegation, especially between Prime Minister Silajdžić and Foreign Minister Sacirbey, also made it difficult for the mediators to elicit clear-cut acceptance of their proposals. Yet it appears that the difficulties lay not only in the social dynamics. The Muslims were emboldened by their recent military success, and hoped that if the war resumed they would win more territory and ultimately a better settlement. They were described as 'lacking any real conviction' about the desirability of an agreement, and as resisting it 'until the very last moment'. No wonder they were ambivalent – the ambiguity of the Dayton agreements made them so.[62]

In trying to bring the parties to agreement the US employed the standard tools of mediators: it exploited the setting, it used its leverage to persuade the parties to change their stance, and it suggested ambiguous wording that each party could interpret as it wished, and in the end – to bring the bargaining to closure – it set a deadline to shut down the conference and blame the parties for its failure.[63]

When examining the use of leverage it is striking that the US committed little of its own material resources to the process. Furthermore the promises and threats of what the US would do directly to the parties were not the only form of persuasion. It was more common for the US to apply its influence indirectly, by moving other actors and by manipulating the international environment in a way that led the disputants to make concessions.

Among the prominent examples of direct leverage was the promise of US financial and material assistance for equipping and training the federation's army. Another was the warning to the Muslims that the US would abandon them to their own devices, if they did not show flexibility.

Equally effective, and no less frequent, were US promises to cause something to happen. The US promised the Muslims that the World Bank would provide reconstruction assistance to the amount of $5 billion, and that additional financial assistance would be granted to them by some Muslim states. It also promised the Muslims that it would persuade its European allies and Russia to agree to the lifting of the UN arms embargo. And it promised the Yugoslavs that it would see that the UN sanctions against their country were lifted. When Milošević found out that the map drawn in the negotiations would leave the Serbian entity with less than the 49 per cent that had been agreed to, the US helped to arrange for the Serbs to be compensated not by the Muslims, but by a side-payment of territorial concessions from the Croats.[64]

Another form of indirect influence was US help in the forming of bilateral alignments, which served as leverage against the third player in the triangle. The road to a tripartite settlement between the Muslims, Croats and Serbs passed through bilateral agreements settling disputes between the Croats and Muslims, the Croats and Serbs, and the Muslims and Serbs. During the Dayton conference the US brokered a Croat–Muslim agreement cementing the fragile federation they had formed under US auspices in March 1994. It also helped to negotiate, jointly with ICFY co-chair Thorvald Stoltenberg, an agreement between Croatia and Yugoslavia for the establishment of Croatian authority over Eastern Slavonia, the last area of Croatia to be controlled by Serbs claiming independence from Croatia. While these agreements were necessary building blocks for the tripartite settlement at Dayton, they were also skilfully used to exert pressure on the Serbs and Muslims respectively. The cementing of the Muslim–Croat Federation, coming on the heels of the coordinated Muslim–Croat military offensive of the summer, was a reminder to the Serbs that the alliance against them might endure. The second agreement, between Croatia and Yugoslavia, helped put pressure on the Muslims to relax their resistance to US proposals by signalling to them the potential revival of the Croat–Serb coalition against them. Even if the Croats and Yugoslavs would not cooperate explicitly, the agreement for the restoration of Eastern Slavonia to Croatia reduced the Croats' motivation to assist the Muslims (as Croatia did by sending its army to Bosnia in the summer of 1995), which would render the Muslims more vulnerable if Serb pressure was resumed.[65]

These examples illustrate not only the role of leverage in mediation, but also the US's unique capabilities in this respect. It is unlikely that any other state or international organisation could have exercised so many diverse forms of influence, applied to fit the particular parties, their concerns and their ambitions. These capabilities stemmed not only from the US's vast economic and military resources, but from its status as the only superpower, unrivalled and unchallenged by any other actor in the system. This status helped to endow its promises and threats with the necessary credibility to shape the disputants' behaviour.

A standard technique used by mediators to bridge the gap between adversaries is ambiguity. It allows parties to form different interpretations of the wording of an agreement. Inconsistencies within the Dayton Accords created ambiguities that played a major role in obtaining the parties' acceptance of the agreement. The documents proclaimed that Bosnia and Herzegovina would be a state under international law, and that it would consist of two entities. But the division of powers between the central government established under the Dayton constitution and those of the entities, and the salience accorded to the inter-entity boundary, opened the accords to contradictory interpretations: that they were meant to reunify Bosnia, or that they confirmed its partition.

Conclusions

The US succeeded in what others had failed to do. Three and a half years of intense effort by skilled and highly regarded diplomats representing the UN, the EU and the Contact Group had failed to persuade the contending parties to alter their policies and accept the compromises suggested to them.

Looking beyond the skilful diplomacy of the mediating team, the US success can be attributed to several important factors. One was clearing the arena of all other mediators to allow for a solo US performance. Unlike the ICFY and the Contact Group, whose efforts were occasionally hampered by the US, the US endeavour encountered no interference.

Much of the US's success derived from its unique status as the sole unrivalled superpower. The US possessed resources that the earlier mediators had lacked. It was able to use the vast economic and military means at its disposal to coerce the disputants, to entice them, to bargain with them and ultimately to persuade them to sign the documents. Moreover, notwithstanding the well-known difficulty of the US governmental machinery to pursue a coherent strategy, it worked far better than an international organisation or a concert-like intergovernmental club such as the Contact Group.

Finally, part of the reason for its success was unrelated to its leverage powers and skill. In some measure the success of the mediation has to be attributed to the change in the US position on an acceptable outcome. After 1994, when the US relaxed its opposition to ethnically defined self-governing units and accepted the Bosnian Croats' claim for self-governance, albeit within a federal structure, it gradually acknowledged the Bosnian Serbs' claim as well and recognised Republika Srpska as an entity within Bosnia. Once the range of outcomes acceptable to the mediator had broadened, it became less difficult to negotiate a settlement.

The conclusion of the Dayton Accords however, raises two questions: one concerns the timing of the intervention, and the other is whether the Accords were brought about by mediation.

Timing involves two factors: the mediator's move to intervene and the readiness of the disputants to make the compromises necessary for a settlement. As we have seen, both of the US mediation initiatives – in 1994, ending the Croat–Muslim war and establishing the federation, and in 1995, concluding the Dayton settlement – were responses to the failure of previous US policies. Both reflected a concern that US leadership of the West was slipping, and both were aimed at reasserting its leadership role. In 1995 an additional concern helped stimulate the US to act – the prospect of having to dispatch US ground forces to Bosnia to help extricate the UNPROFOR troops. This promised to be a far riskier and costlier operation than taking responsibility for brokering a settlement and sending troops to enforce it.

Thus both initiatives teach us about the timing of third-party interventions. These episodes indicate that what matters are the foreign policy needs of the mediator, rather than the fate of the disputants or the assessment that the circumstances are propitious for mediation because the conflict has reached a hurting stalemate.

'Ripeness' refers to the disputants' readiness to change their existing policies and make concessions. The ability of the mediators to persuade the Croats and Muslims to conclude the 1994 federation agreement can in large measure be attributed to ripe circumstances. The Muslims, although successful, were dangerously overextended, simultaneously confronting both Serbs and Croats. The Croats faced the dilemma of whether to extend the involvement of the Croatian army in defiance of the US, Germany and the Security Council, or accept a settlement with the Muslims.

As for the Dayton Accords, the mediator's ability to persuade the parties to conclude them did not stem from propitious timing of the intervention. No hurting stalemate existed when the 1995 mediation began. The Croats did not feel stalemated, having just regained control over much of the Serb-held *krajinas*. The Serbs, although beaten in Croatia, were satisfied with their achievements in Bosnia, and confident about their ability to hold onto their territory. And the Muslims, having equipped and trained their army, were optimistic about their ability to regain territory from the Serbs.

It was the mediator who 'ripened' the conditions, making the parties willing to compromise. It did so by encouraging and helping the Croat and Muslim military campaigns against the Serbs. But when it advised them to cease their advance, it also implied that it would not assist them if they continued.

Thus the mediator did not time its intervention to occur at a naturally propitious moment, but rather created the circumstances that made the disputants ready to compromise.

The second question, whether the process can rightly be called 'mediation', arises because the term refers to a peaceful form of third-party intervention in a conflict. But in the process leading up to the Dayton Accords the US was not only the chief negotiator, bridging the gaps between the parties, but also the leader of the military campaign against the Serbs. So how should the US role be characterised? Did the US impose a settlement, or mediate it?

It did both. It used force to weaken and intimidate the Serbs, and facilitated the redrawing of the front lines so as to approximate the boundaries it wanted to establish. Yet the settlement was also agreed to through negotiation. The final terms, although drafted by the US, represented a common platform that the disputants could accept. They reflected the disputants' position on various issues, and were responsive to some of their concerns. The US actions therefore do not neatly fit in with either mediation or imposing a settlement. They might more appropriately be called 'coercive mediation'.

Like 'coercive diplomacy', coercive mediation involved the employment of limited force to persuade the other to change its terms. But it differed from coercive diplomacy because the coercion was not aimed at changing a disputant's policy towards the third party using coercive means. It was aimed at inducing the disputant to change its policy toward its adversaries and reach an agreement with them. Force was used to inflict painful punishment upon the Serbs, to intimidate them, to redraw the map, and thus to restructure the bargaining situation. This accomplished, the mediator assembled the disputants at the negotiating table. There the mediator's conduct was firm and directive, yet it left some room for negotiation and bargaining. Applying sticks and carrots to all three, it brought the parties to agreement on the terms of a comprehensive settlement.

Will the Dayton settlement endure? The terms agreed to at Dayton did not reconcile the parties' contradictory goals – the Muslims' goal of reuniting the divided parts of Bosnia into a single state, and the desire of most Serbs and Croats to sustain the partition, with the ultimate view of joining their areas to their respective nation-states of Serbia and Croatia. Rather the contradiction was incorporated into the terms of the settlement. The agreements therefore contained inconsistencies: they proclaimed the continued existence of a Bosnian state within its recognised international borders, yet they established frameworks that legalised the existing divisions. Aiming at stability, they prescribed processes of elections, institution building, refugee repatriation and economic integration intended to bring about fluidity, erode the existing divisions and build a new, common Bosnian state. This is the interpretation that has guided the international administrators in charge of implementing the Dayton Accords. In 2000, as these words are being written, the outcome is still uncertain. As long as the disputants continue to adhere to their contradictory objectives, the possibility of renewed warfare cannot been eliminated.

9
Priorities

By 1995 the international efforts had brought an end to the wars in Slovenia, Croatia and Bosnia. Nonetheless the mediation efforts in former Yugoslavia cannot be considered an unqualified success. The attempts in 1991 to bring about a comprehensive settlement of the conflicts were a total failure. The seven months it took to bring about the ceasefire in Croatia, and the three and a half years needed to produce a settlement in Bosnia are hardly examples of effective mediation. While the tortuous process of mediation was taking place, close to 200 000 people were killed and approximately two million were displaced from their homes and turned into refugees.

There are obviously many reasons why the mediation efforts were not more effective; why third parties were unable to bring about agreements to end the wars sooner, thus avoiding much of the killing and destruction that occurred. The analyses in the previous chapters revealed a number of important reasons.

The purpose of this concluding chapter is to call attention to two lessons that emerge from the discussion in the previous chapters. First, the identity of the mediator is of vital importance – mediation is likely to be more effective if conducted by a powerful state than by an intergovernmental entity. Second, the mediator's pursuit of multiple goals, including the pursuit of justice, may hamper its efforts to end a war.

Before elaborating on these points I would like to restate a premise that has guided this study: that mediation is an instrument of foreign policy. Its declared purpose is to assist disputants to reach an agreed settlement of their differences. But this goal is pursued within the context of the mediator's overall policy. Thus the peacemaking activities of states and international organisations often have additional objectives and are constrained by their pursuit of these objectives.[1]

Who should mediate?

Many of the difficulties encountered during the peacemaking efforts in former Yugoslavia can be attributed to the fact that the mediators were collective intergovernmental entities. This is not meant to deny the importance of the roles played by international organisations and other multilateral endeavours in international politics. Rather the observation about the relative ineffectiveness of collective action concerns only one kind of activity – that of mediating conflicts. Moreover the argument is not that collective mediation never succeeds. As we have seen, the EC and UN successfully negotiated the ceasefires in Slovenia and Croatia, and international organisations have been successful in mediating several other disputes in recent years. The point is that intergovernmental entities are by their very nature less suitable than major states for the task of mediating conflicts.[2]

To be sure, there are certain advantages in states channelling peacemaking through international organisations. The most important advantage is that international efforts are endowed with greater legitimacy than those of states acting on their own. Legitimacy is especially significant when outsiders are intervening in a domestic dispute, as was the case in Yugoslavia. Furthermore, if the mediation effort is accompanied by coercion, such action will carry far greater legitimacy if it is conducted under the auspices of an international organisation than if undertaken by a state unilaterally.

Another advantage can be the division of labour. Different governments enjoy varying degrees of access and influence with the disputants. At various points during the Yugoslav conflict, mediation was helped by France's influence on Serbia, Germany's on Slovenia and Croatia, and the US's on the Bosnian Muslims.

Furthermore, by working through an international organisation states can share the risks and responsibilities and limit their own commitment. It is states that make the primary decisions about mediation. When faced with a conflict that may endanger its interests, a major power will often undertake to mediate on its own. But when a conflict appears particularly intractable, great powers may be loath to commit their resources to a risky endeavour and prefer to throw the problem onto the lap of an international organisation. As former UN Secretary-General U Thant has observed: 'Great problems usually come to the United Nations because governments have been unable to think of anything else to do about them. The United Nations is a last-ditch, last resort affair, and it is not surprising that the organization should often be blamed for failing to solve problems that have already been found insoluble by governments'.[3] Mediation through an international organisation can serve as a buffer to protect a state from any damaging consequences of the peacemaking process and allows governments to be less closely identified with the process. If it fails, then the damage to their reputation and prestige is somewhat attenuated. The obvious and glaring example are the mediations in the former Yugoslavia. Most of the public criticisms of the mediation efforts were aimed at the EC/EU, the UN and the ICFY, rather than at the governments that directed the actions of these organisations.

Finally, one cannot overstate the important part played by international organisations in constraining the tendency of states to intervene unilaterally in conflicts. Had France and Germany not been committed to cooperating within the EC/EU, and had the US not been committed to cooperating with its allies and constrained by its membership of the UN Security Council, their divergent attitudes towards the Yugoslav conflicts would probably have caused the rivalry between them to intensify. Criticism of states' resort to collective mediation may be tempered if one views the inefficiency of the collective process as a price to be paid for the sake of averting the intensification of rivalry and the sharpening of tensions that a mediation by a single power, excluding all others, may provoke.

The advantages of collective mediation notwithstanding, the mediation processes in former Yugoslavia highlight the factors that prevent intergovernmental entities from effectively performing this role. One critical disadvantage is their limited capacity to perform an essential function – to exert influence to persuade the disputants to change their stance and agree to terms they are reluctant to accept. To influence disputants, mediators often need to bargain with them: to promise them rewards for following the mediator's suggestions and to threaten them with punishment if they refuse. Furthermore, as mentioned already, mediators often need to induce the disputants to settle, and they do so by helping to create a 'hurting stalemate'.

International organisations are far less effective than powerful states in persuading disputants to change their policies, and in creating stalemates. Doing so requires leverage. Much of a mediator's leverage derives from the economic and military resources it has at its disposal. States, especially great powers, possess such resources. Intergovernmental entities do not, so they depend on the constituent states to provide the resources needed to persuade the disputants to modify their position. It might be argued that the pooling of member-state resources enhances an organisation's bargaining power. But this seldom turns out to be the case. Governments are usually reluctant to commit resources, the negotiations for such commitments are slow and cumbersome, and if resources are made available they are often inadequate. Since these weaknesses are often evident to the disputants, they are likely to doubt whether the promises of assistance or threats of punishment made by negotiators on behalf of an intergovernmental entity will actually be carried out.

As we have seen, the EC's promise of economic assistance when attempting to prevent the break-up of Yugoslavia encountered a sceptical reception because the Yugoslav parties doubted that the individual member states would contribute the necessary funds. Later, during the Croatian ceasefire negotiations and the various Bosnian negotiations, the EC's and UN's lack of influence stemmed in part from the Yugoslav parties' knowledge that the EC and the UN would not be able to enforce a ceasefire or punish the parties militarily for non-cooperation. Even when the member states decided to employ NATO's formidable resources to strike at the Serbs, the lengthy negotiations among NATO members on how to act stimulated doubts about the actual implementation of the decision.

Influence is a function not only of resources but also of credibility, which in turn depends on the capacity to formulate and pursue a coherent policy. The mediator must be able to negotiate dynamically – reacting to events quickly, seizing opportunities and having the necessary flexibility to adjust its position and proposals as the situation unfolds.

States often have difficulty meeting these demanding requirements, but intergovernmental entities tend to find it even more difficult. Policy making always requires trade-offs between contradictory goals, and compromise among the various actors participating in the process. Policy making within international organisations not only adds another layer of bargaining and trade-offs, but is also qualitatively different because there is no ultimate authority to decide between alternative proposals. Voting rules give the appearance of an effective decision-making capacity, but in reality they do not eliminate the need to strive for a consensus. In practice, when trying to mediate conflicts organisations usually adopt only those measures on which consensus is possible. Measures on which unanimity cannot be achieved are thus excluded. Even those decisions which are adopted are likely to be hedged and balanced. They are often ambiguous, reflecting a compromise based on the lowest common denominator.

Collective mediation is further weakened by the inability of the group to speak in a single voice. The efforts of the representatives of the mediating entity need to be backed up by the members. But inevitably the individual member states' communications with the disputants reflect their respective preferences. Inconsistent communications emanating from different parts of a collective mediating entity inevitably detract from the efficiency of the peacemaking process. They are especially damaging to the mediator's efforts to persuade the disputants to change their policies.

Incoherence, contradiction and ambiguity continuously plagued the mediation efforts in the former Yugoslavia. While EC officials were trying to prevent the break-up of the country by offering inducements to persuade the contenders to settle their differences within a reformed Yugoslav framework, the Croat and Slovene leaders were paying greater attention to signals from political circles in Germany that indicated they would be supported if they decided to secede. Subsequently the participants at the EC summit on 27 June, immediately following the secession of Slovenia and Croatia, were unable to agree a common position on the break-up. The EC sent the Troika to Yugoslavia to try to stop the fighting, but without any political guidelines about the attitude it was to take towards the break-up, an omission that the disputants could not fail to notice. Later, while the Council of Ministers was demanding a ceasefire in Croatia, Germany was proclaiming that it would recognise Croatian and Slovenian independence if the fighting continued, thus providing Croatia with an incentive to provoke the JNA in the hope of speeding up recognition. We have also seen how Carrington's efforts to persuade Croatia to grant special status to areas in which there were substantial Serbian populations encountered difficulties because his bargaining position, whereby recognition was conditional on a settlement, was undermined by Germany's insistence on immediate recognition, and the subsequent EC decision to grant recognition without waiting for a settlement. During the Bosnian negotiations, when the ICFY and some governments were trying to persuade the contenders to accept the Vance–Owen Plan and subsequently the *Invincible* Plan, the United States indicated that it did not support these plans, thus encouraging the Muslims to reject them.

The fact that the member states were speaking with different voices prevented the disputants from perceiving the emergence of a stalemate. Thus the German statement that recognition was near encouraged Croatia to withhold the concessions it might have made if it had recognised that the war had reached a stalemate. The US statement that the various peace plans proposed for Bosnia were unfair to the Muslims encouraged the latter to think that the US might support military intervention on their behalf and tilt the balance in their favour. France and Russia's calls for the easing of sanctions on Yugoslavia encouraged the Yugoslav government to expect relief from its predicament without changing its policy on Bosnia.

Thus the incoherence that tends to result from collective mediation deprives peacemaking efforts of the ability to induce a stalemate, or at least to persuade the parties that they have reached a stalemate and should therefore abandon their uncompromising policies.

Another factor that handicaps international organisations is their limited flexibility. Once the members of an organisation have reached agreement on a certain proposal or framework for mediation, the organisation's decision-making process makes it difficult for it to modify its position in response to changing circumstances. The EU's and UN's commitment to the Vance–Owen Plan made it difficult to adapt to the Serbs' rejection of the plan and the need to take a different approach to the problem in the summer of 1993. Also, the arms embargo imposed by the UN Security Council in September 1991 could not be rescinded when the circumstances changed, thus depriving the mediators of useful leverage and making it more difficult for the Muslims to equip their army and defend themselves against the Serb and Croat forces. The task of the UN and the EC was encumbered by a considerable amount of baggage. They were bound not merely by resolutions reflecting the members' consensus on the principles upon which a settlement should be based, but also by the members' fleeting consensus on tactical measures. Such resolutions, 'instead of being pointers to a settlement...become a prison',[4] restricting the mediator's room to manoeuvre.

Lack of resources, together with a cumbersome and uncertain decision-making process, produce an overall image of the mediator as lacking credibility. Besides hindering the bargaining process, lack of credibility can be fatal when the negotiations reach the final stage and guarantees for the implementation of the agreement have to be provided. The disputants will have great difficulty putting their trust in guarantees offered by an international organisation. Guarantees by great powers are likely to be more credible. This was demonstrated at Dayton, when the US guarantee to provide the Muslim-dominated Bosnian government with military assistance helped to persuade the Muslims to accept the settlement.

It seems justified to conclude from this discussion that the mediation efforts in former Yugoslavia were greatly hampered by the fact that they were conducted by intergovernmental entities. As this discussion shows, the problems encountered were embedded in the very nature of joint action by states. Intergovernmental entities have great difficulty performing one of the basic tasks that effective mediators must perform: to persuade the disputants to change their policies. They are short of leverage. Their promises and threats lack credibility. And they are incapable of pursuing coherent, flexible and dynamic negotiations guided by a coherent strategy.

Compared with international organisations and other collective entities, powerful states are better able to mediate. Their main advantage is their ability to influence the disputants' behaviour because their policies are usually more coherent than those of intergovernmental entities, and because they have sufficient economic and military resources at their disposal to use as rewards and punishments. Overall they are seen to have greater credibility than international organisations.

Thus the US mediation efforts that led to the establishment of the Croat–Muslim Federation in 1994 and produced the Dayton Accords in 1995 stand in sharp contrast to the performance of the EC, the UN and the Contact Group. Although the Dayton Accords were formally produced under the aegis of the Contact Group the successful outcome can be ascribed to US leadership, one aspect of which was the US's ability to persuade its partners to step aside. But as far as the disputants were concerned it was not leadership that mattered, it was the US's ability to bring NATO air power to bear against the Serbs. The US was also able to manipulate the Croatian and Muslim armies' offensives against the Serbs, thus preparing the ground for the Dayton negotiations. Its promises and threats at Dayton were credible enough to persuade the disputants to make the concessions necessary for the conclusion of the Dayton agreements.

The record of the mediation efforts in former Yugoslavia demonstrates the difference in effectiveness between mediation by a single major power and collective mediation. The ability of a major power to pursue a coherent policy, to push aside other intervenors and to harness the political, economic and military resources needed to persuade disputants to compromise stands in sharp contrast to the difficulties encountered by collective entities. However, mediation by a powerful state is not always preferable to a collective endeavour. Indeed there are situations in which collective mediation is the more appropriate approach. Nonetheless, while collective action may help third parties avert mutual rivalries, it is not necessarily an effective method for mediating international conflicts. If ending a war is important and urgent, a single major power is likely to accomplish the task more effectively.

Priorities

Mediation is an attractive foreign policy instrument because it serves a dual purpose: it has the ethical purpose of helping disputants to resolve their quarrel, and it can simultaneously serve the interests of the mediator. The mediation efforts in former Yugoslavia show, however, that a lack of clear priorities in the pursuit of a dual goal can detract from the effectiveness of the peacemaking efforts.

There is little doubt that the mediators in former Yugoslavia were strongly motivated to bring the wars to an end. They were appalled by the loss of life and destruction, and feared that the conflicts might spill over into neighbouring states, creating situations that could draw them into the fighting. They were also concerned that the wars might produce large numbers of refugees, with the attendant burden of caring for them and the risk of social unrest in the host countries.

More generally they were apprehensive that the wars might disrupt the peaceful transformation of the European order after the Cold War. All Western states were concerned about the developments in the Soviet Union and its successor states. Before the August 1991 coup in the Soviet Union, most Western states favoured the preservation of a common Yugoslav framework, fearing that its violent disintegration would stimulate groups in the Soviet Union to engage in actions that would result in the violent break-up of the Soviet empire. Such a break-up could have endangered the safety of nuclear weapons, and could have undermined peace and stability in many other ways. Even after the Soviet Union dissolved peacefully at the end of 1991, concerns persisted because of the many unresolved issues that burdened relations among the former Soviet states.

As a result the peacemaking efforts in Yugoslavia at a critical moment were shaped with an eye to the potential Soviet crisis, as if Yugoslavia's break-up were a rehearsal for the disintegration of the Soviet Union. The principles that guided the West's policies towards the Yugoslav crisis were designed in part to fit a potential Soviet crisis. While the US and most European states favoured the preservation of the Yugoslav state, the use of coercive measures to ensure it was strongly opposed. The JNA could not be allowed to act against the pro-independence forces in Croatia and Slovenia not only because of principled opposition to any use of force, but also because it might encourage the Soviet army to attempt to prevent the secession of the Baltic states and Ukraine, an attempt that could have endangered peace in Europe. The policy that the existing internal boundaries must be respected and accorded the status of international borders between sovereign states was intended to serve as a general principle applicable to both disintegrating states.

The members of the EC had additional goals. Besides settling the conflicts in Yugoslavia and helping to prevent violence in the former Soviet domain, mediation in Yugoslavia was also intended to assist in the construction of the European Union. Mediation was seen as a means of institutionalising a common foreign and security policy, and for enhancing the EC/EU's status as a major actor in international politics. The aspiration to raise Europe's status in international politics led the European states to neglect or minimise the need to coordinate with the US. This led to policy differences and tensions that negatively affected the mediation efforts. Moreover France's desire to turn the WEU into a military arm of the European Union, independent from the US, contributed to the delay in the deployment of peacekeeping forces in Croatia and the implementation of the ceasefire there.

Russia's desire to protect its great-power status led to its involvement in the negotiations, and to the assertion of independent policies. Its involvement tended to encourage Serbia, and weakened the West's ability to influence Serb conduct. The restrained Western response to Russia's policies reflected the high priority that the West accorded to stability in Russia and the desire to avoid action that might help Yeltsin's opponents.

The US involvement in the peacemaking efforts also had multiple purposes. In addition to settling the Yugoslav conflicts and helping to stabilise the situation in the former Soviet domain, peacemaking in Yugoslavia had the goal of reasserting US leadership in post-Cold War Europe. It is impossible to tell whether the peaceful transformation of the Soviet Union was facilitated by Western policies toward Yugoslavia. But the other American goal of reasserting its leadership was attained, albeit at the cost of undermining the EC/EU and ICFY mediation efforts.

As mediation became intertwined with additional goals, priorities became blurred. For much of the time the ending of the Yugoslav wars was subordinated to other concerns. Were the principles that guided the EC's efforts in 1991 for a comprehensive settlement aimed at resolving the Yugoslav conflicts, or were they aimed at preventing individual members from pursuing independent policies, or perhaps they represented a signal to actors in the disintegrating Soviet Union? Was the US opposition to ethnically defined entities in Bosnia (1992–1994/95) aimed at facilitating a settlement of the Bosnian wars or at protecting US relations with the Muslim world? One may wonder about the extent to which the pursuit of other objectives interfered with the effectiveness of the mediation efforts, and whether agreements could have been reached earlier if peacemaking had been consistently assigned the highest priority.

The difficulties caused by the multiple goals and interests of the mediators may not be unique to the efforts to settle the conflicts in

the former Yugoslavia, but may hamper peacemaking in other conflicts as well. On the face of it, this problem can be alleviated if
mediators prioritise the ethical obligation of peacemaking over
other foreign policy objectives they seek to accomplish through
mediation. But unfortunately, such a general formulation of ethical
priority does not provide adequate guidance. Peacemaking often
consists of the double task of stopping a war and helping the disputants to arrive at an agreed settlement of the issues in dispute.

Since it can take a long time to settle a conflict in a manner that is
considered fair by the disputants and is thus likely to endure, mediators often face the dilemma of whether to divide their task into two,
giving priority to a ceasefire and postponing the achievement of an
agreed settlement. Put somewhat differently, this choice may be seen
as being between order and justice. To be sure the two objectives are
closely interrelated – justice requires order, and order, if it is to
endure, must be just. But this is a long-term perspective and for
mediators the choice is immediate. Should they pursue both objectives simultaneously, or should they give priority to a ceasefire?

Mediators also often face the dilemma of whether to insist on a
settlement that conforms to the norms and principles of justice
espoused by the international community, or try to facilitate a settlement that reflects the balance of power between the warring sides,
even if it is inconsistent with such norms and principles. The various
mediation efforts in Yugoslavia reflected different answers to this
question.

In Slovenia the mediators chose to give priority to a ceasefire,
postponing a political settlement until later. This may have been
choice by default because the European states were unable to agree
about which of the contradictory norms and principles that they
profess ought to be applied to a political settlement, but by giving
priority to a ceasefire many lives were saved. Although a political
settlement between Slovenia and rump Yugoslavia has still not been
attained, the ceasefire has endured and is likely to continue even
without a formal agreement declaring an end to the conflict between
them. Since the issue over which the war first broke out – the preservation of Yugoslavia – is no longer relevant, the war is unlikely to
be renewed.

The mediators' response to the war in Croatia was to pursue simultaneously both a ceasefire and a political settlement. It took seven

months to conclude the ceasefire, during which time thousands of lives were lost. The tardiness in achieving the ceasefire was caused not only by the attempt to achieve both goals simultaneously, but also by the delay in the dispatch of a peacekeeping force. But a major factor delaying the ceasefire was the dispersal of effort between the two goals. The final push for a ceasefire (in December 1991 and January 1992) did not happen until it was realised that a comprehensive settlement would not be achieved soon.

In the absence of a political settlement, the ceasefire proved unstable, collapsing three years later when Croatia launched a major military operation to establish control over the disputed territories. It is uncertain whether the ceasefire would have been allowed to collapse had this not fitted the West's purpose of defeating the Serbs in order to facilitate a settlement in Bosnia. Be this as it may, the ceasefire in 1992 helped to save many lives. The 1995 war probably caused fewer casualties than would have been the case if in 1992 the mediators had continued to give preference to a comprehensive settlement over the attainment of a ceasefire.

As for the protracted efforts to end the war in Bosnia, a strong case can be made that the insistence that it be linked to a political settlement led to the prolongation of the war. True, the European mediators were at times inclined to recommend a pragmatic settlement, reflecting the existing balance of power and deviating from the principle that Bosnia must be preserved as a multinational state. However the US helped to undermine such a settlement by criticising it as unjust, as legitimising territorial conquest and ethnic cleansing, and thus rewarding aggression. We do not know whether it would have been possible to end the war if the US had supported the endeavour, but it is probable that the insistence on respect for international norms, the insistence that the three national communities should live together side by side in peace and that ethnic partitioning would violate this principle, served to extend the war, at the terrible cost of human life and suffering.

The Dayton Accords were made possible not only by military intervention, but also because they were ambiguous about the conflicting principles of self-determination and the preservation of Bosnia's unity. Had the US allowed such equivocation earlier, it is possible that tens of thousands of lives might have been saved and immense suffering avoided.

This tends to support the view that mediators ought to give priority to stopping a war, rather than to seeking a just political settlement. Granted, it is impossible to arrive at a reliable prediction of which course of action will ultimately cost more: an early ceasefire, which may collapse and be followed by more fighting because the cause of the conflict remains unresolved; or continuation of the war while the search for a just settlement goes on.

Despite this uncertainty, I believe that mediators ought to give greater weight to the likely near-term consequences of their choices because predictions of the near term are generally more reliable than those of the more distant future. Mediators can be certain that an ongoing war will produce casualties. Less certain is the proposition that ceasefires tend to break down, leading to the renewal of war and causing higher casualties in the long term. Many events can intervene between the near and the long term, not all of them negative. A choice based on predictions of the short-term consequences of one's actions therefore seems justifiable in such situations.

Assigning the highest priority to an early cessation of hostilities is justifiable for additional reasons. It is difficult to reach agreement on terms that are perceived by the adversaries as fair and just while the war continues. The emotions generated by an ongoing war make it difficult for the parties to accept that the enemy has valid concerns, and to engage in a joint search for a mutually beneficial outcome, without which no settlement can endure.

Moreover the killings that accompany wars tend to perpetuate hatreds and stimulate vengefulness, thus fuelling the continuation of the conflict. Such emotions not only hinder efforts to settle the conflict, but also make the renewal of war more likely.

A ceasefire that leaves the conflict unresolved may produce a situation that is regarded by one or both sides as unjust. It may leave people subject to alien rule, displaced from their homes or suffering from other violations of their rights. But injustice is reversible; death never is. If people survive to see another day, they can continue their quest for justice.

The twin lessons from the Yugoslav experience – that the mediation of international conflicts is more likely to be effective if conducted by a powerful state, and that mediators ought to give priority to stopping wars over other worthy goals, even the pursuit of justice – have long been known. Unfortunately they need to be relearned. Perhaps it is not too much to hope that these lessons will be heeded by the international community as it addresses the numerous conflicts that are taking place in our time.

Notes and References

1 Introduction

1 The name Bosnia will be used throughout to refer to Bosnia-Herzegovina.
2 The eruption of large-scale violence in Kosovo in 1999 took place after the draft of this book was completed. The unsuccessful diplomacy aimed at preventing the latter tragedy deserves separate treatment.
3 For a review of different approaches to the study of international mediation see Jacob Bercovitch, 'Mediation in International Conflict: An Overview of Theory, A Review of Practice', in I. William Zartman and J. Lewis Rasmussen (eds), *Peacemaking in International Conflict* (Washington, DC: United States Institute of Peace, 1997), pp. 125–53.
4 In the introduction to the volume he edited, Hedley Bull defined intervention as a 'dictatorial or coercive interference'. See Hedley Bull (ed.), *Intervention in World Politics* (Oxford: Clarendon Press, 1984), p. 1.
5 The term mediator refers to a government or an intergovernmental entity, and not to the individuals representing it.
6 For a more detailed discussion of this approach to mediation see I. William Zartman and Saadia Touval, 'Mediation in the Post-Cold War Era', in Chester A. Crocker and Fen Osler Hampson, with Pamela Aall, *Managing Global Chaos* (Washington, DC: United States Institute of Peace, 1996), pp. 445–61.
7 See Saadia Touval, 'Biased Intermediaries: Theoretical and Historical Considerations', *The Jerusalem Journal of International Relations*, vol. 1, no. 1 (1975), pp. 51–69; Peter J. Carnevale and Sharon Arad, 'Bias and Impartiality in International Mediation', in Jacob Bercovitch (ed.), *Resolving International Conflicts* (Boulder, CO: Lynne Rienner, 1996), pp. 39–53.
8 The term 'honest broker' is attributed to Bismarck. When trying to allay suspicions about his motives for convening a conference to settle the disputes between the major European powers following the 1878 Russian–Turkish war, Bismarck described his role as that of an honest broker, or *ehrlicher makler.*
9 Article 3 of the Hague I Convention.
10 Article 2, Section 7 of the UN Charter.
11 See for example Milton J. Esman and Shibley Telhami (eds), *International Organizations and Ethnic Conflict* (Ithaca, NY: Cornell University Press, 1995); Stanley Hoffmann *et al.*, *The Ethics and Politics of Humanitarian Intervention* (Notre Dame, Indiana: University of Notre Dame Press, 1996); Laura W. Reed and Carl Kaysen (eds), *Emerging Norms of Justified Intervention* (Cambridge, MA: American Academy of Arts and Sciences, 1993).

12   See Bercovitch, 'Mediation in International Conflict', op. cit.; Jacob
     Bercovitch and Allison Houston, 'The Study of International Mediation:
     Theoretical Issues and Empirical Evidence', in Bercovitch, *Resolving Inter-
     national Conflicts*, op. cit., pp. 11–35; Marieke Kleiboer, 'Understanding
     Success and Failure of International Mediation', *Journal of Conflict Resolu-
     tion*, vol. 40, no. 2 (1996), pp. 360–89.
13   Mediators' functions have been described in numerous studies, for ex-
     ample Saadia Touval and I. William Zartman, *International Mediation in
     Theory and Practice* (Boulder, CO: Westview Press, 1985); Zartman and
     Touval, 'Mediation', op. cit., pp. 445–61; Louis Kriesberg, 'Varieties of
     Mediating Activities and Mediators in International Relations', in Jacob
     Bercovitch (ed.), *Resolving International Conflicts* (Boulder, CO: Lynne
     Rienner, 1996), pp. 219–233.
14   The European Community (EC) formally became the European Union
     (EU) in November 1993, in conformity with the Maastricht Treaty, con-
     cluded in December 1991.
15   The Contact Group consisted of representatives of Britain, France, Ger-
     many, Russia and the US.
16   This account of the background to the conflict draws on a number of
     sources. Especially useful have been Ivo Banac, *The National Question in
     Yugoslavia* (Ithaca, NY: Cornell University Press, 1984); Lenard J. Cohen,
     Broken Bonds, 2nd edn (Boulder, CO: Westview Press, 1995); Aleksa Djilas,
     The Contested Country (Cambridge, MA: Harvard University Press, 1991);
     John R. Lampe, *Yugoslavia as History* (New York: Cambridge University
     Press, 1996); Sabrina P. Ramet, *Nationalism and Federalism in Yugoslavia,
     1962–1991*, 2nd edn (Bloomington: Indiana University Press, 1992);
     Susan L. Woodward, *Balkan Tragedy* (Washington, DC: Brookings Institu-
     tion, 1995).
17   The term is from Roger Cohen, *Hearts Grown Brutal* (New York: Random
     House, 1998), p. xvi.
18   The precise number of victims and the relative share of the different
     national groups have been a subject of bitter debate. See Christopher
     Bennett, *Yugoslavia's Bloody Collapse* (New York: New York University
     Press, 1995), pp. 45–6.
19   The demographic data (1991 estimates) are from Steven L. Burg, *War or
     Peace?* (New York: New York University Press, 1996), pp. 58–9.
20   To cite only two: Alvin Rabushka and Kenneth A. Shepsle, *Politics in Plural
     Societies* (Columbus, Ohio: Charles E. Merill, 1972), pp. 91, 183–7, 202,
     205–6; Pedro Ramet, 'Yugoslavia and the Threat of Internal and External
     Discontents', *Orbis*, vol. 28, no. 1 (1984), pp. 103–21, especially 114,
     118.
21   *Memorandum Srpske Akademije Nauka i Umetnosti*, Belgrade, September
     1986 (facsimile edition published by the Serbian Literary Association,
     Flushing, NY), p. 45.
22   For details of the developments in Slovenia, see Christopher Cviic,
     'Slovene and Croat Perspectives', in Alex Danchev and Thomas Halverson

(eds), *International Perspectives on the Conflict in Yugoslavia* (London: Macmillan, 1996), pp. 116–23; James Gow, *Legitimacy and the Military: The Yugoslav Crisis* (New York: St. Martin's Press, 1992).

2 Failed Attempts to Prevent War

1 An earlier version of this chapter was published as 'Lessons of Preventive Diplomacy in Yugoslavia', in Chester A. Crocker and Fen Osler Hampson with Pamela Aall, *Managing Global Chaos* (Washington, DC: United States Institute of Peace, 1996), pp. 403–17.

2 'Western' here refers to the United States and the European Community (now the European Union).

3 Quoted in Sabrina Petra Ramet, 'Yugoslavia and the Two Germanys', in Dirk Verheyen and Christian Søe (eds), *The Germans and Their Neighbors* (Boulder, CO: Westview Press, 1993), p. 325.

4 Warren Zimmermann, 'The Last Ambassador', *Foreign Affairs*, vol. 74, no. 2 (1995), p. 2.

5 Ibid., p. 3.

6 For detailed accounts see Lenard J. Cohen, *Broken Bonds* (Boulder, CO: Westview Press, 1995), pp. 79–162; Susan L. Woodward, *Balkan Tragedy* (Washington, DC: Brookings Institution, 1995), pp. 82–145; Aleksa Djilas, 'A Profile of Slobodan Milosevic', *Foreign Affairs*, vol. 72, no. 3, (1993), pp. 81–96; V. P. Gagnon, Jr, 'Ethnic Nationalism and International Conflict: The Case of Serbia', *International Security*, vol. 19, no. 3 (1994/95), pp. 145–8; Sabrina P. Ramet, 'Serbia's Slobodan Milosevic: A Profile', *Orbis*, Winter 1991, pp. 93–95.

7 *New York Times*, 28 November 1990.

8 This is the view of Stipe Mesić, (the Croat representative whose election to the rotating office of President of Yugoslavia was blocked by Serbia) in his *Kako Smo Srušili Jugoslaviju* (How We Brought Down Yugoslavia) (Zagreb: Globus, 1992), pp. 32–3.

9 *Europe*, no. 5505 (5 June 1991), p. 4.

10 David Gompert, 'How to Defeat Serbia', *Foreign Affairs*, vol. 73. no. 4 (1994), pp. 32–5. Gompert served at the time of the crisis as special assistant to the president for national security affairs. See also Don Oberdorfer, 'A Bloody Failure in the Balkans', *Washington Post*, 8 February 1993.

11 David Gompert, 'The United States and Yugoslavia's Wars', in Richard H. Ullman (ed.), *The World and Yugoslavia's Wars* (New York: Council on Foreign Relations, 1996), pp. 127–8. The trade data for 1990 are derived from the table headed 'Principal Trading Partners', *The Europa World Yearbook*, vol. II (London: Europa Publications, 1994), p. 3355.

12 Interview, 12 November 1993. On Lončar's involvements in the diplomacy surrounding the crisis in the Gulf, see *FBIS*, EEU edition, 4 December 1990; Lawrence Freedman and Efraim Karsh, *The Gulf Conflict 1990–1991* (Princeton, NJ: Princeton University Press, 1993), p. 262.

13 Zimmermann, 'The Last Ambassador', op. cit., pp. 3–11; Gompert, 'How to Defeat Serbia', op. cit., pp. 33–5; interviews 13 April and 20 June 1994.

14 Warren Zimmermann, *Origins of a Catastrophe* (New York: Times Books, 1996), pp. 126–31.

15 Ibid., pp. 101, 109–10, 123; James Gow, 'Deconstructing Yugoslavia', *Survival*, vol. 33, no. 4 (1991), p. 306.

16 Zimmermann, *Origins of a Catastrophe*, op. cit., pp. 126–7, 131.

17 *New York Times*, 28 November 1990; Zimmermann, *Origins of a Catastrophe*, op. cit., p. 131.

18 Interview, 13 April 1994. Support for these perceptions was also provided in an editorial by Jerry Laber and Kenneth Anderson, 'Why Keep Yugoslavia One Country?', *New York Times*, 10 November 1990.

19 FBIS-EEU, 13 February 1991.

20 On this visit see Zimmermann, *Origins of a Catastrophe*, op. cit., p. 103; Woodward, *Balkan Tragedy*, op. cit., pp. 156–7.

21 'United States Policy Toward Yugoslavia', statement released by State Department spokesperson Margaret Tutwiler, 24 May 1991. *Dispatch*, 3 June 1991, pp. 395–6.

22 For more details see James A. Baker III with Thomas M. DeFrank, *The Politics of Diplomacy* (New York: G.P. Putnam's Sons, 1995), pp. 479–83; Zimmermann, *Origins of a Catastrophe*, op. cit., pp. 133–7; Mesić, *Kako Smo Srušili Jugoslaviju*, op. cit., pp. 34–9.

23 Interviews, 22 February and 13 April 1994.

24 John Newhouse, 'The Diplomatic Round', *The New Yorker*, 24 August 1992, p. 62.

25 Baker, *The Politics of Diplomacy*, op. cit., p. 482.

26 Hans Stark, 'Dissonances franco-allemandes sur fond de guerre serbo-croate', *Politique Étrangère* (2/1992), pp. 340–1; Woodward, *Balkan Tragedy*, op. cit., pp. 148–9, 153.

27 Quoted in Stark, 'Dissonances franco-allemandes', op. cit., pp. 339–40. On the impact of Napoleonic France, see John R. Lampe, *Yugoslavia as History* (New York: Cambridge University Press, 1996), pp. 41–4.

28 EEC–Yugoslavia Cooperation Council press release, Brussels, 18 December 1990.

29 Agence Internationale d'Information Pour la Presse, *Europe*, no. 5425 (6 February 1991), pp. 4–5.

30 *Europe*, no. 5433 (16 February 1991), pp. 7–8; Michael Libal, *Limits of Persuasion: Germany and the Yugoslav Crisis, 1991–1992* (Westport: Praeger, 1997), p. 6. Libal was head of the Southeast European Department of the German Foreign Ministry from 1991 to 1995.

31 *Europe*, no. 5461 (28 March 1991), p. 5; no. 5466 (6 April 1991) p. 10.

32 *Europe*, no. 5447 (8 March 1991), pp. 7–8; no. 5461 (28 March 1991), p. 5; no. 5466 (6 April 1991), p. 10; no. 5502 (31 May 1991), p. 3; no. 5503 (1 June 1991), p. 7; no. 5505 (5 June 1991), p. 4; no. 5510 (12 June 1991), p. 5.

33 *Europe*, no. 5519 (24/25 June 1991), pp. 4–5. See also no. 5489 (11 May 1991).

34 Cohen, *Broken Bonds*, op. cit., p. 219.

35 Quoted in Pia Christina Wood, 'European Political Cooperation: Lessons From the Gulf War and Yugoslavia', in Alan W. Cafruny and Glenda G. Rosenthal (eds), *The State of the European Community*, vol. 2 (Boulder, CO: Lynne Rienner, 1993), p. 233.

36 Quoted in Gow, 'Deconstructing Yugoslavia', op. cit., p. 308. For a subsequent statement by the European Parliament supporting the Croat and Slovene aspiration for independence, see *Europe*, 17 May 1991.

37 *Europe*, no. 5431 (14 February 1991), p. 4.

38 *Archiv der Gegenwart*, vol. 61, no. 14 (1991), pp. 35795–6; Libal, *Limits of Persuasion*, op. cit., pp. 6–7.

39 Mesić, *Kako Smo Srušili Jugoslaviju*, op. cit., pp. 18, 40.

40 Ibid., p. 44.

41 Ibid., pp. 32–3.

42 James Gow, *Legitimacy and the Military: the Yugoslav Crisis* (New York: St. Martin's Press, 1992), p. 132; Sabrina P. Ramet, *Nationalism and Federalism in Yugoslavia, 1962–1991* (Bloomington: Indiana University Press, 1992), p. 246.

43 On Croat expectations about the West's reactions to Serbian use of force see Norman Cigar, 'The Serbo-Croatian War, 1991: Political and Military Dimensions', *The Journal of Strategic Studies*, vol. 16, no. 3 (1993), p. 311.

44 The disclaimers are reported in *Europe*, Agence Internationale d'Information Pour la Presse, no. 5490 (13/14 May 1991), p. 3; no. 5505 (1 June 1991), p. 7. For the offer to help in constitutional talks see *Europe*, no. 5519 (25/25 June 1991), p. 4.

45 Zimmermann, *Origins of a Catastrophe*, op. cit., pp. 146–7; Gow, 'Deconstructing Yugoslavia', op. cit., p. 304; *Europe*, May 1991, p. 6/7; interview, 13 and 14 May 1994.

3   The Entry of Mediators

1 The European Council consists of the EC heads of government. The Troika consists of the current president of the Council and his or her predecessor and successor, or their representatives.

2 The summit of seven major industrial countries: Britain, Canada, France, Germany, Italy, Japan and the US.

3 Stipe Mesić, *Kako Smo Srušili Jugoslaviju* (How We Brought Down Yugoslavia) (Zagreb: Globus, 1992), pp. 75, 77, 81–2; Susan L. Woodward, *Balkan Tragedy* (Washington, DC: The Brookings Institution, 1995), p. 174.

4 James A. Baker III, with Thomas M. DeFrank, *The Politics of Diplomacy* (New York: G.P. Putnam's Sons, 1995), pp. 637–8.

5 Michael Libal, *Limits of Persuasion: Germany and the Yugoslav Crisis, 1991–1992* (Westport: Praeger, 1997), pp. 14, 16–19. Libal was head of the Southeast Europe Department of the German Foreign Ministry from 1991–95. See also Hans-Dietrich Genscher, *Erinnerungen* (Berlin: Siedler, 1995), pp. 934, 941–2; James B. Steinberg 'International Involvement in

the Yugoslav Conflict', in Lori Fisler Damrosch (ed.), *Enforcing Restraint* (New York: Council on Foreign Relations Press, 1993), p. 35; Marc Weller, 'Current Developments: The International Response to the Dissolution of the Socialist Federal Republic of Yugoslavia', *The American Journal of International Law*, (vol. 86) (1992), pp. 572–573; Richard Weitz, 'The CSCE and the Yugoslav Conflict', *RFE/RL Research Report*, 31 January 1992, pp. 24–5.

6   Libal, *Limits of Persuasion*, op. cit., p. 19.
7   The evolution of CSCE mechanisms and procedures is discussed in Steven L. Burg, *War or Peace?* (New York: New York University Press, 1996), pp. 45–50.
8   Libal, *Limits of Persuasion*, op. cit., p. 18.
9   Baker, *The Politics of Diplomacy*, op. cit., pp. 636–7; interview, 8 September 1994.
10 Mesić (op. cit., passim) provides many details about attitudes towards particular intervention initiatives and the debates on them. See also Mihailo Crnobrnja, *The Yugoslav Drama* (Montreal: McGill-Queen's University Press, 1994), pp. 190–1.
11 *Financial Times*, 20 September 1991; Genscher, *Erinnerungen*, op. cit., pp. 948–9; Stanley Hoffmann, 'Yugoslavia: Implications for Europe and for International Institutions', in Richard H. Ullman, *The World and Yugoslavia's Wars* (New York: Council on Foreign Relations Press, 1996), p. 108.
12 Security Council Resolution 713, 25 September 1991. For Lončar's speech and the statements by other delegations, see S/PV.3009, 25 September 1991. See also Weller, 'Current Developments', op. cit., pp. 577–581.
13 On the contribution of mediation to the dissolution of Yugoslavia see Susan L. Woodward, 'Redrawing Borders in a Period of Systemic Transition', in Milton J. Esman and Shibley Telhami (eds), *International Organizations and Ethnic Conflict* (Ithaca, NY: Cornell University Press, 1995), p. 210.

4   The Ceasefire in Slovenia

1   For more detailed accounts of these events see Laura Silber and Allan Little, *Yugoslavia: Death of a Nation* (New York: TV Books, 1995), pp. 154–8; Susan L. Woodward, *Balkan Tragedy* (Washington, DC: Brookings Institution, 1995), pp. 162–8; Warren Zimmermann, *Origins of a Catastrophe* (New York: Times Books, 1996), pp. 142–5.
2   Alan Riding, *New York Times*, 29 June 1991.
3   *New York Times*, 29 June 1991.
4   Viktor Meier, *Wie Jugoslawien verspielt wurde* (Munich: C.H. Beck, 1995), p. 392.
5   This account of the 28 June mission is based on Stipe Mesić, *Kako Smo Srušili Jugoslaviju* (How We Brought Down Yugoslavia) (Zagreb: Globus, 1992), pp. 50–5; Woodward, *Balkan Tragedy*, op. cit., pp. 162–3, 168.
6   Zimmermann, *Origins of a Catastrophe*, op. cit., pp. 147–8; Silber and Little, *Yugoslavia*, op. cit., p. 162; and Mesić, *Kako Smo Srušili Jugoslaviju*, op. cit., pp. 58–64, provides a detailed summary of the proceedings.

7 Michael Libal, *Limits of Persuasion: Germany and the Yugoslav Crisis, 1991–1992* (Westport: Praeger, 1997), p. 16.
8 Mesić, *Kako Smo Srušili Jugoslaviju*, op. cit., p. 74.
9 On this and similar problems stemming from the agreements, see James Gow and James D.D. Smith, *Peace-making, Peace-keeping: European Security and the Yugoslav Wars* (London: University of London Centre for Defence Studies, 1992), p. 16.
10 Statement by the office of the spokesman, Brussels, 5 July 1991 (mimeo); *Europe*, no. 5529 (6 July 1991); *New York Times*, 6 July 1991; *Financial Times*, 6 July 1991. See also Libal, *Limits of Persuasion*, op. cit., pp. 19–20.
11 Lenard J. Cohen, *Broken Bonds*, 2nd edn (Boulder, CO: Westview Press, 1995), p. 205.
12 Mesić, *Kako Smo Srušili Jugoslaviju* op. cit., pp. 86–92; Silber and Little, *Yugoslavia*, op. cit., pp. 164–6; Meier, *Wie Jugoslawien verspielt wurde*, op. cit., p. 380; *Europe*, no. 5530 (8/9 July 1991); *European Report*, 10 July 1991.
13 The full text is reproduced in the *Review of International Affairs*, vol. 42, no. 995–7 (Belgrade, 5 October–5 November, 1991), pp. 20–1.
14 Mesić, *Kako Smo Srušili Jugoslaviju*, op. cit., pp. 105–17, 122–4.
15 On the gradual change of the JNA from being dedicated to the protection of Yugoslavia to becoming an instrument of Serbia, see V.C. Gagnon Jr, 'Historical Roots of the Yugoslav Conflict', in Esman and Telhami (eds), *International Organizations and Ethnic Conflict*, (Ithaca, NY: Cornell University Press, 1995), pp. 194–6. See also Cohen, *Broken Bonds*, op. cit., pp. 172–83. The population figures are from Steven L. Burg, *War or Peace?* (New York: New York University Press, 1996), p. 59.
16 Zimmermann, *Origins*, op. cit., p. 149. On Serbian attitudes and rumoured contacts between Milošević and Kučan, see Steven L. Burg, 'The International Community and the Yugoslav Crisis', in Esman and Telhami, *International Organizations*, op. cit., pp. 241–2; Cohen, *Broken Bonds*, op. cit., p. 210 and n. 23, p. 223; Silber and Little, *Yugoslavia*, op. cit., p. 166; Zimmermann, *Origins*, op. cit., p. 144.
17 Interview, 13 May 1994.

5 The Search for a Comprehensive Settlement

1 Stanley Hoffmann, 'Yugoslavia: Implications for Europe and for European Institutions', in Richard H. Ullman (ed.), *The World and Yugoslavia's Wars* (New York: Council on Foreign Relations, 1996), p. 111.
2 Alan Riding, *New York Times*, 29 June 1991.
3 See Chapter 4, pp. 59–60.
4 Henry Wynaendts, *L'engrenage* (Paris: Editions Denoël, 1993), pp. 50, 68–9; Michael Libal, *Limits of Persuasion*, op. cit., p. 22ff.
5 On Croatian hopes, see Mihailo Crnobrnja, *The Yugoslav Drama* (Montreal & Kingston: McGill-Queen's University Press, 1994), p. 194; Warren Zimmermann, *Origins of a Catastrophe*, op. cit., p. 154.

6 These phrases appear in the Lake Ohrid Statement, reproduced in *Review of International Affairs* (Belgrade), vol. 42, nos 995–7 (1991), p. 6. See also Zimmermann, *Origins*, op. cit., p. 153.

7 Stipe Mesić, *Kako Smo Srušili Jugoslaviju* (How We Brought Down Yugoslavia) (Zagreb: Globus, 1992), p. 179.

8 *Review of International Affairs* (Belgrade), vol. 42, nos 995–7 (1991), p. 8. For a detailed description of the meetings see Mesić, *Kako Smo Srušili Jugoslaviju*, op. cit., pp. 131–2, 172–9.

9 Mesić, ibid., pp. 224–6.

10 The Council of Ministers' decision was circulated as UN Security Council document S/22902 (7 August 1991).

11 Libal, *Limits of Persuasion*, op. cit., pp. 39–40. On the atmosphere among EC officials after the coup see *Europe* no. 5553 (26/27 August 1991), pp. 3–4.

12 Hans-Dietrich Genscher, *Erinnerungen* (Berlin: Siedler, 1995), pp. 946–7; Geoffrey Edwards, 'The Potential Limits of the CFSP: The Yugoslav Example', in Elfriede Regelsberger, Philippe de Schoutheete de Tervarent and Wolfgang Wessels (eds.), *Foreign Policy of the European Union* (Boulder, co: Lynne Rienner, 1997), p. 176.

13 These Council of Ministers decisions were circulated as UN Security Council documents S/22991 (29 August 1991) and S/23010 (4 September 1991).

14 Donald Rothchild, *Managing Ethnic Conflict in Africa* (Washington, DC: The Brookings Institution, 1997), p. 174. See also Stephen John Stedman, *Peacemaking in Civil War: International Mediation in Zimbabwe, 1974–1980* (Boulder, CO: Lynne Rienner, 1991), p. 199.

15 Conférence de Presse Conjointe de M. le Président de la République et de M. Richard von Weizsäcker, Président de la République Fédéral d'Allemagne, mimeo (Château de Weimar, 20 September 1991).

16 Zimmermann, *Origins*, op. cit., pp. 154–5, 162, 164; Genscher, *Erinnerungen*, op. cit., pp. 947–8; Javier Pérez de Cuéllar, *Pilgrimage for Peace* (New York: St. Martin's Press, 1997), pp. 483–4.

17 For descriptions of this drama see Mesić, *Kako Smo Srušili Jugoslaviju*, op. cit., pp. 207–11, and Wynaendts, *L'engrenage*, op. cit., pp. 75–77. The text of the ultimatum is reproduced in UNSC S/22991, 29 August 1991.

18 Quoted in the *Christian Science Monitor*, 6 September 1991. For Delors' and van den Broek's views see *European Report*, no. 1701 (7 September 1991). See also James Gow, *Triumph of the Lack of Will* (New York: Columbia University Press, 1997), pp. 53–5.

19 UN document S/23059, 20 September 1991; Mesić, *Kako Smo Srušili Jugoslaviju*, op. cit., pp. 246–7; Wynaendts, *L'engrenage*, op. cit., pp. 100–3.

20 *Financial Times*, 24 June 1991.

21 *New York Times*, 29 June 1991.

22 Interview, 8 September 1994.

23 The statement is reproduced in the *Review of International Affairs* (Belgrade), vol. 42, nos 995–7 (1991), p. 19. For press reports on the policy

disagreements during this period see *Washington Post*, 2 July; *New York Times*, 2 July; *The Times*, 4 July, p. 5; *Europe* (no. 5529 6 July); *European Report*, 6 July.

24 David Owen, *Balkan Odyssey* (New York: Harcourt Brace & Co., 1995), pp. 31–3. The quotations are taken from Owen's reproduction of van den Broek's memorandum.

25 Ibid., p. 33.

26 For texts, see *Review of International Affairs*, (Belgrade), Vol. 42, nos. 995–7 (1991), pp. 23, 27. The EC declarations of 6 August, 27 August, 3 September and 19 September are reproduced as UN Security Council documents S/22902 (7 August 1991), S/22991 (29 August 1991), S/23010 (4 September 1991) and S/23059 (20 September 1991) respectively. On Germany's role in the development of these principles see Libal, *Limits of Persuasion*, op. cit., pp. 24–38.

27 Libal, *Limits of Persuasion*, op. cit., pp. 28–9.

28 FBIS-WEU-91–197, 10 October 1991, pp. 1, 12.

29 UN document S/23169, 25 October 1991, Annex II.

30 For more on the events surrounding the conference and the proceedings see Susan L. Woodward, *Balkan Tragedy* (Washington, DC: Brookings Institution, 1995), pp. 173–82; Wynaendts, *L'engrenage*, op. cit., pp. 117–31.

31 The quotes are taken from UN document S/23169, 25 October 1991, Annex VII.

32 For the debate on the word 'nation' see Mesić, *Kako Smo Srušili Jugoslaviju*, op. cit., pp. 306–7.

33 S/23169, 25 October 1991, Annex VI, Para. 2.5.

34 18 October – Section 2.7; 25 October – Article 2.6.

35 Steven L. Burg and Paul S. Shoup, *The War in Bosnia and Herzegovina* (Armonk, NY and London: M.E. Sharpe, 1999), pp. 89–91.

36 *The Times*, 16 November 1991, p. 11.

37 Laura Silber and Allan Little, *Yugoslavia: Death of a Nation* (New York: TV Books, 1995), pp. 194–5.

38 Opinion 1, *International Legal Materials*, vol. 31, no. 6 (1992) pp. 1494–7.

39 Opinion 2, *International Legal Materials*, vol. 31, no. 6 (1992), pp. 1497–9.

40 Ibid., Opinion 3, pp. 1499–500. For a critique of the Commission's opinion, arguing that it misapplied the *uti possidetis* principle regarding the validity of inherited colonial borders to the internal boundaries of disintegrating states, see Steven R. Ratner, 'Drawing a Better Line: Uti Possidetis and the Borders of New States', *American Journal of International Law*, vol. 90, no. 4 (1996), pp. 590–624.

41 S/23203, 8 November 1991.

42 Libal, *Limits of Persuasion*, op. cit., pp. 76–9; Wynaendts, *L'engrenage*, op. cit., p. 149; Mesić, *Kako Smo Srušili Jugoslaviju*, op. cit., p. 312.

43 S/23203, 8 November 1991.

44 S/23280, 11 December 1991, Annex IV; Pérez de Cuéllar, *Pilgrimage*, op. cit., pp. 492–4; Wynaendts, *L'engrenage*, op. cit., pp. 150–1.

45　Pérez de Cuéllar, *Pilgrimage*, op. cit., p. 493.
46　Interview, 17 May 1994.
47　For detailed analyses see Beverly Crawford, 'Domestic Pressures and Multilateral Mistrust: Why Germany Unilaterally Recognized Croatia in 1991', *German Politics and Society*, vol. 13, no. 2 (1995), pp. 1–34; Marie-Janine Calic, 'German Perspectives', in Alex Danchev and Thomas Halverson (eds), *International Perspectives on the Yugoslav Conflict* (New York: St. Martin's Press, 1996), pp. 52–75.
48　The German Foreign Office. 'Zur Frage der Anerkennung der jugoslawischen Nachfolgestaaten', mimeo.
49　S/23293, 17 December 1991, Annex II.
50　Resolution S/724, 15 December 1991, para. 7.
51　Interview, London, 9 May 1994; Hoffmann, 'Yugoslavia', op. cit., p. 111; 'The Deal is Done', *The Economist*, 14 December 1991, p. 51; 'Wreckognition', *The Economist*, 18 January 1992, p. 49.
52　S/23293, 17 December 1991, Annex I.
53　Genscher, *Erinnerungen*, op. cit., p. 961; Libal, *Limits of Persuasion*, op. cit., pp. 79–80.
54　Opinions 4, 5, 6, 7, 11 January 1992, *International Legal Materials*, vol. 31, no. 6 (1992), p. 1501 ff.
55　European Report, no. 1735 (15 January 1992); *Europe*, no. 5647 (16 January 1992).
56　Genscher (*Erinnerungen*, op. cit., pp. 964–8) claims that it had beneficial effects.
57　Further Report of the Secretary-General Pursuant to Security Council Resolution 721 (1991), S/23513, 4 February 1992, para. 13.
58　Pérez de Cuéllar, *Pilgrimage*, op. cit., pp. 494–5.
59　Owen, *Balkan Odyssey*, op. cit., p. 343; Wynaendts, *L'engrenage*, op. cit., pp. 149–50; Lord Carrington, 'Turmoil in Balkans', *RUSI Journal*, vol. 137, no. 5 (1992), pp. 1–2.
60　A similar criticism is offered by Zimmermann, *Origins*, op. cit., pp. 161–2.
61　These were former Secretary of State James Baker's words. See James A. Baker III, with Thomas M. DeFrank, *The Politics of Diplomacy* (New York: G.P. Putnam's Sons, 1995), p. 638.
62　EC Council of Ministers' declarations on Yugoslavia of 7 August (S/22902) and 27 August (S/22991).
63　Carrington may have been influenced by his experience as mediator in the Rhodesia/Zimbabwe settlement in the late 1970s, when he was able to obtain concessions from Robert Mugabe's Patriotic Front by threatening that Britain would formally recognise a government headed by its rival, Bishop Abel Muzorewa.

6　The Ceasefire in Croatia

1　*The Europa World Yearbook 1994* (London: Europa Publications, 1994), p. 861; Lenard J. Cohen, *Broken Bonds*, 2nd edn (Boulder, CO: Westview Press, 1995), pp. 127–9.

2 Cohen, *Broken Bonds*, op. cit., pp. 129–35; Misha Glenny, *The Fall of Yugoslavia* (London: Penguin Books, 1992), pp. 1–30, 75–92; Susan L. Woodward, *Balkan Tragedy* (Washington, DC: Brookings Institution, 1995), pp. 102–3, 133–4. There is controversy over the question of whether Croat and Serb are separate languages, or merely dialects of the same language. The alphabets are respectively rooted in the Roman Catholic and the Greek Orthodox religions.

3 Cohen, *Broken Bonds*, op. cit., pp. 132–5; Glenny, *The Fall of Yugoslavia*, op. cit., pp. 1–31, 75–92.

4 Woodward, *Balkan Tragedy*, op. cit., pp. 173–4; *The Europa World Yearbook 1994* (London: Europa Publications, 1994), p. 859.

5 This was the number reported by the UN secretary-general, S/23280, 11 December 1991, p. 6.

6 This number was cited by General Kadijević. See Warren Zimmermann, *Origins of a Catastrophe* (New York: Times Books, 1996), p. 160.

7 Quoted by Michael Libal in *Limits of Persuasion* (Westport: Praeger, 1997), p. 45. See also Mihailo Crnobrnja, *The Yugoslav Drama* (Montreal: McGill-Queen's University Press, 1994), pp. 167–8; Jonathan Eyal, *Europe and Yugoslavia: Lessons From a Failure* (London: Royal United Services Institute for Defence Studies, 1993), p. 37.

8 Eyal, *Europe and Yugoslavia*, op. cit., p. 38.

9 Henry Wynaendts, *L'engrenage* (Paris: Editions Denoël, 1993), p. 100.

10 S/23169, 25 October 1991, pp. 4–5.

11 For the text of the two documents see *Review of International Affairs* (Belgrade), nos 995–7 (5.x-5.xi, 1991).

12 Wynaendts, *L'engrenage*, op. cit., p. 63.

13 Ibid., p. 68.

14 S/22991, 29 August 1991.

15 Wynaendts, *L'engrenage*, op. cit., p. 77. For descriptions of the drama, see Wynaendts, ibid., pp. 70–77; Stipe Mesić, *Kako Smo Srušili Jugoslaviju* (How We Brought Down Yugoslavia) (Zagreb: Globus, 1992), pp. 208–11.

16 Elfriede Regelsberger, Philippe de Schoutheete de Tervarent and Wolfgang Wessels (eds), *Foreign Policy of the European Union* (Boulder, CO: Lynne Rienner, 1997), passim, and especially the chapter by Philippe de Schoutheete de Tervarent, 'The Creation of the Common Foreign and Security Policy', pp. 41–63.

17 Eyal, *Europe and Yugoslavia*, op. cit., pp. 32–4; Geoffrey Edwards, 'The Potential Limits of the CFSP: The Yugoslav Example', in Regelsberger *et al.*, *Foreign Policy*, op. cit., pp. 186–7; James E. Goodby, 'Peacekeeping in the New Europe', *The Washington Quarterly*, Spring 1992, pp. 157–9.

18 Hans-Dietrich Genscher, *Erinnerungen* (Berlin: Siedler, 1995), p. 948.

19 Warren Zimmermann, *Origins of a Catastrophe* (New York: Times Books, 1996) p. 160; Laura Silber and Allan Little, *Yugoslavia: Death of a Nation* (New York: TV Books, 1995), pp. 197–8.

20 Steven L. Burg and Paul S. Shoup, *The War in Bosnia-Herzegovina* (Armonk, NY, and London: M.E. Sharpe, 1999), pp. 83–4, 88–9; Norman Cigar, 'The

Serbo-Croatian War, 1991: Political and Military Dimensions', *Journal of Strategic Studies* vol. 16, no. 3 (1993), pp. 317–22, 325–8; Zimmermann, *Origins*, op. cit., p. 160.

21 Mesić, *Kako Smo Srušili Jugoslaviju*, op. cit., pp. 308–9; Javier Pérez de Cuéllar, *Pilgrimage for Peace* (New York: St. Martin's Press, 1997), p. 487.

22 Wynaendts, *L'engrenage*, op. cit., p. 136.

23 S/23239, 24 November 1991.

24 'Concept for a United Nations peace-keeping operation in Yugoslavia, as discussed with Yugoslav leaders by the Honourable Cyrus R. Vance, Personal Envoy of the Secretary-General and Marrack Goulding, Under-Secretary-General for Special Political Affairs', published as Annex III of the secretary-general's report to the Security Council, S/23280, 11 December 1991.

25 S/23513, 4 February 1992, p. 5.

26 For a description of a dramatic encounter between Carrington and Tudjman see Wynaendts, *L'engrenage*, op. cit., pp. 142–3.

27 Security Council Resolution 743, 21 February 1992.

28 On the problems encountered in implementing the Vance Plan see William J. Durch and James A. Schear, 'Faultlines: UN Operations in the Former Yugoslavia', in William J. Durch (ed.), *UN Peacekeeping, American Politics, and the Uncivil Wars of the 1990s* (New York: St. Martin's Press, 1996), pp. 206–23. On the transfer of Eastern Slavonia to Croatian control, see UN Security Council Resolutions S/1023 (22 November 1995) and S/1037 (15 January 1996).

29 According to Wynaendts (*L'engrenage*, op. cit., p. 153), Milošević told Carrington that he expected the UN to allow a referendum to take place.

30 S/23363, 5 January 1992.

31 S/23513, 4 February 1992.

32 Milošević's conversation with Vance on 13 October 1991, S/23169, 25 October 1991, p.11.

33 Genscher (*Erinnerungen*, op. cit., p. 964), claims credit for persuading Tudjman.

34 Zimmermann, *Origins*, op. cit., pp. 159–60; interview, 23 November 1993.

35 John Zametica, *The Yugoslav Conflict*, Adelphi Paper 270 (London: International Institute of Strategic Studies, 1992), p. 67; Pérez de Cuéllar, *Pilgrimage*, op. cit., p. 486.

36 Genscher, *Erinnerungen*, op. cit., pp. 965–6; James Gow, *Triumph of the Lack of Will* (New York: Columbia University Press, 1997), pp. 62–4; Crnobrnja, *The Yugoslav Drama*, op. cit., p. 207.

7   Collective Mediation in Bosnia, 1992–94

1 A reminder: I use the term Bosnia to refer to the Republic of Bosnia-Herzegovina.

2 *Europa Yearbook, 1994*, (London: Europa Publications, 1994), p. 556.

3 Interview, 13 May 1994.

4 For a comprehensive discussion of the background to the war, see Steven L. Burg and Paul S. Shoup, *The War in Bosnia-Herzegovina* (Armonk, NY, and London: M.E. Sharpe, 1999), pp. 16–61; Ivo Banac, 'Bosnian Muslims: From Religious Community to Socialist Nationhood and Post-Communist Nationhood, 1918–1992', in Mark Pinson (ed.), *The Muslims of Bosnia-Herzegovina* (Cambridge, Mass.: Harvard University Press, 1993), pp. 141–4.

5 Sabrina P. Ramet, *Nationalism and Federalism in Yugoslavia, 1962–1991*, 2nd edn (Bloomington: Indiana University Press, 1992), pp. 177–81.

6 Lenard J. Cohen, *Broken Bonds*, 2nd edn (Boulder, CO: Westview Press, 1995), pp. 139–47.

7 Ibid., pp. 241–2.

8 Among the publicised meetings at which Serb–Croat cooperation over Bosnia is believed to have been discussed were those between Milošević and Tudjman at Karadjordjevo in March 1991, between Tudjman and the Bosnian Serb politician Nikola Koljević in January 1992, and between Karadžić and Boban in Graz in May 1992. See Burg and Shoup, *The War*, op. cit., p. 82; Cohen, *Broken Bonds*, op. cit., pp. 207–9, 248–9; Warren Zimmermann, *Origins of a Catastrophe* (New York: Times Books, 1996), pp. 178–84.

9 Burg and Shoup, *The War*, op. cit., pp. 71–3.

10 Zimmermann, *Origins*, op. cit., pp. 173–4, 177–8.

11 'Opinion No. 4: On International Recognition of the Socialist Republic of Bosnia-Herzegovina by the European Community and its Member States', 11 January 1992, *ILM*, vol. 31, no. 6 (1992), pp. 1501–3.

12 Cohen, *Broken Bonds*, op. cit., p. 242.

13 Burg and Shoup, *The War*, op. cit., pp. 108–12. The text of the Statement of Principles, dated 18 March 1992, is reproduced in the *Review of International Affairs* (Belgrade), no. 1003 (1 April 1992), pp. 15–16. For the Lisbon draft of 23 February, see the *Review of International Affairs*, no. 1002 (1 March, 1992), pp. 14–15.

14 Lord Carrington, 'Turmoil in the Balkans', *RUSI Journal*, vol. 137, no. 5 (1992), p. 2. The article was based on Carrington's presentation to the Institute on 6 July.

15 For more details and commentary see Paul C. Szasz, 'The Quest for a Bosnian Constitution: Legal Aspects of Constitutional Proposals Relating to Bosnia', *Fordham International Law Journal*, vol. 19, no. 2 (1995), pp. 363–407. Paul Szasz was the legal adviser to the International Conference on the Former Yugoslavia.

16 Burg and Shoup, *The War*, op. cit., pp. 111–12.

17 Interview, 17 May 1994.

18 Zimmermann, *Origins*, op. cit., pp. 188–90.

19 Interview, 26 September 1995; Burg and Shoup, *The War*, op. cit., pp. 113–16; Susan L. Woodward, *Balkan Tragedy* (Washington, DC: Brookings Institution, 1995), pp. 280–1; James A. Baker III, with Thomas M. DeFrank, *The Politics of Diplomacy* (New York: G.P. Putnam's Sons, 1995),

pp. 639–43; David Gompert, 'How to Defeat Serbia', *Foreign Affairs*, vol. 73, no. 4 (1994), p. 37; *Financial Times*, 10 March 1992. See also David Binder's reconstruction of this period in the *New York Times*, 29 August 1993, p. 10.

20   Resolution 757, 30 May 1992.

21   UN Document S/24100, 15 June 1992. See also S/23836, 24 April 1992.

22   Baker, *The Politics*, op. cit., pp. 644–51; David C. Gompert, 'The United States and Yugoslavia's Wars', in Richard H. Ullman (ed.), *The World and Yugoslavia's Wars* (New York: Council on Foreign Relations, 1996), pp. 130–3; *The Times*, 3, 26 and 29 June 1992.

23   S/23900, 12 May 1992; S/24333, 21 July 1992; Henry Wynaendts, *L'engrenage* (Paris: Editions Denoël, 1993), pp. 178–80; interview, 23 November 1993.

24   Michael Libal, *Limits of Persuasion* (Westport: Praeger, 1997), p. 94; Patrick Moore, 'A New Phase in the Bosnian Crisis?', *RFE/RL Research Report*, vol 31, no. 1 (1992), pp. 2–3.

25   *New York Times* and *Washington Post*, 26 August 1992.

26   *ILM*, vol. 31, no. 6 (1992), pp. 1534–5; S/24795, 11 November 1992.

27   *Financial Times*, 1 July 1992.

28   For a brief review of these tasks see S/24795, 11 November 1992.

29   On US sensitivity to the concerns of the Islamic world see Elizabeth Drew, *On the Edge* (New York: Simon & Schuster, 1994), p. 144.

30   Michael Libal, *Limits of Persuasion*, op. cit., p. 91. Libal was one of the principal architects of German policy on Yugoslavia.

31   Lord Owen's speech to the Security Council, 13 November 1992, S/PV.3134.

32   *ILM*, vol. 31, no. 6 (1992), pp. 1527–48.

33   Cohen, *Broken Bonds*, op. cit., pp. 257, 352; Laura Silber and Alan Little, *Yugoslavia: Death of a Nation* (New York: TV Books, 1996), pp. 258–64.

34   For Owen's description of this dilemma, see his speech to the Security Council, S/PV.3134, 13 November 1992. See also David Owen, *Balkan Odyssey* (New York: Harcourt, Brace & Co., 1995), p. 63; Gompert, 'The United States', op. cit., p. 134.

35   Owen, *Balkan Odyssey*, op. cit., pp. 48–9.

36   UN document S/PV.3134, p. 31.

37   The discussion that follows draws heavily on Paul C. Szasz, 'The Quest for a Bosnian Constitution: Legal Aspects of Constitutional Proposals Relating to Bosnia', op. cit., pp. 363–407.

38   S/25403, 12 March 1993.

39   Szasz, 'The Quest', op. cit., passim; Owen, *Balkan Odyssey*, op. cit., p. 211.

40   S/24795, 11 November 1992.

41   The course of the negotiations is reflected in reports to the Security Council. See S/24795, 11 November 1992; S/25050, 6 January 1993; S/25100, 14 January 1993; S/25221, 2 February 1993; S/25248, 8 February 1993; S/25403, 12 March 1993; S/25479, 26 March 1993. For details of behind the scene activities see Owen, *Balkan Odyssey*, op. cit., pp. 89–149.

42 Szasz, 'The Quest', op. cit., pp. 368–9; Silber and Little, *Yugoslavia*, op. cit., p. 277; Owen, *Balkan Odyssey*, op. cit., p. 91.

43 S/25221, 2 February 1993, Annex A (p. 41). See also Owen, *Balkan Odyssey*, op. cit., p. 90.

44 Zimmermann, *Origins*, op. cit., p. 222; Silber and Little, *Yugoslavia*, op. cit., pp. 276–7. For a detailed description of the negotiations see Burg and Shoup, *The War*, op. cit., pp. 214–250.

45 S/25221, 2 February 1993; interview, 11 May 1994.

46 S/25479, 26 March 1993.

47 Cohen *Broken Bonds*, op. cit., p. 252; Silber and Little, *Yugoslavia*, op. cit., p. 276.

48 For a description of the efforts to persuade the Serbs and the accompanying drama see Owen, *Balkan Odyssey*, op. cit., pp. 136–49, 153–8; Silber and Little, *Yugoslavia*, op. cit., pp. 279–87.

49 Owen, *Balkan Odyssey*, op. cit., pp. 89–184.

50 For a description of the breach between Vance and the Clinton administration see ibid., pp. 69, 107–8.

51 Ibid., pp. 124–5, 140–4; Silber and Little, *Yugoslavia*, op. cit., pp. 277–80.

52 Interview, 20 May 1994; Owen, *Balkan Odyssey*, op. cit., pp. 123–6.

53 *Washington Post*, 13 December 1992, 4 February 1993; *New York Times*, 3 and 4 February 1993; Owen, *Balkan Odyssey*, op. cit., pp. 94, 102, 105, 110, 116.

54 Gompert, 'The United States', op. cit., pp. 131–3; Owen, *Balkan Odyssey*, op. cit., pp. 116, 129–30, 132, 146, 151–3.

55 Owen, *Balkan Odyssey*, op. cit., pp. 191–3, 208, 210, 213.

56 Ibid., pp. 193–4, 221–2; Cohen, *Broken Bonds*, op. cit., p. 287; *New York Times*, 22 and 27 June 1993.

57 S/26337, 20 August 1993.

58 S/26486, 23 September 1993; Owen, *Balkan Odyssey*, op. cit., pp. 193–217.

59 Owen, *Balkan Odyssey*, op. cit., pp. 217–21; Cohen, *Broken Bonds*, op. cit., pp. 286–96.

60 Owen, *Balkan Odyssey*, op. cit., p. 213; Burg and Shoup, *The War*, op. cit., pp. 280–281.

61 Article J of the Treaty on European Union – providing for the development of a Common Foreign and Security Policy, to replace the European Political Cooperation mechanism followed by the EC – entered into force on 1 November 1993.

62 Owen, *Balkan Odyssey*, op. cit., p. 213.

63 Ibid., pp. 225, 227–9.

64 Ibid., p. 238.

65 Szasz, 'The Quest', op. cit., pp. 370–1, 380; Owen, *Balkan Odyssey*, op. cit., pp. 236–7.

66 Owen, *Balkan Odyssey*, op. cit., pp. 240–54.

67 Ibid., pp. 229, 231, 234.

68 Ibid., pp. 249–54; Silber and Little, *Yugoslavia*, op. cit., pp. 319–21.

69 Owen, *Balkan Odyssey*, op. cit., pp. 275–8; Pauline Neville-Jones, 'Dayton, IFOR and Alliance Relations in Bosnia', *Survival*, vol. 38, no. 4 (1996–7), pp. 46–7; Burg and Shoup, *The War*, op. cit., pp. 265, 300.

70 Owen, *Balkan Odyssey*, op. cit., pp. 278–9, 311–12 and passim; Neville-Jones, 'Dayton', op. cit.; Burg and Shoup, *The War*, op. cit., pp. 301–5.

71 Interviews, 13 May and 18 May 1994.

72 Owen, *Balkan Odyssey*, op. cit., pp. 278–9, 281–2, 284–7.

73 Szasz, 'The Quest', op. cit., pp. 383–4, 387, 396; Owen, *Balkan Odyssey*, op. cit., p. 285; Carl Bildt, *Peace Journey* (London: Weidenfeld and Nicolson, 1998), p. 18.

74 S/1994/916, 1 August 1994; Owen, *Balkan Odyssey*, op. cit., p. 286.

75 Owen, *Balkan Odyssey*, op. cit., pp. 290, 293–7, Cohen, *Broken Bonds*, op. cit., pp. 312–17.

76 I. William Zartman and Saadia Touval, 'International Mediation in the Post-Cold War Era', in Chester A. Crocker and Fen Osler Hampson with Pamela Aall, *Managing Global Chaos* (Washington, DC: United States Institute of Peace, 1996), pp. 452–3.

77 Gompert, 'The United States', op. cit., p. 134; Owen, *Balkan Odyssey*, op. cit., p. 63.

8 US Policy and the Making of the Dayton Accords

1 This chapter is based on my article 'Coercive Mediation on the Road to Dayton', *International Negotiation*, vol. 1, no. 3 (1996), pp. 547–70.

2 I. William Zartman and Saadia Touval, 'International Mediation in the Post-Cold War Era', in Chester A. Crocker and Fen Osler Hampson, with Pamela Aall (eds), *Managing Global Chaos* (Washington, DC: United States Institute of Peace, 1996), pp. 452–7.

3 See Chapter 2.

4 For other interpretations of US policies see James E. Goodby, 'When War Won Out: Bosnian Peace Plans Before Dayton', *International Negotiation* vol. 1, no. 3 (1996), pp. 501–23; Wayne Bert, *The Reluctant Superpower* (New York: St. Martin's Press, 1997).

5 David Gompert, 'The United States and Yugoslavia's Wars', in Richard H. Ullman (ed.), *The World and Yugoslavia's Wars* (New York: Council on Foreign Relations, 1996), p. 127; Robert L. Hutchings, *American Diplomacy and the End of the Cold War* (Washington, DC, and Baltimore, MD: The Woodrow Wilson Center Press and The Johns Hopkins University Press, 1997), p. 307.

6 James A. Baker III with Thomas M. DeFrank, *The Politics of Diplomacy* (New York: G.P. Putnam's Sons, 1995), pp. 636–7.

7 David Gompert, 'How to Defeat Serbia', *Foreign Affairs*, vol. 73, no. 4 (1994), p. 37. David Gompert was senior director for Europe and Eurasia in the National Security Council at the time of recognition. See also Baker, *The Politics*, op. cit., pp. 639–44.

8 Baker, ibid., p. 640, quoting a letter by Eagleburger.

9 Ibid., p. 640.

10 Duygu Bazoglu Sezer, 'Turkey's Political and Security Interests and Policies in the New Geostrategic Environment of the Expanded Middle East', Occasional Paper no. 19 (Washington: The Henry L. Stimson Center, July 1994), pp. 17–19. On Turkish interest in the Bosnian problem see also Kemal Kirisci, 'The End of the Cold War in Turkish Foreign Policy Behavior', and Ali Fuat Borovali, 'The Bosnian Crisis and Turkish Foreign Policy', both in *Foreign Policy* (The Quarterly Review of the Turkish Foreign Policy Institute), vol. xviii, nos. 3–4 (1993), pp. 17–20 and 74–80 respectively.

11 Hutchings, *American Diplomacy*, op. cit., p. 315.

12 Peter W. Galbraith, 'Diplomacy Helps Contain the Bosnian Conflict', *SAIS Review*, vol. 15, no. 2 (1995), pp. 115–17.

13 George Rudman, 'Backtracking to Reformulate: Establishing the Bosnian Federation', *International Negotiation*, vol. 1, no. 3 (1996), pp. 525–45. On US policy regarding arms shipments to the Muslims see *Washington Post*, 12 May 1996, pp. A1, A26; Richard Holbrooke, *To End a War* (New York: Random House, 1998), pp. 50–1.

14 Rudman, 'Backtracking', op. cit; Galbraith, 'Diplomacy', op. cit., pp. 113–15; Steven L. Burg and Paul S. Shoup, *The War in Bosnia-Herzegovina* (Armonk, NY and London: M. E. Sharpe, 1999), pp. 292–8; David Owen, *Balkan Odyssey* (New York: Harcourt Brace & Co., 1995), pp. 268–71; Laura Silber and Allan Little, *Yugoslavia: Death of a Nation* (New York: TV Books, 1995), pp. 219–23.

15 Silber and Little, *Yugoslavia*, op. cit., pp. 327–8.

16 Holbrooke, *To End a War*, op. cit., pp. 65–7; *New York Times*, 1 June 1995, p. A10, 2 June 1995, p. A1, 4 June 1995, p. A1.

17 *New York Times*, 28 May 1995, p. A12; *Washington Post*, 30 May 1995, p. A14.

18 *International Herald Tribune*, 25 July 1995, p. 7; *Washington Post*, 24 August 1995, p. A21.

19 For a detailed account see Ivo H. Daalder, *Getting to Dayton: The Making of America's Bosnia Policy* (Washington, DC: Brookings Institution Press, 2000), pp. 81–111. See also Holbrooke, *To End a War*, op. cit., pp. 66, 71–2; Burg and Shoup, *The War*, op. cit., pp. 323–7; *Washington Post*, 11 September 1995, pp. A1, A16.

20 Burg and Shoup, *The War*, op. cit., pp. 322, 330–1; Owen, *Balkan Odyssey*, op. cit., p. 322; Holbrooke, *To End a War*, op. cit., pp. 63, 88.

21 Burg and Shoup, *The War*, op. cit., pp. 307–9, 313–14, 327, 338–40, 346–7, 352–3; Daniel Serwer, 'A Bosnian Federation Memoir', in Chester A. Crocker, Fen Osler Hampson and Pamela Aall (eds), *Herding Cats: Multiparty Mediation in a Complex World* (Washington, DC: United States Institute of Peace, 1999), pp. 561–7.

22 Quoted in Holbrooke, *To End a War*, op. cit., p. 73. see also ibid., pp. 51n., 62–3; Daalder, *Getting to Dayton*, op. cit., pp. 119–27.

23 Daalder, ibid., p. 136, n.49.

24 1 September 1995, quoted in Holbrooke, *To End a War*, op. cit., pp. 102–3.

25   *Washington Post*, 1 September 1995, p. A26, 13 September 1995, p. A1, 15 November 1995, p. 1, and November 16, 1995, p. 1.
26   Carl Bildt, 'Holbrooke's History', *Survival*, vol. 40, no. 3 (1998), pp. 187–90.
27   Owen, *Balkan Odyssey*, op. cit., pp. 312, 330; Holbrooke, *To End a War*, op. cit., pp. 74–5; Daalder, *Getting to Dayton*, op. cit., pp. 110–14.
28   Holbrooke, *To End a War*, op. cit., p. 84.
29   Ibid., pp. 4–5; Owen, *Balkan Odyssey*, op. cit., pp. 320–1.
30   Holbrooke, *To End a War*, op. cit., pp. 105–6; *Washington Post*, 31 August 1995, p. A31, 1 September 1995, p. A1.
31   Owen, *Balkan Odyssey*, op. cit., pp. 238–9, 254, 281.
32   Burg and Shoup, *The War*, op. cit., pp. 294–8.
33   Holbrooke, *To End a War*, op. cit., pp. 159–62, 164–7, 172–3, 191, 193–6, 199. See also *New York Times*, 19 September 1995, p. 1A, 20 September 1995, p. 14A; *Washington Post*, 19 September 1995, p. 1A, 20 September 1995, p. 1A.
34   *Washington Post*, 25 September 1995, p. A13.
35   Holbrooke, *To End a War*, op. cit., pp. 181–4.
36   I. William Zartman and Maureen R. Berman, *The Practical Negotiator* (New Haven, CT: Yale University Press, 1982).
37   Silber and Little, *Yugoslavia*, op. cit., pp. 307–8.
38   Owen, *Balkan Odyssey*, op. cit., p. 211.
39   The text is reproduced in *New York Times*, 9 September 1995, pp. 1, 4. On the negotiations leading up to the agreement see Holbrooke, *To End a War*, op. cit., pp. 133–41; Carl Bildt, *Peace Journey* (London: Weidenfeld and Nicolson, 1998), pp. 99–101.
40   *New York Times*, 27 September 1995, pp. 1A, 10A. On the negotiations see Holbrooke, *To End a War*, op. cit., pp. 169–84; Bildt, *Peace Journey*, op. cit., pp. 107–8.
41   *New York Times*, 6 October 1995, pp. A1, A8, 11 October 1995, p. A23, 15 October 1995, p. 10. On the negotiations for the ceasefire agreement, see Holbrooke, *To End a War*, op. cit., pp. 195–8.
42   Holbrooke, *To End a War*, op. cit., pp. 305–9; *New York Times* and *Washington Post*, 23 November 1995.
43   For an account of the negotiations among the Contact Group states see Bildt, *Peace Journey*, op. cit., pp. 113–19, 136–8.
44   Holbrooke, *To End a War*, op. cit., pp. 96–8.
45   Ibid., p. 240; Pauline Neville-Jones, 'Dayton, IFOR and Alliance Relations in Bosnia', *Survival*, vol. 38, no. 4 Winter (1996–7), pp. 48–9.
46   Bildt, *Peace Journey*, op. cit., pp. 132–3; Holbrooke, *To End a War*, op. cit., pp. 251–2; Neville-Jones, 'Dayton', op. cit., p. 52; Interview, 6 June 1997.
47   *Washington Post*, 20 November 1995, pp. A1, A16, 22 November 1995, p. A22; Holbrooke, *To End a War*, op. cit., pp. 276–8; Neville-Jones, 'Dayton', op. cit., p. 51.
48   Holbrooke, *To End a War*, op. cit., p. 301.
49   Ibid., pp. 87, 251, 274.

50   Ibid., pp. 87–8, 250. 252.
51   Ibid., pp. 215–23, 253–4, 258, 260, 270–1, 275–8; interview, 18 June 1996. See also Daalder, *Getting to Dayton*, op. cit., pp. 140–9.
52   Holbrooke, *To End a War*, op. cit., pp. 238–9.
53   Ibid., pp. 237–40, 248–9, 264–8; *New York Times*, 2 November 1995, p. A8, 13 November 1995, p. 1, 23 November 1995, pp. A1, A10; *Washington Post*, 23 November 1995, p. A1.
54   Serwer, 'A Bosnian Federation', op. cit., pp. 547–86; Holbrooke, *To End a War*, op. cit., pp. 236, 240, 256, 262–4; Burg and Shoup, *The War*, op. cit., pp. 373–7.
55   Holbrooke, *To End a War*, op. cit., pp. 289–90, 309; *New York Times*, 3 November 1995, p. A12, 6 November 1995, p. A6, 18 November 1995, p. 5, and 19 November 1995, p. 10; Burg and Shoup, *The War*, op. cit., pp. 367–73.
56   Holbrooke, *To End a War*, op. cit., pp. 294–309.
57   Ibid., pp. 272–3, 281–3, 294–309; *New York Times*, 16 November 1995, p. A14, 17 November 1995, p. 13, 20 November 1995, p. A1, 21 November 1995, p. A8; *Washington Post*, 20 November 1995, p. A1.
58   *Washington Post*, 6 March 1999, p. A15.
59   Holbrooke, *To End a War*, op. cit., pp. 234, 306–8.
60   Ibid., p. 285.
61   *New York Times*, 23 November 1995, pp. A1, A12; *Washington Post*, 19 November 1995, p. A23, and 23 November 1995, pp. A32, A35.
62   *New York Times*, 23 November 1995, p. A10; *Washington Post*, 19 November 1995, p. A23.
63   Holbrooke, *To End a War*, op. cit., pp. 288–309.
64   Ibid., pp. 274–5, 294–303; *New York Times*, 23 November 1995, p. A10.
65   *Washington Post*, 13 November 1995, p. A1; *New York Times*, 15 November 1995, p. A8, and 19 November 1995, p. 1.

9   Priorities

1   Fred Ikle's discussion of 'negotiating for side effects' is of relevance here. See his *How Nations Negotiate* (New York: Praeger, 1964), pp. 42–58.
2   For other perspectives on this issue see Chester A. Crocker, Fen Osler Hampson and Pamela Aall (eds), *Herding Cats: Multiparty Mediation in a Complex World* (Washington, DC: United States Institute of Peace, 1999), pp. 668–77; Jeffrey Z. Rubin, 'Conclusion: International Mediation in Context', in Jacob Bercovitch and Jeffrey Z. Rubin, *Mediation in International Relations* (New York: St. Martin's Press, 1992), pp. 249–72.
3   U Thant, *View From the UN* (Garden City, NY: Doubleday, 1978), p. 32.
4   Sydney D. Bailey, *How Wars End: The United Nations and the Termination of Armed Conflict, 1946–1964*, vol. I (Oxford: Clarendon Press, 1982), p. 168.

Index

Printed in the United States
67065LVS00002B/12